D0958613

About the Writers

Irving Hexham is professor of religious studies at the University of Calgary, Alberta, Canada. He obtained his Ph.D. in history from the University of Bristol and is the author of seven books, including two written with his wife, Karla Poewe.

Lothar Henry Kope was born in Germany. Before retiring, he was the principal of a private language school for German, and he taught German at the University of Calgary in Alberta, Canada.

http://www.christian-travelers-guides.com

Visit our Web site for even more information. You'll find:

- Links to many of the cities and sites listed in our guidebooks
- Information about Christian hotels and bed and breakfasts
- Lists of English-speaking churches so you can plan where to worship
- Information about evangelical organizations in each country
- Diagrams comparing different architectural styles
- Examples of Christian art
- Brief essays on topics of interest to Christian scholars and travelers
- Readings from key historical texts
- Suggested readings for daily devotions as you travel around Europe

Plan your next trip with
http://www.christian-travelers-guides.com

"In an era that often overlooks the significance of the past as such, and certainly the Christian past, Professor Hexham's well-crafted guides for heritage tourists truly fill a gap. Don't leave home without one!"

J. I. Packer
professor, Regent College, Vancouver
author of *Knowing God*

"Using vacations to discover the riches of the Christian tradition is a great idea that's long overdue."

Bruce Waltke,
professor, Regent College, Reformed Theological Seminary
and a member of the *NIV* translation team

"At last! A guidebook which treats churches as windows onto the living faith of Christianity and not just as museums or graveyards. These books bring church history alive."

David V. Day
principal, St. John's College, University of Durham
and frequent broadcaster on the BBC

"Excellent...we can all learn from these books."

Terry Muck
professor, former editor-in-chief of *Christianity Today*

THE
CHRISTIAN
TRAVELERS GUIDE TO
GERMANY

IRVING HEXHAM, GENERAL EDITOR
written by **IRVING HEXHAM AND LOTHAR HENRY KOPE**

ZondervanPublishingHouse
Grand Rapids, Michigan

A Division of HarperCollins*Publishers*

This series of books is an unintended consequence of serious academic research
financed by both the University of Calgary and the Social Sciences and Humanities
Research Council of Canada. Both institutions need to be thanked for the support
they gave to the original academic research that allowed some of the authors to visit
many of the places discussed in these books.

The Christian Travelers Guide to Germany
Copyright © 2001 by Irving Hexham and Lothar Henry Köpe

Requests for information should be addressed to:

📖 ZondervanPublishingHouse
Grand Rapids, Michigan 49530

Library of Congress Cataloging-in-Publication Data
Hexham, Irving.
    The Christian travelers guide to Germany / Irving Hexham and Lothar Henry Kope.
       p. cm.
    Includes bibliographical references.
    ISBN: 0-310-22539-6 (softcover)
    1. Christians—Travel—Germany—Guidebooks. 2. Germany—Guidebooks.
I. Kope, Lothar Henry. II. Title.
DD16.H47 2001
914.304'88'024204-dc 00
                                      00-043727
                                      CIP

All Scripture quotations, unless otherwise indicated, are taken from the *Holy Bible: New
International Version*®. NIV®. Copyright © 1973, 1978, 1984 by International Bible
Society. Used by permission of Zondervan Publishing House. All rights reserved.

All rights reserved. No part of this publication may be reproduced, stored in a
retrieval system, or transmitted in any form or by any means—electronic, mechanical, photocopy, recording, or any other—except for brief quotations in printed
reviews, without the prior permission of the publisher.

Interior design by Todd Sprague

Printed in the United States of America

01 02 03 04 05 /❖ DC/ 10 9 8 7 6 5 4 3 2 1

Contents

PREFACE

Remember how the Lord your God led you.

Deuteronomy 8:2

The task of history . . . is to establish the truth of this world.

Karl Marx (1955:42)

Memories of paintings, sculptures, museums, churches last a lifetime.

Edith Schaeffer—*The Tapestry*

Our series of books is designed to awaken an awareness of Europe's Christian heritage among evangelical Christians, although we hope all Christians and others who are simply interested in Christianity will also find them helpful. Anyone visiting a large bookstore will quickly discover that it is possible to buy travel guides with titles like *Pagan Europe, Occult France, Magical Britain,* and *The Traveler's Guide to Jewish Germany,* alongside more traditional travel guides which attempt to take in everything worth seeing. Yet even books like the *Frommer's, Fodor's,* and *Rough* guides, although they mention Christian places and events, tend to underplay the Christian contribution to Western Civilization through neglect or a negative tone. Therefore, our guides have been written to correct what we see as a major oversight in existing works.

Our series is concerned with people and events of historical significance through their association with particular places. Thus we attempt to locate the development of ideas which have changed the world through their relationship with people and places. Consequently, we suggest visits to particular places, because by visiting them you can gain a better understanding of the times when important events took place.

The central theme of these books is the contribution of Christianity to Europe and the world. But not everyone discussed in these books was Christian. Indeed, many of the people we mention were strongly anti-Christian. Such people are included because it is impossible to understand our own times without appreciating the destructive forces that have attempted to replace Christianity by secularism and neopagan religions.

HISTORY AND MEMORY

Christianity is rooted in history. The New Testament begins with a genealogical table that most modern readers find almost incomprehensible (Matthew 1:1–17). The purpose of this genealogy is to locate the birth of Jesus in space and time according to the standards of Jewish history. The appeal to "the first eye-witnesses," in the prologue to the gospel of Luke, is also clearly intended to engage the skepticism of Greco-Roman readers by providing specific historical data against which ancient readers could weigh the writer's claims (Luke 3:1–2). The Gospels contain many references to historical data and specific geographic locations. So important is historical truth that its denial becomes a mark of heresy for New Testament authors (1 Corinthians 15:1–8; 1 John 4:1–3).

Clearly, the Bible is steeped in history and the remembrance of history. Both the Old and New Testaments constantly reminded their readers about particular historical events (cf. Deuteronomy 4:9–14; Acts 7). Thus, parents are commanded to teach their children the significance of history (Deuteronomy 6:4–25) both by retelling the story and through commemorations which enact the central acts of salvation (Exodus 13:3–16; 1 Corinthians 11:23–26). Further, an appeal is frequently made to visible memorials that remind people of God's wonderful deeds (Acts 2:29–36). We also find both Jews and early Christians visiting historic sites as acts of devotion (Luke 2:21–41; Acts 21:17–27).

The importance of history, and the way in which we remember past events, is recognized by many influential opponents of Christianity. Karl Marx, for example, argued that the ability to control history, or rather the interpretation of history, was an essential step in the abolition of religion. Almost a century later, Adolf Hitler made a similar appeal to history and historical necessity. Both Marx and Hitler, following in the footsteps of Enlightenment skeptics like Tom Paine, sought to establish the truth of their revolutions by denying the validity of Christian history.

Our books are, we hope, a small contribution to the reestablishment of a sense of history and cultural pride among Christians. Following the biblical model, we believe that visiting places and seeing where great events took place help people remember and understand the present as well as the past (Joshua 4:1–7).

Anyone involved in education knows that people remember things by association. The act of visiting a historic site creates associations that simply reading about it does not. Through the engagement of all our senses, we are able to make associations which enable us to remember the importance of events and ideas that would otherwise seem dead and dreary facts with little connection to our present life.

For example, a visit to Wittenberg has an immediacy which makes the work of Martin Luther live in ways that no book can fully convey to the reader. Walking around Luther's home, seeing the chairs he sat in, visiting his wife's garden, observing where he debated with his students, recognizing the hardships he endured, make the Reformation real to the visitor. Many thoughts are only fully realized when all of our senses are engaged by the specifics of a particular place.

It is our hope that these books will bring history alive, and with a sense of history a growing awareness of the realities of faith in our world. As Francis Schaeffer repeatedly loved to point out, there is a flow to history because Christian faith is rooted in space and time. To forget our history is the first step to the abandonment of our faith, the triumph of secularism, the ascendancy of New Age spirituality, and the rebirth of paganism.

SEEKING SPIRITUAL ROOTS

The great truth of the New Testament is that Christians are children of God by adoption. Today many people have forgotten that the New Testament preaches the revolutionary doctrine that our relationship to God is not through physical descent, but by adoption (Romans 8:23; Galatians 4:5; Ephesians 1:5).

The implications of this doctrine are profound. All Christians are united by bonds of faith and love, not physical relationships (Ephesians 2). Thus, Christianity is not a tribal religion rooted in local communities bound by kinship bonds. Rather, it is a world faith that unites all believers.

Repeatedly, both the Old and New Testaments point to examples of faith which we are encouraged to follow and remember (Joshua 4; Luke 11:29–32; Acts 7; Hebrews 12). Remembering acts of courage and obedience to God strengthens our own faith. This fact was long recognized by the leaders of the church. Throughout history, Christians have told and retold stories of courage and faith. Yet today these stories are all but forgotten. Lives of the saints which were once standard texts for every educated person and pious believer are now rarely read, and books like *Foxe's Book of Martyrs* (1563) are left unopened.

Today, Christians are quickly forgetting their rich spiritual heritage as Christian biographies are replaced in popular culture by secular gossip. Popular magazines, radio, and television are full of "lives." But they are the lives of pop singers, film stars, television personalities, and secular politicians. Instead of teaching spiritual lessons, they repeat trivia and revel in scandal. Something has been lost. And it is this something that can be recaptured by Christians who begin to search for their spiritual roots.

Visiting Germany to learn about great acts of faith can be a rewarding experience, and it is something all Christians, regardless of race or nationality, can find profitable. This spiritual quest helps us see our own lives in perspective and understand our times against a much greater backdrop than tonight's television news. That is the quest this book encourages you to begin.

Part I

GERMAN HISTORY

AN OVERVIEW OF GERMAN HISTORY

Before 1890, what we now know as Germany did not exist. Instead, there were several large states, such as Bavaria, Prussia, and Saxony, plus around three hundred minor states and free cities—like Bremen and Hamburg—with constantly changing borders. Several events stand out in what should really be called the history of German-speaking peoples, which begins in recorded time with the Roman invasion, occupation of large areas, and the founding of cities like Augsburg, Bonn, and Trier.

After the fall of the Western Roman Empire in A.D. 474, a period of chaos engulfed the whole of western Europe. Things really began to change with the establishment of Charlemagne's (742–814) empire in A.D. 800 and the conversion of the Saxons. From then on we see a gradual recovery of towns and cities,

the growth of monasteries, and a general improvement in material life.

The next major event in German history is the Reformation led by an obscure Augustinian professor of theology, Martin Luther (1483–1546). Whatever else Luther achieved, his work resulted in the division of German-speaking peoples between Protestants and Roman Catholics. This division led to the Thirty Years' War (1618–48), when Germany was invaded first by the imperial armies of Austria and later by the Swedish army, which came to the aid of the Protestants. This war led to an almost complete breakdown of civil society in many areas and death rates of up to two-thirds of the population through warfare, famine, and plague. For a good history of the period up to the French Revolution see Frank Eyck's *Religion and Politics in German History*.

After the German states recovered from the Thirty Years' War, the State of Prussia slowly came to dominate northern

Germany as the leader of the Protestant states. Frederick II, the Great (1712–86), succeeded in making Prussia the predominant military force on the continent. However, the German-speaking lands were quickly overrun by the armies of Napoleon Bonaparte (1769–1821) in the late 18th century. French occupation led to extensive administrative reforms and the abolition of many smaller states, principalities, and monastic institutions. The *de facto* imposition of French as the official language led to a strong nationalist reaction which found expression in the writings of the Kantian philosopher Johann Gottlieb Fichte (1762–1814). Napoleon's defeat in 1814 led to the partial reorganization of German states and, as was the case elsewhere in Europe, a strong conservative reaction.

In 1848 a group of liberals and freethinkers from all over the German-speaking world set up the ill-fated Frankfurt Parliament. After endless discussions, they appealed to the king of Prussia to accept the German crown and unify all German-speaking areas except Austria and Switzerland. The king refused and, encouraged by Austria, sent in Prussian troops to crush this flowering nationalist movement and uphold the existing order. Twenty-two years later, Otto von Bismarck (1815–98) unified Germany under Prussian rule, to the dismay of the Prussian king, who preferred Prussia to a greater German empire. In the same year the Prussian army defeated France in the Franco-Prussian war and

asserted German military dominance on the continent. Until the creation of a unified state, the Germans were usually portrayed as a peaceful, artistic, philosophical, and music-loving people. But after the birth of modern Germany, the image of Germans in the British press changed to one of a militaristic nation that threatened British interests through their industrial success.

The assassination of the heir to the Austrian throne at Sarajevo and the refusal of Serbia to extradite the assassins led to the First World War. Historians argue about the ultimate cause and intent of the combatants. But there is no doubt that from the German viewpoint the war was fought to end terrorism. From the outbreak of this war the British controlled the trans-Atlantic cable. Therefore, Americans heard the British side of things at least two weeks before the Germans were able to respond with their version of events. Consequently, it came as no surprise when, in 1917, America entered the war on the British side. American entry into the war resulted from the sinking of the Lusitania (1915), which at the time was depicted as an act of German barbarism. Recently, historians have confirmed that the Lusitania was indeed carrying munitions for the British, making it a legitimate target in any conflict.

Despite their propaganda about German barbarism and violations of international law, it was the British who actually violated international law by imposing a total naval blockade on

German ports in an effort to starve German civilians into submission. This policy was greatly aided by a devastating potato blight that destroyed the German potato harvest from 1916 onwards. The blockade lasted until 1920—for two years after the German surrender—causing widespread starvation, which in turn helped create popularity for the newly formed Nazi party.

During the 1920s, German society was devastated by runaway inflation, which wiped out the middle class. The economic recovery began in the late 1920s but was shattered by the Wall Street crash of 1929 and the Great Depression, which left one in three Germans unemployed. Hitler (1889–1945) came to power in 1933 as the head of a Government of National Unity. The Reichstag fire of March 1933 provided him with the excuse to declare a state of emergency and force through the Enabling Act. At that time there were 120 Socialists, 81 Communists, and 74 members of the Center Party facing 288 Nazis supported by 52 Nationalists in Parliament. The Socialist and Communist parties were banned, and many of their supporters were sent to the newly created concentration camps that were modeled on the British concentration camps of the Second Anglo-Boer War (1899–1902). Now Hitler had supreme power. Within a year, unemployment had drastically fallen through government programs of road building, public works, and government aid to families with small children.

Holger Herweg's *Hammer or Anvil? Modern German History 1648–present* provides an excellent overview of this fateful time.

The Nürnberg Laws of 1935 formalized what until then had been the informal persecution of Jews through boycotts of Jewish shops and businesses. Now Jews were banned from professions such as the civil service, law, medicine, and university teaching, and they were eventually sent to death camps. Leni Yahil's award-winning *The Holocaust* offers readers a good place to begin a study of this highly disturbing topic. For theological reflections by a Jewish theologian see *After Auschwitz* and *Approaches to Auschwitz: The Holocaust and Its Legacy* by Richard Rubenstein.

At this point it is important to note that most of the six million Jews whom the Nazis murdered did not live in Germany, where there were less than 250,000 Jews in 1939. Therefore, to a limited extent Nazis were able to hide their crimes from many ordinary people living in Germany. This fact does not excuse the Holocaust, but it does explain the lack of resistance to it among German civilians.

At the same time neopagan movements, which arose in the 19th century, received official and semiofficial encouragement through the Ministry of Education and various other institutes and organizations set up by the chief Nazi theoretician Alfred Rosenberg (1893–1946) and Hitler's chief of police

Heinrich Himmler (1900–1945). Secular rituals, which were relatively successful, were introduced to replace baptism, confirmation, marriage, and burial services. Attempts to downgrade and even replace Christmas with a neo-pagan midwinter festival and Easter by a festival of new birth were far less successful and abandoned toward the end of the war for fear of further alienating the population. Nevertheless, the Nazis were remarkably successful in destroying Christian influence in German society and encouraging the growth of new religions. Numerous books are available on this issue in German, but in English the choice is very limited. Richard Noll's *The Aryan Christ* remains one of the most accessible.

Eventually, the invasion of Poland led to the Second World War. The harsh realities of the war are summed up in British historian Clive Ponting's *Armageddon*.

To understand modern Germans, it is necessary to realize that while the Blitz killed 51,000 British civilians, the British wrought a terrible revenge, killing over 600,000 German civilians in bombing raids that concentrated on destroying the homes of ordinary people. It is also important to know that, at the end of the war, Germany lay in ruin. It lost half of its territory to Poland, Russia, and Czechoslovakia and was flooded with over ten million German refugees. The refugees were victims of ethnic cleansing who were expelled from eastern lands, including territories like East Prussia, which had been German for over a 1,000 years. Alfred-Maurice de Zayas's *A Terrible Revenge* provides a dramatic overview of these events. The Roman Catholic Church also published *The Tragedy of Selesia,* a detailed account of Russian atrocities and the persecution of Christians.

Following the end of hostilities, Germany was divided into four military zones: the American, British, French, and Soviet, with the capital, Berlin, being placed under joint control. Further, although American and British troops had occupied parts of what became the Soviet Zone, they were required to withdraw and hand their territories over to Russian troops. In the Western Zones, food was scarce, and widespread starvation lasted until 1948.

But, in the East, the Russians proceeded to go on a rampage of rape and destruction that lasted until at least 1949. Any industrial plant that had survived the war was dismantled and shipped to Russia as part of Soviet war reparations. Former concentration camps were reopened, this time for German prisoners, and a reign of terror ensued. Ironically, in handing over the Harz mountain region, the Americans also gave the Soviets the uranium mines they needed to build their atomic bomb. All of this is described in graphic detail in Norman M. Naimark's excellent *The Russians in Germany*.

The onset of the Cold War in 1948 and the Berlin Blockade (which lasted from June 23, 1948 to May 12, 1949) changed the international situation dramatically. During this time people in the western sectors of Berlin were supplied with food, fuel, and clothing through a massive airlift. The Western Allies proceeded to create the Federal Republic of Germany in May 1949 with its capital in Bonn. Elections were held and the Roman Catholic anti-fascist mayor of Köln, Konrad Adenauer, (1876-1967) became the first West German chancellor. Stalin responded in October 1949 by creating the Deutsche Demokratische Republik (German Democratic Republic), the DDR, in the Soviet Zone with its capital in East Berlin.

Economic recovery was slow, but gradual. With the aid of the Marshall Plan, Germany began to regain its industrial strength. The success of Western Germany led to a flight of refugees from East Germany, where conditions had worsened, leading to a workers' uprising in East Berlin in 1953. It was ruthlessly crushed by the Red Army. The failure of this revolt plus growing prosperity in the West—where by the mid-1960s people were talking about the post-war "economic miracle"—led to increased migration from the DDR. To stop people voting with their feet, Walter Ulbricht (1893-1973) sealed the borders of the DDR and erected barriers between the Eastern and Western Zones of Berlin in July 1961. Within a few weeks, a high concrete wall had been built to seal East Berlin. Anyone attempting to cross the Berlin Wall was shot.

In 1969, the West German government embarked on a highly successful policy of détente with Communist governments in Eastern Europe, which became known as Germany's "Eastern Policy." This initiative led to a softening of attitudes in the DDR and a gradual relaxing of tension in Berlin. Twenty years later, just as suddenly as it had been erected, the Berlin Wall was torn down after popular protests that originated in church-based prayer meetings, forcing the government of the DDR to resign. Finally, on October 3, 1990, a treaty was signed reuniting the two Germanys.

CHRISTIANITY IN GERMANY

There is evidence of early Christian activity in archaeological sites along the Rhine and Danube in towns such as Aachen, Köln, and Trier. The evangelization of Germany began through the conversion of Roman soldiers, traders, and settlers. Consequently, by the 2nd century there was widespread evidence of Christian activity throughout the Roman areas of modern Germany. Irenaeus (130–202) wrote "the German Churches," and Tertullian (160–225) mentions the Germans as people who had "bowed their neck to Christ." According to the Roman Ammianus (330–390), the majority of the citizens of Mainz were Christian in 368. During the 4th century the Christian traditions and communities that these converts established were disrupted or destroyed by barbarian invaders.

By the 7th century, the small Christian communities scattered throughout German-speaking lands were often led by illiterate, frequently heretical, priests. Consequently, a new missionary initiative was launched to convert and reconvert people living in German-speaking lands. This enterprise spread north from Italy and southern Europe and east from England and is usually associated with the work of Wynfrith (680–754), better known as Boniface, who organized an extensive mission work in German-speaking lands. He was greatly strengthened by the support of the Frankish rulers Karl Martel (688–741), who saved Europe from Moslem invasion by defeating Arab armies at the battle of Tours in 732, and his son Pippin the Short (715–758). Pippin was succeeded by his son Charlemagne (742–814), who was crowned Holy Roman Emperor on Christmas Day 800. He sought to reestablish Christianity and scholarship throughout his realm. Once again English scholars, particularly Alcuin of York (735–804), were recruited to assist in establishing the faith through the creation of schools and other centers of learning. Charlemagne also subdued the pagan Saxons through a series of long wars which began in 772. According to Einhard's (770–844) *Life of Charlemagne,*

written around 820, the Saxons first invaded Christian lands in 755, causing devastation to many communities. Under Charlemagne they were defeated and forcibly converted. Thus, by the 9th century Christianity extended from the Rhine near Köln, to Passau with the Hessians, Thuringians, and Bavarians professing faith. The art and architecture of this period is known as Carolingian and is closely linked to earlier Christian forms of church building.

Following the death of Charlemagne, his kingdom, which included modern France, was divided between his sons. This division eventually led to the separation of German- and French-speaking areas. Civil war and the ravages of Viking invasions threw Charlemagne's empire and German-speaking lands once more into chaos. But Christianity, and to a lesser extent learning, had been restored. Despite considerable confusion, towns and cities began to grow so that by the 10th century relative stability led to a rebirth of learning. Massive Christian missionary campaigns and church building projects began in the north and east of German lands. The art and architecture of this period is known as Romanesque.

The aim of these efforts was to convert Slavic peoples, particularly the Wends who lived between the rivers Elbe, Oder, and Saale. Three other missionary bishops were consecrated by Albrecht (939–997), bishop of Magdeburg, on Christmas Day, 968. These men included the "Apostle to the Wends," Boso (d. 970), bishop of Merseburg, who was a Benedictine monk. Although these missions were particularly successful, numerous rebellions often destroyed churches and slaughtered clergy before the country was finally Christianized in the 12th century.

A mission to Pomerania, which lies along the Baltic coast of former East Germany and modern Poland, was started in the 12th century by the Polish duke Boleslav III (1085–1138) after he first conquered the area and captured its capital Stettin. Due to the savagery with which Boleslav had subdued the area, executing thousands of people, the Polish bishops wisely declined to undertake mission work among a people embittered by conquest. But a Spanish monk named Bernard, who was a simple hermit, undertook the task without any knowledge of the people's language or customs. At first his efforts were rejected and his poverty scorned. He then retired to Bamberg where he convinced Bishop Otto (1060–1139) to continue the Pomeranian mission, avoiding the mistakes he had made. Therefore, Otto arrived in Pomerania surrounded by great wealth, numerous retainers, and obvious power, although his personal habits were simple and austere. The people accepted Otto as a great man and responded to his preaching, and after several months the whole area became Christian. Thus Otto, who never spoke a word of Pomeranian, became one of the most successful missionaries of the Middle Ages.

From the 10th century on, German missionaries were also active further east in Prussia, Latvia, Estonia, and Lithuania. These missions saw mixed results, and it took over two hundred years before the Prussians converted to Christianity. This is known as the high Middle Ages or Gothic period in art and architecture.

By the early 14th century, all of the German-speaking lands and many adjacent territories were Christian. A mere two hundred years hence, Germany was engulfed by the Reformation and a series of devastating religious wars. During the reign of the 218th pope, Leo X (1475–1521), the disputes which led to the breakup of Christendom began. These theological and social conflicts are associated with Martin Luther (1483–1546), whose preaching and publications provoked what became known as the Reformation. This period also saw the growth of new church music. After a short period of social and political unrest caused by the new teachings, a peace was established in 1555. It lasted until 1618. In that year the foolish elector Friedrich V of the palatinate, the son-in-law of James I of England, accepted the crown of Bohemia. His brief rule in Prague outraged the Habsburg monarchy, leading to a short war in which his forces were defeated and he was forced to flee. These hostilities marked the outbreak of the Thirty Years' War, one of the most devastating conflicts in European history during which large areas of Germany were devastated and, in some places, up to two-thirds of the population died.

The Swedish king and brilliant general, Gustavus Adolphus (1594–1632), entered the war in 1530 to rescue Protestant fortunes, only to be killed, possibly by friendly fire, two years later. The war ended with the Peace of Westphalia in 1648, leaving behind a devastated country with deep psychic wounds and a loathing for religious conflict.

This revulsion against violence and religious fanaticism found expression in the mediating theologies of the following century and the desire to distance faith from dogmatism. At the same time, a religious revival occurred in both Protestant and Roman Catholic areas of Germany. The Roman Catholic revival was part of the Counter-Reformation which saw the founding of new monastic orders such as the Capuchins, a branch of the Franciscans (1525), Jesuits (1534), and Oratorians (1577). All of these groups played a major role in reviving both Christian education and piety in Roman Catholic German-speaking lands. The Council of Trent which opened in 1545 further added to the revival of Catholicism, which found expression in the development of new pilgrimage sites, the restoration of older ones, and the erection of numerous new churches in what became known as the Baroque style. Among Protestants the revival—inspired in part by Roman Catholic devotional writings—was known as Pietism and made a major impact on Germany and the world.

By the end of the 18th century, church life in Protestant Germany had reached a low ebb while Catholic areas were still enjoying the flowering of Baroque culture (see Würzburg). Soon, however, both Protestant and Catholic areas of Germany were engulfed by a growing rationalism and anti-Christian spirit encouraged by the Enlightenment and French Revolution. Consequently, in the late 18th and early 19th century, a new spirit of criticism was encouraged by the example of English Deism, a revival of interest in the writings of Spinoza (1632–1677), and the translation of Tom Paine's (1737–1809) *The Age of Reason* (1794–1796). This new spirit took root in German intellectual circles.

Against this torrent of rationalist polemics, Friedrich Schleiermacher (1768–1834) attempted to save Christian faith by retreating from the realm of traditional apologetics to that of subjective feeling. His work was severely criticized by Ludwig Feuerbach (1804–72), who in turn prepared the way for Karl Marx (1818–83). Simultaneously, Ferdinand Christian Baur (1792–1860), Bruno Bauer (1809–82), and David Friedrich Strauss (1808–74) laid the foundation for the new Higher Criticism, which distorted traditional views of the Bible. It found expression in the work of Paul de Lagaard (1827–91), his pupil Julius

Wellhausen (1844–1918), and numerous others who, following the example of Tom Paine, seemed motivated by a virulent anti-Semitism.

In theology Albrecht Ritschl (1822–89) and later Adolf von Harnack (1851–1930), in their different ways, developed new liberal theologies in the light of their understanding of scientific progress. Conservative theology was kept alive by people like Friedrich August Tholuck (1799–1877), August Neander (1789–1850), Johann Cristoph Blumhardt (1805–80), his son Christopher Friedrich Blumhardt (1842–1919), and Martin Kähler (1835–1912).

The late 19th century saw what became known as the *Kulturkampf,* or struggle for civilization. This was a concerted attack on the Roman Catholic Church by Chancellor Otto von Bismarck. It lasted from 1873–79, and for Bismarck represented the age-old struggle between priestcraft and freedom. The government of Bismarck disliked the mainly Roman Catholic Center Party for its sympathy toward Poles living in East Prussia and other parts of Germany. To weaken the Center Party, Bismarck attacked the Roman Catholic Church with the full support of political liberals. The attack began with restrictions on Catholic schools and educational institutions. A "pulpit paragraph" was then added to the civil code that prohibited clergy from discussing political matters in their sermons or church publications. Then in 1872 laws were passed outlawing the Jesuits. Finally, in May 1873, the independence of the Catholic Church was restricted by new laws which required all ministers to pass state-administered exams in government schools and universities.

Pope Pius IX declared these acts and the accompanying legislation illegal and

JOHANN CRISTOPH BLUMHARDT (1805–80) was educated at Tübingen before becoming a teacher at the Missionary Training Institute of the Basil Mission. Blumhardt moved to a parish in 1842 where he was asked to pray for a mentally ill child. To everyone's amazement, the child was cured. Other cures followed, and Blumhardt moved to the small town of Bad Boll, where he established a healing ministry and clinic that was later taken over by his son Christopher Friedrich (1842–1919). Through his emphasis on the power of God in an age of increasing rationalism and skepticism about the miraculous, Blumhardt helped revive 19th-century German churches. The best known person to acknowledge his influence is the Swiss theologian Karl Barth (1886–1968).

urged Catholics to resist. Consequently, by 1877, half of all Catholic bishops had been deposed from their sees and 1,400 parishes were priestless. But the people resisted and the number of Center Party delegates elected to Parliament increased significantly. Finally, in 1878, Bismarck realized the growing opposition to his policies and relaxed the application of the laws, although many were not removed from legislation until 1917.

The Kulturkampf significantly weakened the Roman Catholic Church and its influence in Germany. It weakened all other churches as well, because most of the laws also applied to them even though they were not as rigorously enforced. Further, it laid the groundwork for future persecution of churches during the Third Reich. Finally, one of the side effects was the promotion of radical and strongly liberal theologians to university posts.

The 20th century saw writers like Ernst Troeltsch (1865–1923) and his friend and colleague Max Weber (1864–1920) develop the sociology of religion and comparative religion, while Rudolf Otto (1869–1937) developed a new understanding of world religions similar to ideas laid down by Schleiermacher. Rudolf Bultmann (1884–1976) and Paul Tillich (1886–1965) represented the new wave of radical theology, which led to the development of various forms of liberation theology, while Adolf Schlatter (1852–1938), Karl Heim (1874–1959), Karl Barth (1886–1968),

HABILITATION. In German-speaking countries, the "habilitation degree," or second graduate thesis, is far more important than the Ph.D. To teach in a German university you must habilitate before you can possibly be considered for a permanent academic position. The habilitation process involves writing a second, and more rigorous doctoral thesis. This is a highly political process that requires the complete agreement of an entire faculty that the candidate is worthy of being allowed the honor to teach in a university before the degree can be conferred. Consequently, it is very easy to prevent someone from habilitating by playing academic politics. Practically, this means that it has been possible to exclude anyone holding conservative evangelical views about the Bible from key theological posts in Protestant theological faculties. The two main exceptions to this exclusion are practical theology and the study of missions. The last German conservative scholar—whose views about the Bible were similar to those of F. F. Bruce—to hold a professorship in New Testament was Adolf Schlatter (1852–1938), who retired from Tübingen in 1922. Since then North American–type evangelicals have been effectively shut out of German Protestant faculties of theology.

and Helmut Thielicke (1908–85) represented the more conservative wing of German theology. More recently Klaus Bockmühl (1931–1989), Gerhard Maier (1937–), and Rainer Riesner (1944–) have given strong academic leadership to evangelical Christians in Germany, even though none of them have held a university professorship in Germany due to habilitation.

The Nazis encouraged the various German Protestant Churches to merge into one Evangelical Church in 1933 while at the same time slowly stepping up restrictions on Christian activity. In reaction, a breakaway Confessing Church was formed by Karl Barth (1886–1968), Dietrich Bonhoeffer (1906–45), Otto Dibelius (1880–1967), Martin Niemöller (1892–1984), and others. It issued the Barmen Declaration in 1934 which attacked Nazi policies. To break Protestant resistance, seven hundred pastors were arrested and sent to concentration camps.

The Roman Catholic Church also came into conflict with the Nazis despite a concordat, or diplomatic agreement, signed between the pope and the Nazi government in 1933. Conflict occurred over the control of youth movements, Christian schools, Nazi teachings in state schools, abortion, and euthanasia. Catholic opposition was led by Cardinal Faulhaber (1869–1952) of Munich and Bishop Galen (1879–1946) of Münster. In 1937, the Nazis smashed Roman Catholic resistance through a press campaign followed by a series of spectacular show trials where priests were charged with gross immorality, financial corruption, and similar crimes. John Conway's *The Nazi Persecution of the Churches* (1968) remains the standard work on this topic.

Since World War II, mainline Christian churches have played an important role in German social life. But evangelical Christianity in the British and North American sense has been very weak. In recent years, the charismatic movement has made significant inroads in Germany, with the result that today the largest active congregations are inevitably independent charismatic churches like the Church on the Way in Berlin.

Part 2

GERMAN LITERATURE, MUSIC, ART, AND ARCHITECTURE

GERMAN LITERATURE

All we can do in this short introduction is to give a few excerpts and examples from different epochs to provide a taste of German literary styles. To fully appreciate these works, the reader needs to know something about German history, culture, and above all the influence of Christianity in central Europe.

From the earliest times until the mid-18th century, German poetry and literature were deeply Christian and often very pious. All of this changed with the revolution of thought known in Germany as the Aufklärung, or Enlightenment, which swept through Europe in the 18th century and fed the anti-Christian movements of the 19th century, such as Marxism, nationalism, nihilism, and destructive biblical criticism.

German literary history encompasses eleven major epochs, which we explore below.

1. GERMAN POETRY (ANCIENT TO mid-8TH CENTURY)

The earliest German literary fragments come from the 4th century, but it was not until the mid-8th century that poetry and other works began to appear in German. This epoch reflects an age of migration when the Wends, Franks, and Huns occupied large areas of the former Roman Empire as well as lands to the east. It is the age of sagas, including the Edda, Hildebrandlied, Merseburger Zaubersprüche (a book of magic spells), and the Bible translations of Ulfila. Some fragments of Ulfila's (311–83) translation of the Bible into German still exist.

2. SPIRITUAL POETRY OF THE EARLY MIDDLE AGES (800–1150)

The Carolingian reforms initiated by Charlemagne around 800 made Germany a center of learning and began the second epoch of German literature. Here is a short excerpt from the Wessobrunner Gebet, an epic prayer:

That I learned as the greatest wonder
  That neither earth nor heaven was
Neither tree nor mountain was
  Nor sun was shining . . .

At this time the Gospels were in Latin; however, for the Ezzo and the Annolied the vernacular was used. These works rhymed in a form known as Stabreim, where two short verses are connected through the alliteration of the initial syllables of two significant words. This technique gives each stanza a heaviness. Here is a selection from the Annolied:

We listened often to songs of worldly matters;
  How fast swords fought,
How strong castles went down,
How dear friends parted,
How mighty kings perished—
  Now it is time that we give thought,
How we will end.

In this period we also find the many poems which express strong devotion to Mary.

3. POETRY IN THE AGE OF CHIVALRY (1150–1250)

This period of German literature is associated with medieval courts like that of Barbarossa. From this time we get the *Nibelungenlied,* a collection of fairy-tale-like legends associated with the destruction of the Burgundian kingdom of Worms by the Huns in 436, and the heroic adventures of Siegfried. Another epic from this era is Wolfram von Eschenbach's *Parzival,* consisting of 16 books and over 20,000 verses. It relates the faith of a child, his growth to knowledge, appreciation of ethics, and love of God. The poem closes with the following words:

Whoever ends his life in such a manner
  That he has not offended God
By lust for worldly things,
  But also has proved himself
With honor in this world,
  He has lived right.

About 70 of von Eschenbach's manuscripts survive, as have many other examples of knightly lyrics such as the following love poem:

You are mine, I am yours;
  You can be certain of that
You are locked
  In my heart,
Lost is the key
  You have to be always there.

4. THE GROWTH OF POPULAR POETRY (1250–1500)

With the decline of Imperial power in the period 1250–1500, cities grew in importance and local lords became stronger. The first German university was founded at this time in Prague (1348), followed by Erfurt (1379), and Heidelberg (1385). This period of literature drew to a close with the discovery of the Americas in 1492 by Christopher Columbus (1451–1506). Some popular poetry and prose associated with the common people exists from this period. So too does the *Visionsbuch,* or *Book of Visions* by Mechthild von Magdeburg, which tells about her longing for Christ. She called it "the flowing light of Godliness." Another Christian poet of this period was the knightly Meister Eckhart von Hochheim (1260–1327), who taught the need to renounce worldly possessions and strive for God. During his lifetime, Eckhart, who was the provincial of the Dominican order and a respected university teacher, was accused of heresy. He died before he could defend himself. Actually, only 28 sentences in his writings were eventually censured by the pope. Eckhart's work was rediscovered in the early 19th century by Romantic writers, who portrayed him as a pantheist. Later authors hailed him as a forerunner of German religion and precursor of National Socialism. Fragments of his works, often mistranslated, were used by the Nazis to promote their own form of esoteric nationalism. Modern scholars, however, agree that Eckhart was actually an orthodox Dominican whose works have been badly misused by New Age writers.

Volkslied is an anonymous collection of popular songs of unknown origin, and the *Volksbuch* is a collection of stories, epics, knightly adventures and misadventures. Tales of tricksters, jesters, magicians, traveling entertainers, and actors also became popular at this time. The best known of these works are the humorous adventures of the *Schildbürger,* citizens of Schildau, and the strange tricks of Till Eulenspiegel. Some of these German tales are used by Christopher Marlowe (1564–93) in his *Doctor Faustus,* which later inspired Johann Wolfgang von Goethe (1749–1832).

5. THE RENAISSANCE, HUMANISM, AND REFORMATION (16TH CENTURY)

The Renaissance and Reformation of the 16th century was a time of turmoil and social and intellectual ferment. The writings of Martin Luther (1483–1546), particularly his translation of the Bible, dominated this period. In fact, it was Luther who pioneered and shaped the new High German as a written language.

6. THE COUNTER-REFORMATION, PIETISM, AND THE BAROQUE (17TH–18TH CENTURIES)

The Counter-Reformation and Age of the Baroque during the 17th century saw the devastation of the Thirty Years' War (1618–48), followed by an outpouring of literature, much of which was highly spiritual, such as the works of Andreas Gryphius (1616–64). The era begins with Martin Opitz (1597–1639) publishing the *Buch von der deutschen Poeterey* or *German Poetry Book* (1624). Gryphius's poems and plays recall the reader to God by reminding everyone of their dependence on him. In his tragedy *Catherina von Georgien,* Gryphius deals with the reality of faith in the face of suffering and death. His comedies *Horibilcribrifax* and *Herr Peter Squentz* mock youthful folly while exposing the differences between illusion and reality. Angelus Silesius (1624–77) is an interesting figure who wrote poems for both Roman Catholic and Protestant readers. Paul Gerhardt (1607–77), on the other hand, was one of the great Protestant hymn writers whose "O sacred head, now wounded" was incorporated into one of J. S. Bach's oratorios. Friedrich von Spee (1591–1635) and Paul Fleming (1609–40) represented the Roman Catholic Counter-Reformation through their deeply devotional poetry.

Baroque novels, often long tedious affairs hundreds of pages in length, relate happenings at court, the lives of noble families, and adventures in exotic lands. Love stories with long, bombastic, and complex footnotes that refer the reader to classical texts are also a feature of this period. So too is the novel *Der abenteuerliche Simplicissimus* by Hans Jakob von Grimmelshausen (1620–76), which combines fairy tales, adventures, and vivid accounts of the misery of the Thirty Years' War.

7. THE AUFKLÄRUNG, OR ENLIGHTENMENT, ROCOCO, AND STURM UND DRANG (1700–1775)

The Enlightenment and late Baroque or rococo era begins with the age of the devout and industrious Pietist king Friedrich Wilhelm I (1688–1740) of Prussia. He was succeeded by his better known apostate son Friedrich II (1744–97), who is known as Frederick the Great as a result of his military victories. It is the period of Prussian consolidation and expansion under a skeptical king who scorned the religion of his father. The loser in this military struggle was the devout Roman Catholic Empress Maria Theresa of Austria (1717–80).

The poetry and prose of this age is didactic, intended to teach lessons of self-improvement and the importance of rational thought in a world where God plays the role of a distant watchman. Gottfried Wilhelm Leibniz (1646–1716) set the tone of the age with his view that language is the mirror of the mind, with an emphasis on mathematical certainty. Immanuel Kant (1724–1804) typifies the period. He defined the Enlightenment, known in Germany as the *Aufklärung,* in terms of his dictum, "Dare to be wise. Think for yourself."

The philosopher Johann Christoph Gottsched (1700–1766) helped redirect the sensitivies of the age through his reformation of the theater and insistence on the serious nature and dignity of theatrical productions. Gotthold Ephraim Lessing (1729–81) reflected the tolerance of Enlightenment thought through plays like *Nathan the Wise* (1779), which extols the virtues of a Jewish father and religious tolerance at the expense of confessional orthodoxy. His play *Emilia Galotti* deals with the struggles of the citizen against the tyranny of the absolutist prince. Lessing believed that "Not truth—but the sincere pain—to acquire truth gives value to mankind." He also helped popularize William Shakespeare, 22 of whose works were translated by Christoph Martin Wieland (1733–1813), a talented writer in his own right.

This was also a period of strong reaction against traditional Christian themes encouraged by the rationalism of Frederick the Great and his patronage of Enlightenment ideals. Pantheism, which ultimately was derived from the philosophy of Spinoza (1632–77), became a popular worldview, and a definite anti-Pietistic tone enters into the works of many writers. The hostility to biblical Christianity of this time is well documented by Wilhelm E. Petig in his informative *Literary Antipietism in Germany* (1984).

These developments led into the period of *Sturm und Drang*, 1760–85, often mistranslated as "Storm and Stress." Actually, *Sturm und Drang* means "storm and pressure, or thrust" or even "creativity." This time was ushered in by writers like Friedrich Gottlieb Klopstock (1724–1803), who kept alive the older tradition of piety through his poems which stress friendship, the love of God, and a consciousness of death and eternity. The period takes its name from a drama by Friedrich Maximilian Klinger (1752–1831) and was inspired by the writings of Jean Jacques Rousseau (1712–79), whose treaties *The Social Contract* (1762)

and *Emile* (1762) inspired a revolutionary age. The greatest writers of this period are Johann Gottfried von Herder (1744–1803), Goethe's mentor, whose work gave birth to modern anthropology and historical research. Klinger, Heinrich Leopold Wagner (1747–79), Michael Reinhold Lenz (1751–92), Matthias Claudius (1740–1815), Gottfried August Bürger (1747–94), Christian Daniel Schubart (1739–91), Ludwig Hölty (1748–76), and Johann Heinrich Voss (1751–1826) all produced sentimental poetry full of tenderness and emotion that captured the ethos of the times.

8. CLASSICISM: GOETHE AND SCHILLER (1775–1832)

The next major literary epoch, Classicism (1775–1832), saw an intensification of the rejection of biblical Christianity and a turning towards Greece and, to a lesser extent Rome, for inspiration from ancient paganism. It is associated with Johann Wolfgang von Goethe (1749–1832), who grew up in a Pietist home before turning towards a form of pantheism, and Friedrich Schiller (1759–1805), who retained a more orthodox Lutheran outlook. Goethe is best known for his epic play *Faust* (1808 and 1832) and *The Sorrows of Young Werther* (1774), which was credited with initiating a string of suicides in imitation of the "heroic" deed of the play's hero. He also wrote the poems *Prometheus* and *Ganymed* which reflect a turning from Pietism to pantheism. Schiller, who was professor of history at the University of Jena, wrote poetry, historical romances, and moving plays as well as historical texts. At the beginning of this period both Goethe and Schiller were influenced by and influenced Romanticism.

9. ROMANTICISM (1797–1830)

Romanticism is a highly complex artistic movement that is often confused with Neoclassicism. This period of German literature was a reaction against what was seen as the sterility of the Enlightenment's emphasis on reason. It is marked by a longing for historical traditions, the rise of modern nationalism, a hunger for the miraculous and marvelous, a sense of destiny, demonism, and mysticism. The Romantic period saw a turning towards the imagined unity of medieval life guided by the Roman Catholic Church. Fairy tales, fantasy, the unreal, make-believe, legends, saga, and fables all occupied people's imagination. In English this style of writing was best represented by Sir Walter Scott's classic tale *Ivanhoe* (1819). An exception to this trend was Matthias Claudius (1740–1815), who defended a traditional evangelical faith in an age of skepticism and mysticism.

Friedrich Schleiermacher (1768–1834) represents the spirit of the Romantic movement in theology through his *Speeches on Religion* (1799). Politically, Romanticism found expression in Fichte's *Address to the German Nation* (1808–9). Arthur Schopenhauer (1788–1860) gave Romanticism a slant towards India and Eastern religions which profoundly influenced the development of German thought. This was also the period of Friedrich Schlegel (1772–1829), August Wilhelm Schlegel (1767–1845), Caroline Schlegel-Schelling (1763–1809), and Joseph von Eichendorff (1788–1857).

The Grimm brothers, Jacob (1785–1863) and Wilhelm (1786–1859), deserve particular attention because of their well-known fairy tales which mark a move from seeking inspiration in the paganism of classical antiquity to that of the German past. Although the Grimms asserted that they were publishing authentic German sagas and traditional fairy tales which they claimed to have collected from peasants, recent research has cast doubt on the truthfulness of their claim. Like the Scottish writer James Macpherson (1736–96), whose immensely popular *Works of Ossian* (1765) were a forgery, so it seems that the Grimms invented most of their "traditional" tales or borrowed them from French sources (cf. John M. Ellis, *One Fairy Story Too Many: The Brothers Grimm and their Tales,* 1983).

The works of the Grimm brothers are also important because they represent a conscious attempt to popularize pre- or anti-Christian stories in an increasingly secular age where anti-Semitism was on the rise. Thus, their work may be seen as part of an attempt to replace traditional Christian stories and biblical narrative with "authentic" German folk tales of pagan origin. Certainly, their work played a major role in the creation of a new paganism towards the end of the 19th and in the early 20th centuries. The anti-Christian nature of the Grimm tales is noted by various writers, although usually in passing as something which is more a lack of Christian content than an actual attack on Christian foundations. The German Christian author Siegfried Fritsch has, however, made a strong case that the Grimms systematically undermined Christian beliefs and values through their numerous writings (Fritsch's book *Märchen und Sagen* is only available in German).

10. NIHILISTIC, NEO-GOTHIC, HISTORICAL, AND REGIONAL LITERATURE (19TH CENTURY)

The philosopher Georg Wilhelm Friedrich Hegel (1770–1831) profoundly influenced the development of 19th-century literature and philosophy even though Schopenhauer regarded him as a conservative reactionary whose fame depended on his support for the State. Later other philosophers, like Friedrich Nietzsche (1844–1900), had an equally powerful, and many would argue detrimental, influence on German authors. As a mature writer, Hegel outwardly paid lip service to Christianity, but his early works show the decidedly anti-Christian turn of this thought. Nietzsche was anti-Christian from the beginning and gave later German writers a nihilistic edge, which led many to embrace National Socialism. Defenders of Nietzsche argue that although his work was promoted by National Socialist propagandists, his views are at variance with the creed of this totalitarian movement. Actually, the issue is complicated, because while Nietzsche's work is ambiguous, there is no doubt that his published writings did lead many to embrace anti-Semitism, fascism, neopaganism, and National Socialism.

This period saw the development of neo-Gothic styles in the writings of people like Christian Dietrich Grabbe (1813–36), and later Ernst Theodor Amadeus Hoffmann (1776–1822), whose ghostly works are similar to Edgar Alan Poe's writings (1809–49). Other writers like Heinrich Heine (1797–1856) wrote anti-German and anti-Christian polemics before turning to mystical forms of Catholicism. Some of Heine's essays, such as his *The Romantic School,* are among the most powerful critiques of 19th-century culture to be found. Another representative of the times is Eduard Mörike (1804–75), who wrote warmhearted poems and moving prose.

The 19th century also saw the rise of the historical novel, which gained great popularity in Germany as the study of history became a science under the able guidance of scholars like Leopold von Ranke (1795–1886). Joseph Viktor von Scheffel (1826–86) and Konrad Ferdinand Meyer (1825–98) were masters of this style. Another development was the regional novel best represented by men like Jeremias Gotthelf (1797–1854) and Berthold Auerbach (1812–82), who immortalized the Black Forest region. Fritz Reuter (1810–74), Theodor Storm (1817–88), and Theodor Fontane (1819–98) also wrote in this style, often with a depressing melancholy inherited from Romanticism that portrayed the futility of middle-class life and ended in tragedy.

Two writers stand out in a class of their own. First is Wilhelm Busch (1832–1908), a humorist who is best known for his children's book *Max and Moritz* (1865) and later anticlerical satires like *Der Heilige Antonius (St. Anthony)*. Busch's work is generally admired.

The other immensely popular German writer is the controversial novelist Karl May (1842–1912), whose work is largely ignored by literary scholars and conspicuously absent in books about German literature. Nevertheless, May, who was a prolific writer of adventure novels, is Germany's all-time bestselling author and the hero of every German schoolboy even today.

Superficially an adventure writer, May also produced some profound works on inter-religious dialogue, showed great respect for non-Western cultures, and promoted multiracial marriages. A Roman Catholic by upbringing, May wrote from a broadly Christian perspective, similar to that of C. S. Lewis, in his early works. He seems to have moved away from Christianity after numerous vicious attacks upon his person and work by conservative Catholics and narrow-minded Protestants. Later his writings gave expression in popular form to the ideas of philosophers like Feuerbach (1804–72). May's classic novel about Native Americans, *Winnetou* (1892), was written from a Christian perspective and is available in English. His later works *Ardistan* and *Der Mir von Dschinnistan* (1907–8), which show a move away from Christianity under the influence of Feuerbach's philosophy, are also translated. Both books were published in English in 1977.

11. FASCIST AND ANTIFASCIST LITERATURE (20TH CENTURY)

For Germans, the 20th century has been an age of turmoil, revolutionary fervor, defeat, and disillusionment. The result has been the outpouring of numerous literary works by antifascists like Heinrich Böll (1917–85); Bertolt Brecht (1898–1956), famous for his *Threepenny Opera* (1928); and Thomas Mann (1875–1955), whose *Buddenbrooks* saga continues the 19th-century tradition of depressing melancholy and criticism of middle-class life.

Others, like Stefan George (1868–1933), Ernst Jünger (1895–1998), and

Hans Grimm (1875–1959), the author of *People Without Space* (1928–30), produced a heroic nihilism. The works of these men played a key role in popularizing National Socialism and fascist ideas. Their work shows the literary sophistication of fascism and its intellectual underpinnings, which most popular accounts tend to ignore.

On a more positive note, there were a number of outstanding Christian writers, many of whom were Roman Catholic or Catholic converts. Unfortunately, few of these writers, who produced moving works depicting the plight of the individual in a totalitarian state, had their works translated into English. An exception is Erich Maria Remarque (1898–1970), whose *All Quiet on the Western Front* (1929) is an antiwar classic.

GERMAN MUSIC

Leipzig is above all remembered as the city of Bach. But few Christians realize that Germany has a long musical tradition. Archaeological finds in Northern Germany show that a musical tradition existed among the pre-Christian Germanic tribes who played a wind instrument known as the luren. A number of splendidly crafted bronze instruments of this kind have now been discovered. The Roman historian Ammianus Marcellinus (330–90) says that when German slaves were brought to Rome, they carried with them wind instruments.

Songs and poetry dealing with the Roman Catholic practice of penance and healing are found in the *Ezzolied,* from 1060, which is named after a canon of Bamberg Dom. It describes the biblical story of the creation, fall, and redemption through Christ's atoning death, and urges the hearer to contemplate God's love and do penance. Another song cycle, the *Annolied,* dating from 1100, tells the story of Archbishop Anno II (1056–75) of Köln and his expulsion from the city in 1074.

Apart from these clearly religious songs, there are numerous medieval minstrels known to have created complex song cycles on secular and religious themes. Among them Walther von der Vogelweide (1160–1227), Hartmann von Aue (1127–1210), and Wolfram von Eschenbach (1170–1220) are remembered as particularly important musicians. Their songs told the story of courtly loves, knightly ideals, and religious devotion. In 1935, Carl Orff (1895–1982) set a number of 13th-century songs to music in his cantata *Carmina Burana.*

By 850 all Western churches, with the exception of those in Spain, accepted the use of one-voice chants. Only slowly did polyphonic, or multivoice singing, develop. By the time of Luther, the older choral tunes, which he loved, and newer prayer songs were in vogue. The *Lünenburgische Gesangbuch* (Lünenburg Songbook) of 1661 clearly distinguishes between the older chants and newer spiritual songs or hymns. Before the Reformation, the actual singing of hymns and chants was the work of choirs of monks, leaving the congregation mute spectators.

Martin Luther's courageous response at the Diet of Worms, "Here I stand, I can do no other," is well known. But few people know that Luther was a great lover of music and a talented musician in his own right. His sayings "Comforter Music" and "I have always been fond of music, singing does not have anything to do with the world" clearly state his attitude, as do the many hymns and tunes that he composed. Luther also insisted, as part of his reforms, that the congregation must once more participate in worship and the singing of spiritual songs. To this end, he composed numerous hymns, the best-known of which is "A Mighty Fortress Is Our God." Luther and his students also created the earliest German chorales, which were adapted from Gregorian chants to be sung in German as part of normal church services. This form of music was brought to perfection by Johann Sebastian Bach (1685–1750).

Following the Reformation there was an outpouring of Christian music in both Protestant and Roman Catholic parts of Germany. This revival of the musical tradition led to formal works composed for choirs and many new hymns written for congregational singing. Among the greatest of German hymnwriters are Philip Nicolai (1556–1601), Paul Gerhardt (1607–76), Paul Fleming (1609–40), Andreas Gryphius (1616–64), Johan Neander (1640–80), and Nikolaus von Zinzendorf (1700–1760).

The church organ came into its own after the Reformation. Known as the "queen of instruments," the organ gave artists and musicians the opportunity to express their skill in numerous ways. Composers such as Johann Walther (1496–1570), Hans Hassler (1564–1612), Michael Praetorius (1571–1621), Heinrich Schütz, the Swede (1585–1672), Dietrich Buxtehude (1637–1707), Handel's teacher F. W. Achau (1663–1712), Johann Sebastian Bach (1685–1750), and George Frideric Handel (1685–1759) all produced marvelous organ and other Christian works often strongly influenced by Pietism. This great tradition came to an end with the work of Johann Christian Bach (1735–82), who eventually settled in England as a composer at the court of George III.

Ludwig van Beethoven (1770–1827), who was born in Bonn, initiated a new phase in German music. Although Beethoven wrote some beautiful Christian works, the thrust of his work is secular and in keeping with the revolutionary times into which he was born. Franz Schubert (1797–1827) and Robert Schumann (1810–56) continued the drift away from Christian themes with their beautiful romantic works and interest in German folk songs. An exception to this secular trend was Felix Mendelssohn-Bartholdy (1809–47), who developed the new Romanticism in a Christian direction following his conversion from Judaism. His powerfully moving works *Paulus* and *Elijah* vividly bring alive God's call to obedience. But the future of German music lay with Richard Wagner (1813–83), whom many scholars see as the evil genius of 19th-century anti-Semitism. Together with his followers, Wagner created an intellectual ethos that gloried in Germanic paganism and despised biblical Christianity, even though his later works embrace a form of mystical Christianity.

It comes as no surprise, therefore, that in 1820 the English traveler Thomas Hodgekins could write, "Music is to the Germans what moral and political reasoning is to us—the great thing to which all the talents of the people are directed."

GERMAN ART

The earliest German paintings come from the time of Charlemagne (742–814), who, in addition to encouraging education, strongly supported the arts. To do this, he imported Byzantine and Italian artists to work on his numerous church building programs and to train local German artists. This flowering of artistic culture was centered on Charlemagne's main palace in Aachen. Unfortunately, only a few of the many church wall paintings created during this era of 8th-century creativity survive in places like the Trier church of St. Maximun. Illuminated manuscripts were also produced at the court of Charlemagne and his successors similar to those produced in England around the same time.

Following the decline of Charlemagne's dynasty, opportunities for the creation of German art seem to have waned. Only with the reign of Emperor Otto I (912–973) did an artistic revival take place in the late 10th century known to many historians as the "Ottonian Renaissance." Otto married a Byzantine princess, and like Charlemagne, he imported artists from Byzantium who created some great monastic works in places like Fulda, Köln, and Trier. Although similar to the earlier Carolingian style that emerged from the Court of Charlemagne, the new art was closer to what became known as the Gothic style with a heightened sense of spirituality and otherworldly dignity. The Ottonians also produced some wonderfully crafted illustrated manuscripts including the *Bamberg Apocalypse* and the *Trier Gospels*. Strangely enough, after the first outbursts of Ottonian art, the style of painting tended to lose its Gothic elements reverting to what we generally call the Romanesque. This style continued until the 12th century and saw the production of some outstanding frescoes and illuminated manuscripts.

An early form of what became known as Gothic art began to emerge in the 12th century under the influence of French artists. This is first seen in the flowing robes of men and women in stained glass windows and sculptures. Later it came to be seen in wall paintings and illuminated manuscripts. By the 14th century, the Gothic style was in full bloom, and the painting of wood panels replaced illuminated manuscripts, becoming the main means of artistic expression for painters. The earliest painted panels were made for devotional purposes as a part of church altars, but later they were used to decorate walls and became what today we would call a painting.

Painting on wood gradually led to the invention of the woodcut or print, which was originally used to make playing cards. Woodcuts were later used to illustrate printed books and pamphlets or to provide artists with a means of reproducing the same pattern at will.

By the 15th century the style sometimes known as "international Gothic" was firmly established. It represented an idealized image often reflecting great spirituality or some other virtue. With the development of Gothic went a fascination with nature and natural shapes, such as leaves and vines, which were used to ornament. One of the major centers for this mature style was Köln, where artists created devotional works. Few individual artists are known by name from this time. Instead, they are known, or recognized, by their work, which became their name. Consequently, art historians speak about "the Master of St. Veronica" who worked in Köln and "Master Bertram" who worked in Hamburg. By the 16th century Gothic art had developed a rich typology where each flower, each bird, and even the colors of the garments people wore all had their own meaning.

Around the end of the 15th century things started to change. Through his greater sense of realism and space, the Dutch artist Jan van Eyck (1390–1441) began to influence German painters. Once again, as a result of its location near the Netherlands, Köln became a center for the development of the new style. In places like Wittenberg and Augsburg, in east and south Germany, Italian influences mingled with those of the Dutch, resulting in the work of such great artists as Hans Baldung also called Grien (1484–1545), Lucas Cranach (1472–1553), Albrecht Altdorfer (1480–1538), and Albrecht Dürer (1471–1528). Of these, Cranach, who was a close personal friend of Martin Luther, was probably the most committed Christian artist in the Protestant tradition.

Although Lutherans continued to use and appreciate altar pieces, few new ones were produced in Protestant lands, and Calvinists positively rejected such art. Consequently, many popular writers on art, including a lot of travel books, claim that the Reformation curtailed the development of German art. What these writers overlook is the fact that, while many Protestants either rejected or did not greatly value church art, they gave secular painting a major impetus with the result that the production of landscapes and portrait painting developed at an unprecedented rate in Protestant lands. In reality, the greatest setback to the development of painting and art in general, following the Reformation, was the devastation caused by the Thirty Years' War, which raged from 1618–1648.

The Jesuit Church St. Michael was built in Renaissance style between 1583–1597. It prefigures the development of the Baroque that flowered, particularly in southern Germany, following the Peace of Westphalia in 1648. Baroque churches are a mass of light colors, painted walls, and decorated ceilings. After a while one may tire of winged cherubs and flying angels, but the Baroque gave painters endless opportunities to develop their talents, as the profusion of decorated rooms show in the Residenz, or the Bishop's Palace in Würzburg, designed by Balthasar Neumann (1687–1753). The playful Baroque gave way to the frivolous rococo, which some critics describe as "Baroque gone to seed," but which nevertheless has a charm of its own as can be seen in numerous Bavarian churches, stately homes, in parts of the Schloss Charlottenburg in Berlin, at the Sanssouci Palace Complex in Potsdam, or at the Zwinger in Dresden.

These peaceful styles gave way in the late 18th century to neoclassicism, which had already deeply influenced art and architecture in England and France. Inspired by the art and literature of ancient Greece and Rome, a new school of artists arose that produced some very beautiful works of art. Yet behind the beauty was an increased emphasis on heroic values and a warrior tradition, as the work of the great artist and architect Karl Friedrich Schinkel (1781–1841)

graphically shows. During the 19th century a school of "Nazarene" painters arose led by Friedrich Overbeck (1789–1869). They were inspired by the Christian work of Dürer and Raphael (1483–1520) and were similar to the British Pre-Raphaelite school. They particularly enjoyed frescoes like *The Story of Joseph,* which can be seen in Berlin.

Closely associated with the impulse that inspired both neoclassicism and the Nazarenes was the German Romantic movement led by men like Caspar David Friedrich (1774–1840). A superb collection of works by German Romantic painters is on show in the Gallery of the Romantic in Berlin. Like the Nazarenes, many Romantics appreciated Christianity and painted Christian themes. But their work also represented a flight from the emerging realities of industrial society, and in its later phase gives way to a general mysticism.

Realistic painting also made a comeback in the 19th century largely through the work of artists like Adolf von Menzel (1815–1905), who was a keen observer of daily life and painted some interesting factory scenes. By the end of the century and into the 20th century, realism developed a critical edge with artists like Käthe Kollwitz (1867–1945), whose antiwar cartoons and sculpture make her one of Germany's great prophetic artists. Expressionism and a whole range of artistic styles flourished in Germany during the 1920s only to be abruptly curtailed with the Nazi takeover in 1933. Before then, many leading modern artists lived and worked in Germany, including Paul Klee (1879–1940), who lived in Germany from 1898–1933, Vasily Kandinsky (1866–1944), who fled to Germany after the Russian Revolution in 1921, and Lyonel Feininger (1871–1956), who was born and died in New York but lived in Germany from 1887 to 1936. Some artists fled the Nazis; others simply lay low to emerge again in the ruins of post-war Germany as leaders of a new democratic and deeply secular culture that incorporated many elements of American pop art.

ARCHITECTURE STYLES
THE EARLIEST CHURCHES (TO 800)

Christians originally met in private homes or secret hiding places. Eventually, when Christianity became an accepted religion in the Roman Empire, Christians adapted the Roman basilica, or assembly hall, as their meeting place. From the 2nd century to the 6th century the basilica was the standard form of church building in Western Europe.

Separate from the main building there was usually a tower, as shown in Figure 1.

Later, during the Middle Ages, the simple style of the basilica formed a basis for the basic form of church buildings, as shown in Figure 2.

In 313, with the Edict of Milan, Emperor Constantine granted toleration and the protection of the state to Christianity. Following this development, the Roman Empire, which until then had sporadically persecuted Christians, gradually became Christian. Consequently, many formerly pagan buildings and places of worship were converted into

Figure 1

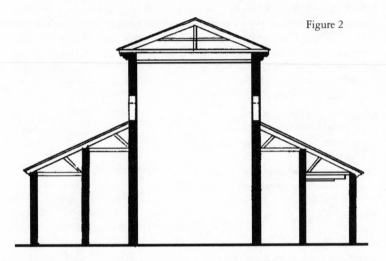

Figure 2

churches. One such architectural conversion was the Roman temple of the Pantheon in Rome.

The circular plan of the Pantheon and similar buildings provided Christian architects with the basic layout of many churches. Thus, the circular church became the basis of what was later to be known as the Byzantine style. This circular style became very popular throughout the Eastern Roman Empire, providing the basis for the ground plan of the Church of the Holy Sepulcher in Jerusalem and the greatest of all Byzantine churches, Hagia Sophia, in Constantinople. This pattern was adopted in Germany around 785, when Charlemagne (742–814) instructed his architects to construct the Dom (cathedral) in Aachen using a circular plan.

THE ROMANESQUE STYLE (9TH–13TH CENTURIES)

Strange as it may seem, the other great inspiration for the development of churches in northern Europe was the abundance of Roman ruins, such as the Colosseum in Rome, which inspired awe in all who saw its magnificent ruins. Thus for over a millennium, ancient Rome provided the inspiration and often the materials for Christian architects and builders. The basic designs were incorporated into church buildings to create what became known as the Romanesque style.

The Worms Dom is typical of what is called Romanesque. Notice the massive nature of the stonework, the rounded arches, and the few windows.

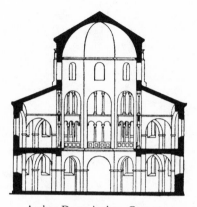

Aachen Dom, Aachen, Germany

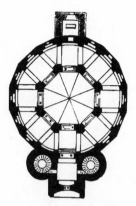

Floor plan of Aachen Dom

Romanesque churches have very thick walls reinforced by buttresses. Buttresses are specially thickened sections of wall which look like a smaller second wall. They are necessary to help carry the weight of the walls and roof. Although the Romans knew how to make concrete, the secret of this valuable aid to building was lost from the 4th century to the early 19th century.

Therefore, medieval builders had to rely on porous mortar and carefully placed stone slabs which interlocked with each other.

Most Romanesque churches were built to a cruciform plan. Normally the altar, or communion table, in such churches always faced east while the entrance, known as the West End, is at the other end of the church.

Worms Dom, Worms, Germany

Romanesque shapes for arches, doors, roofing, and windows were very distinctive. If you learn to recognize these shapes, you will soon know whether a church or part of a church is Romanesque. Below are several examples of typical Romanesque shapes.

THE GOTHIC STYLE (12TH–16TH CENTURIES)

"Gothic" was originally used as a term of contempt by the Italian art historian Giorgio Vasari (1511–74) for what he regarded as the "barbaric" nature of northern European architecture. By associating this style with the ancient Goths who had helped destroy ancient Rome, Vasari implied that it was unworthy of civilized people. Today, the Gothic style is regarded as one of the greatest architectural achievements of the Middle Ages and the high point of Christian civilization. The overall impression created by Gothic buildings is one of unbelievable lightness. The whole structure points to heaven and reminds the worshiper of God.

Flying buttresses are erected on the outside of the church building. These are the arches used to strengthen the upper walls of the nave. They deflect the weight of the roof from the nave walls to the outer walls, making it possible to build the walls both higher and thinner. Along the roof you will find gutters and open spouts that conduct rain water well away from the walls. These spouts are often decorated with animal figures and heads known as gargoyles.

Köln (Cologne) Dom, Köln, Germany

Several phases of the Gothic style can be distinguished: the Early, High, and Late, plus the Gothic revival of the late 18th and early 19th century. Gothic cathedrals were built over centuries; consequently, the styles often changed even within one building. When visiting a Gothic dom, look for the roof supports, which have veins like those of a fan. This is often very beautiful and a masterpiece of craftsmanship.

Gothic churches are recognizable by their pointed arches and windows. The following diagram provides some examples to help you recognize them.

Finally, below is the west front, or facade, of a typical Gothic cathedral or dom. Note the names of the key features.

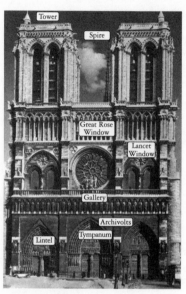

THE RENAISSANCE STYLE (14TH–17TH CENTURIES)

From the mid-14th century to the late 17th century, a style best described as Renaissance art and architecture developed in Italy and spread to the rest of Europe. The Renaissance style combines straight lines, corners, and curves in a far more sophisticated manner than the heavy solidity found in northern European buildings of the same period.

Like the Byzantine style, Renaissance churches tended toward circular or semi-circular floor plans. In Roman Catholic Renaissance churches, the style allowed the altar to be placed in the center of the church. In Protestant churches it allowed the pulpit to be placed prominently on one side, bringing the congregations closer to the preacher. Thus in both Roman Catholic and Protestant churches, this new style served a theological purpose.

Following the Reformation in the 16th century, Protestants failed to develop their own unique style of art and architecture. Rather, they adapted existing styles to their own needs, replacing the ritual of the Mass with an emphasis on preaching "the Word." Consequently, the number of altars were drastically reduced, often from over fifty to two or three in large churches. At the same time that the pulpit became the central feature, congregational worship replaced professional choirs of monks. The Reformers also removed the altar screens which separated the laypeople from the chancel. When visiting a German Protestant church, take a close look at the pulpit. It is often very impressive and a later addition to the original building.

THE BAROQUE STYLE (17TH–18TH CENTURIES)

For many years, Baroque was used as a term of contempt for what was thought to be a degenerate form of art. Such attitudes were changed by the Swiss art historian and critic Jacob Burckhardt (1818–97), who argued that contrary to popular opinion, particularly in Protestant northern Europe, Baroque was an important artistic movement and a legitimate development of the Renaissance style. In many ways, Baroque can be described as sophisticated Disney, because entering a Baroque church is like entering Disneyland. In fact, it is clear that Walt Disney borrowed many of his ideas for films like *Snow White* from Baroque artists.

The Baroque style proper was essentially found among Roman Catholics. Protestants, however, adopted the general layout and external appearance of Baroque churches without the elaborate decoration. The other major change was the adaptation of the ground plan of Baroque churches for preaching purposes.

Baroque churches are intended to symbolize the Holy Trinity and God's revelation of himself in the world. It is almost impossible to provide a cross-section of a typical Baroque church. Similarly, one cannot point to specific Baroque designs except to say that they involve twists and turns, cherubs and angels, in a profusion of colors. The Age of the Baroque coincided with both a revival of Roman Catholicism and Protestant Pietism and also with the flowering of a rich musical tradition that saw such outstanding composers as Johann Sebastian Bach (1685–1750) and George Frideric Handel (1685–1759).

Below is a picture of the great Protestant Baroque church, the Frauenkirche in Dresden, Germany. It was destroyed during a disastrous bombing raid during World War II, but is presently being reconstructed and is due to be reopened in 2002. Note the way the floor plan is adapted to the needs of a preacher.

NEOCLASSICISM AND NOSTALGIC NATIONALISM (18TH–20TH CENTURIES)

In his *A History of Architecture,* Sir Banister Fletcher points out that in Europe the neoclassical style of the 19th century, which was inspired by Greek temples, was closely connected with a growing nationalism and a form of neo-paganism.

The new master problem for late 18th-century and early 19th-century architects was the creation of civic pride and national consciousness through museums and cultural monuments. The rediscovery, even reinvention, of ancient Greek culture coincided with a decline in church construction in favor of secular buildings that proclaim the rise of humanity and national pride. Instead of creating great churches to the glory of God, aspiring architects were busy creating temples to man.

This transition is perhaps best seen in the work of one of Germany's greatest architects, Karl Schinkel (1781–1841). His National Museum is a masterpiece of the neoclassical style.

Neoclassicism was also adapted into monuments of military glory and national

Frauenkirche, Dresden, Germany

Floor plan of Frauenkirche

41

National Museum, Berlin, Germany

pride. The Greek influence and neopagan themes—as seen in Carl Gotthard Langhans's Brandenburger Tor (1788–91)—were directly inspired by the Acropolis in Athens.

Johann Gottfried Schadow's (1764–1850) bronze statue of Quadriga sits on top of the gate. It was added two years after the construction of the gate, in 1793, and depicts an ancient war chariot drawn by four horses. In it Victoria, the goddess of victory, triumphantly carries a staff tipped by a wreath of oak and a Prussian eagle. After the defeat of Napoleon in 1814, an Iron Cross was placed within the oak wreath. Originally, following Greek convention, the goddess was nude. But this outraged public opinion and the sculptor was forced to clothe her in a robe of copper. Here it is impor-

Brandenburger Tor, Berlin, Germany

The Returning Warrior, Rüdesheim, Germany

tant to recognize that the implicit militarism of the new style was not a German invention. If anything, it was far more developed in France and England than Germany and came to Italy even later.

Pagan mythology inspired many public monuments throughout the late 18th and 19th century, usually depicting gods and goddesses of war and victory such as Johann Schilling's (1828–1910) *The Returning Warrior.*

Statue of Quadriga

Heinrich Heine, a German-Jewish poet and Christian convert who lived most of his adult life in France, looked upon this new art form with growing apprehension. He feared the return of an old, yet new, paganism that would glorify war and scorn Christianity. The relief seen above reflects Heine's concerns and the essence of late neoclassicalism. In 1834, Heine aptly summed up the times when he wrote:

> ... philosophy is a serious affair, which concerns all mankind. . . . These doctrines have developed revolutionary forces which only await the day to break forth and fill the world with terror and astonishment ... the philosopher of Nature will be terrible because it will appear in alliance with the primitive powers of Nature, able to evoke the demonic energies of the old Germanic Pantheism. . . . It is the fairest merit of Christianity that it somewhat mitigated that brutal paganism. And should that subduing talisman the Cross, break, then will come crashing and roaring forth the wild

43

madness of the old champions, the insane Berserker rage, of which Northern poets say and sing. . . . The old stone gods will rise from long forgotten ruin, and rub the dust of a thousand years out of their eyes, and Thor, leaping to life with his giant hammer, will crush the Gothic Doms. . . .

Today these words sound more like a prophecy than anything else.

HOW TO ENJOY YOUR VISIT TO A GERMAN CHURCH

Visiting German churches can be quite confusing for anyone used to thinking about a church as somewhere to hear a sermon and meet fellow Christians. Even guidebooks are often not very helpful because they are full of unfamiliar terms like *chancel, sanctuary,* and *transept*. Unless you grew up in Europe, you will probably be overwhelmed with this mass of information and seemingly endless detail. So to make things easy, we have provided a brief introduction to the layout of a typical church and cathedral.

Here is the layout of a typical parish church:

The structure of this church is familiar to most people. There is a **tower** and **main doorway,** or **narthex,** a baptismal area represented by the **font,** the main body of the church known as the **nave,** and a place for the communion table, or **altar,** known as the **chancel**. Finally there is a **crypt,** or underground chapel used for burying people. Although this structure looks familiar, the way it was understood by medieval people is far from familiar.

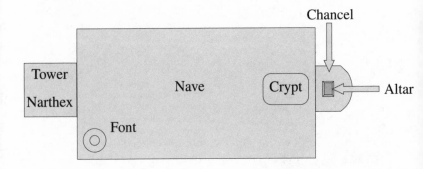

Now let us examine a more advanced and complex design:

To the basic church design, transepts have been added, the tower has been moved, and the narthex is also called the **porch.** There are also two altars plus an **altar screen,** which separates the nave from the chancel, where the choir is now located. The screen also separated lay-people from the monks and priests who sang in the choir. The **vestry** was a small room used by the priest to change from his ordinary clothing into the special church clothing, or vestments, used during the service. The color and design of his vestments would change during the year to visibly indicate what part of Christ's life was to be remembered.

Now we must look at the most developed version of a church, which would be found in a cathedral (in German, called a *Dom*). It is important to remember that in medieval churches the altar, not the pulpit, was the focus of worship. The congregation were separated from the high altar by a screen and could not even see what was happening. Most people stood in the nave or aisles,

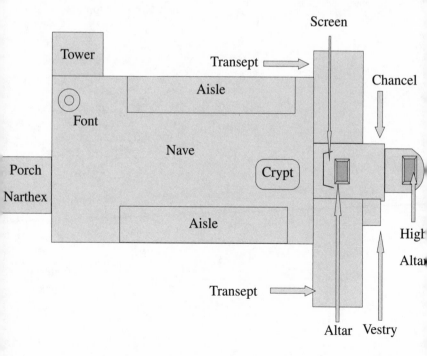

often conducting daily business or exchanging gossip while the priests performed the Mass. Pews were not added until after the Reformation, when people sat to hear the preaching of the Word.

Here is the layout of a typical cathedral church:

Now let us go through these various areas in turn. First the worshiper entered the church through a doorway with a porch or **narthex**. In Roman basilicas, the narthex was a long porch at the west end of the church. It was the place where women, people awaiting baptism, or those who were under some form of discipline waited before being allowed into the church itself. Symbolically the narthex was associated with the cleansing waters of baptism and the womb where the child waits before its birth.

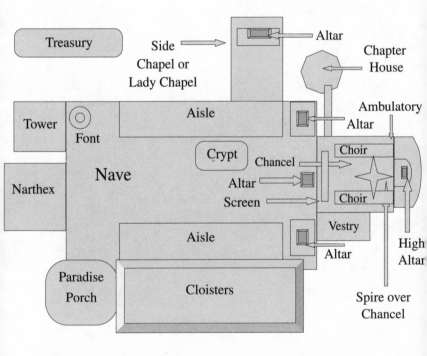

In some churches there is also a **paradise porch**. It is so named because it was decorated with sculptures and frescoes, or wall paintings, of the Garden of Eden. It often contained a fountain where unbaptized people and sinners could wash themselves before entering the church.

Beyond the narthex one enters the **nave**. This is the main body of the church and is the Latin word for "ship." It represents the ship of salvation, Noah's Ark, and the invisible church of Christ to which all saved souls belong and where humans are protected from the storms of life and material temptations. The nave was both a place of worship and general meeting place. Not until after the Reformation were seats added. Before then everyone had to stand, and people often wandered around selling food and other goods in winter.

In large churches there may be more than one nave and most have **aisles**, which are separated from the nave by pillars.

Near the nave is a **baptismal font**. Originally these were wide, low stone basins where new converts stood while water was poured over them. Later, as the general population became Christian, fonts were smaller, raised vessels suitable for baptism.

Near the font and the narthex there is often at least one, sometimes two **towers**. These functioned both as landmarks and watchtowers in isolated villages. Bells were added to call people to worship and warn of danger.

At the end of the nave was an **altar**, where the death of Christ was ritually reenacted with each service.

There are other **side altars**. Until the 10th century, worshipers partook in communion before the altar where they received both bread and wine. Later they received only bread. Originally this change seems to have come about to prevent drunkenness, but later it gained theological importance as only priests were allowed to receive communion in both kinds, bread and wine.

Beyond the altar was a **screen**, which prevented ordinary people from entering the chancel.

The **chancel** is where the choir, which consisted of men only, was located. The **choir stalls** are often richly decorated with wood carvings.

Beyond the chancel was the **high altar**, where the most solemn Masses were performed. In medieval churches the celebration of the Mass was the central event.

Near the altar or even the high altar is the **crypt**. Originally crypts were underground chambers where Christians met for worship in secret and where they buried their dead. Crypts are often the earliest part of a church building.

The **vestry** is the small room where priests changed from their normal garb into ecclesiastical robes, which were selected on the basis of their color depending on the season in the church year.

Many large churches have a walkway leading behind the choir, chancel, and the high altar. This is known as the **ambulatory** and was used, particularly in pilgrimage churches, to allow worshipers to file past relics.

The **Lady Chapel**, which is often located behind the high altar, was devoted to the Virgin Mary. It was often the most important side altar in a church and usually survived after the Reformation, when many altars were removed from churches

To one side of large churches, usually the south side, one finds the **cloisters**. This is an enclosed rectangle with a high outside wall and roof, often with very beautiful stonework and ceiling vaulting, surrounding an open garden, usually a grassy lawn, that is enclosed by a low wall and pillars. Here monks and other clergy could walk in bad weather, reciting the Scriptures or praying. In time cloisters became more elaborate and served both as a general meeting place for monks and a place where copyists transcribed the Scriptures or wrote sacred theological treatises.

Above the chancel it became the practice to build a tall church **spire**. The spire served as a local landmark and replaced, or at least supplemented, church towers.

Cathedrals and doms also have a **chapter house**, which is the meeting place of clergy during synods and other important functions. Here the business of a dioscese was discussed.

Finally, don't miss the **treasury**. In some churches, like Aachen Dom, the treasury is housed in a separate building. In others, like Bamberg Dom, it adjoins the church itself. Here the treasures of the church are kept, such as ancient crosses, Scriptures, rare books, relics, and vestments.

Part 3

CHRISTIAN HERITAGE SITES IN GERMANY

TOP 10 CHRISTIAN SITES IN GERMANY

1. **TRIER:** Once, for a short time, the capital of the Roman Empire, this city has some of the oldest Christian sites in Germany, including a magnificent 4th-century basilica church.

2. **AUGSBURG:** Another ancient Roman town where Christianity originated in German-speaking lands and later the site of the Augsburg Confession.

3. **FULDA:** The main missionary base for St. Boniface, who evangelized Germany and the Netherlands in the 7th century.

4. **KÖLN:** Apart from its magnificent Gothic cathedral, there are a remarkable number of excellent medieval churches that provide vivid insights into pre-Reformation Christianity. Here you can see every major architectural style including Romanesque, Gothic, and Baroque churches, all within easy walking distance of each other.

5. **WITTENBERG:** The site of Martin Luther's Reformation where there are many historical items, including rare printed books.

6. **MÜNSTER:** The capital of German Anabaptism and scene of a gruesome revolt that was savagely suppressed in the 16th century.

7. **MARBURG AN DER LAHN:** Here one finds the world's first Protestant university, Germany's earliest Gothic church, and a beautiful medieval old town.

8. **HALLE:** Where German Pietism, which is closely related to Methodism, developed in the 17th century.

9. **BAMBERG:** Wonderful medieval town with an important Romanesque cathedral modified by Gothic features. From Bamberg one can also visit Lichtenfels and the Vierzehnheiligen pilgrimage church, one of Germany's most important Baroque churches.

10. **BERLIN:** Germany's capital city. It houses some of the world's best

archaeological museums that are rich in biblical materials. The city is equally rich in terms of both the Enlightenment and modern Christian history.

SITES FROM THE LIFE OF MARTIN LUTHER

Germany, particularly former East Germany, is full of Luther monuments and places where he preached, slept, or ate a meal. Therefore, to help you plan a "Luther tour," we have listed some of the main places, in chronological order, that are well worth visiting.

LUTHERSTADT-EISLEBEN: Here you can visit the house where Luther was born on November 10, 1483, as well as the house where he died on February 18, 1546.

EISENACH is where Luther lived as a young student. Later, from May 4, 1521–March 6, 1522, he took refuge in the nearby Wartburg Castle disguised as Junker Jörg, gentleman Jörg. During his stay in the Wartburg, he translated the New Testament into German.

ERFURT is where Luther was a university student from 1507 to 1511.

DRESDEN was visited by Luther in 1516 and 1518 when his teachings were welcomed. Later the local ruler turned against Luther and banned his books.

WITTENBERG is the birthplace of the Reformation, where Luther posted his 95 Theses on November 1, 1517.

WÜRZBURG: Martin Luther was a guest at the Augustinian Monastery here in 1518. In the palaces of the prince bishop, one sees something of the pomp of Roman Catholic clerics, against which Luther revolted.

COBURG is where Luther preached in 1518; later, in 1530, he preached here again before taking refuge from Imperial troops in Coburg Castle.

WEIMAR: Martin Luther stopped at Weimar during his travels in 1518 and 1521. Later he visited again, giving sermons in the ducal palace and in the St. Peter and St. Paul Church.

LEIPZIG is where Luther debated John Eck (1486–1543) between June 27 and July 16, 1519. The result of this debate led to the papal ban of June 15, 1520.

WORMS was the scene of the famous Diet, or Council, where Luther defended his views before the Emperor Charles V (1500–1558) on April 17 and 18, 1521.

JENA: Here in the Stadtkirche St. Michael, the Parish Church of St. Michael, you can view Luther's original tombstone, which was brought here when Catholic armies threatened Wittenberg during the Thirty Years' War.

If you have limited time, the most important Luther towns are Eisleben, Wittenberg, and Eisenach. If you have time to visit all of these Luther towns we suggest the following order based on their geographic location: Eisleben, Wittenberg, Leipzig, Dresden, Jena, Weimar, Erfurt, Coburg, Würzburg, Eisenach, and Worms.

KEY TO THE TEXTS

All entries in the Christian Travelers Guides are written according to the following outline.

The name of each place is given in alphabetical order. Places are listed according to the local spelling, followed by the English spelling if needed, e.g., **München (Munich)**.

Background: A short history of the area explains its religious, cultural, and intellectual significance.

Places to visit: Individual sites are mentioned with recommendations about things that deserve close attention. Different places are identified in **bold**.

Throughout the text we have given people's names using the German spelling because when you look for a tomb, or at an inscription, what you will see is the German spelling. The main exceptions to this usage are the names of **Karl der Große** (Karl the Great), who is generally know as **Charlemagne,** and **Bonifatius,** whose English name is St. **Boniface**. In German there is always a full stop after Roman numerals, as in Friedrich II. But this causes some confusion in an English sentence so we have omitted it for the sake of clarity. Most dates are A.D. and are given as a plain number, e.g., 800. Only when there might be some doubt about the exact time are B.C. or A.D. used.

Finally, throughout the text we follow modern German usage by referring to the former Communist State of East Germany, the Deutsche Demokratische Republik (DDR), as the DDR.

MAP OF KEY CHRISTIAN
HERITAGE SITES IN GERMANY

Baltic Sea

Netherlands

Poland

Hamburg

Rostock

Stendal
Tangermünde
Jerichow
Wolfenbüttel
Berlin
Potsdam Frankfurt/Oder
Magdeburg
Wittenberg
Quedlinburg
Eisleben Halle
Osnabrück
Münster
Xanten Externsteine
Essen Paderborn
Leipzig
Naumburg
Dresden
Bautzen
Köln
Eisenach
Erfurt Weimar Jena
Herrnhut
Aachen
Bonn Marburg
Maria-Laach
Zittau
Fulda
Bingen
Mainz Frankfurt am Main
Coburg
Lichtenfels
Bamberg
Trier Worms
Würzburg Erlangen
Heidelberg Rothenburg o.d. Tauber Nürnberg
Maulbronn Marbach
Speyer
Eichstätt Regensburg
Tübingen Ingolstadt
Augsburg
Ulm
Altötting
Freiburg
München
Oberammergau
Berchtesgaden

Belgium

Luxembourg

France

Czech Republic

Switzerland

Austria

AACHEN

Few places rank beside Aachen in the history of Christian Europe. Here 32 Holy Roman kings and queens were crowned. Here too a cultural and educational revolution began in the 8th century which saved Europe from barbarism. No wonder that today the annual Charlemagne prize is awarded in the Rathaus (town hall) to the person deemed to have made the greatest contribution to European unity.

Aachen is a city rich in history, symbolism, and treasures. Known to the Romans as Aquis Granum, after the Celtic god of grain, Granus, it was later named Bad Aachen after its famed hot springs, which once attracted Roman legions. The town was also called Aix-la-Chapelle because of its famous cathedral. Medieval Aachen was founded by the Frankish king Pippin III, the Short (715–58), who enjoyed the healing waters of the hot springs. During the reign of his son Karl the Great, better known as Charlemagne (742–814), Aachen became the center of his newly restored Holy Roman Empire.

Fortunately, Lewis Thorpe has published an excellent translation of the earliest accounts of Charlemagne's life by two priests, Einhard (770–840) and Notker the Stammerer (840–912), a monk from the Swiss monastary of St. Gall or Gallen. The stories found in *Two Lives of Charlemagne* (1969) provide us with vivid insights into the rebirth of

CHARLEMAGNE (742–814) was king of the Franks, a Germanic tribe of the Rhine region, and the first Holy Roman Emperor. His conquests greatly extended his kingdom, stemming the spread of Islam, and reducing Viking raids into Europe. He is remembered for the enlightened reforms, revival of learning, and extensive building program by which he began the slow restoration of Europe after centuries of chaos and barbarism.

HOLY ROMAN EMPIRE. A complex but remarkably loose and flexible political organization tracing its origins to the coronation of Charlemagne in 800. It was formalized with the coronation of Otto I in 962 and united Western Europe along the lines of the Western Roman Empire. Its rulers claimed to be the legitimate successors of Rome's ancient rulers. It was finally abolished as a political entity by Napoleon Bonaparte in 1806.

European civilization after the devastation following the destruction of the Western Empire in the 6th century.

For centuries Aachen was looked upon as "the Rome of the North" and was one of the richest cities for relics in Europe. Thus Aachen became a holy city and center of pilgrimage where people flocked to visit Charlemagne's tomb and such alleged wonders as the swaddling clothes of Jesus, St. John the Baptist's leather belt, and a gown worn by Mary, the mother of Jesus.

Places to Visit

Aachen Dom (Aachen Cathedral) was built in 790–800 as Charlemagne's palace chapel. The original church, designed in Byzantine style by the architect Odo of Metz (8th century), is an octagonal structure with a vast domed roof richly decorated with mosaics and a first-floor gallery. The design of this church reflects that of Imperial Roman churches, symbolizing the continuity between Charlemagne and the Christian emperors of the late Roman period.

According to legend, the CHAPEL was consecrated on the feast of the Epiphany, January 6, 805, by Pope Leo III (750–816), who dedicated it to Christ the Redeemer and his mother, Mary. Built onto the original structure is the Gothic choir constructed between 1355 and 1414. These central areas are surrounded by various smaller chapels. These are all rich in art and history.

After its consecration the dom took another thousand years to complete.

The Carolingian high altar, "The Pala d'oro," dating from 1020, is decorated with scenes of Christ's Passion and majesty. Behind it is a richly decorated shrine, built 1182–1215, containing a reliquary, with the bones of Charlemagne, who was canonized in 1165.

You can only visit the gallery by joining a tour. On the balcony you see the throne of Charlemagne, which was used in the coronation of 30 German kings between 936 and 1531. It is made from white marble said to have been quarried in the Holy Land. The marble of the throne turned yellow from contamination while in storage during World War II. From this level you can look down on the visitors below just as the king surveyed his subjects.

If you look up, above you are huge mosaics, restored in the 19th century, depicting chapter 5 from the book of Revelation with God and his angels looking down upon the king. Below this magnificent scene are mosaics of Mary, John the Baptist, and other biblical figures plus Charlemagne kneeling with a model of his Dom, and Pope Leo III, who is also kneeling. These latter figures were added in 1901 by the artist Hermann Schaper (b. 1880).

In the central mosaic we have a wonderful example of the way the Bible has influenced Western political thought. Just as David was judged by Nathan for his adultery with Bathsheba and his role in her husband's death (2 Samuel), so too the king sits under the judgment of God. The mosaics are explicitly intended to remind the monarchs that while they may judge their subjects, their own deeds are judged by God. No one, not even kings or presidents, is above the Law of God.

The dom TREASURY is the richest in northern Europe. It is located across a narrow alley within the Dom grounds. Here you will find the magnificent gold cross of King Lothar (1075–1135) dated from shortly after the year one thousand. Notice its centerpiece, a fine Roman cameo of the Emperor Augustus, during whose reign Christ was born. Nearby is a marble Roman sarcophagus, of pagan origin, dating from the 2nd century. It was used to store the bones of Charlemagne for almost four hundred years.

Most stunning of all is the imposing bust of Charlemagne in silver and gold which was created for Karl IV (1316–78) in 1350 and presented to him at his coronation along with his crown, thus emphasizing the importance of continuity and tradition in European views of kingship. Another important item in the treasury is a blue velvet chasuble, a vestment which belonged to Bernard of Clairvaux (1090–1153), who made a pilgrimage to Aachen in 1147.

MARKTPLATZ contains the Rathaus (Town Hall), which was built in 1349 on the site of Charlemagne's palace. Almost completely destroyed in World War II, along with 80 percent of the city, the Rathaus was reconstructed following the war. Outside you see a carving of Charlemagne and Pope Leo kneeling before Christ. Inside, in the Council Chamber, are five surviving frescoes out of eight depicting scenes from Charlemagne's life. The Rathaus also houses copies of Charlemagne's crown jewels; the originals were taken to Paderborn and later to Vienna during the ravages of the French Revolution. The Nazis took them to the island of Norderney, but after the end of the war they were returned to Vienna, where they have remained until today. There are also some valuable copies of the Gospels, weapons, and various other items of interest.

INTERNATIONALES ZEITUNGSMUSEUM (International Museum of Journalism), Marktplatz 13, contains a wonderful collection of over 120,000 newspapers, including many Christian and Jewish ones. Not far away, at 117 Pontstrasse, you can see the house where Paul Julius Reuter (1816–99), a Jewish convert to Christianity, founded Reuter's News Agency.

ALTÖTTING

The first documented mention of Altötting is in 748. There are two explanations for the origin of the name: Ötting, or Otinga, was the Carolingian king's place in the Palatinate in 788. Perhaps the town of Altötting (old Ötting) grew around this palace. The other suggestion is that Altötting derives from the name of an old clock with the picture of a scythe-swinging "Tod von Edling" (Death of Edling) and that the name "Edling" changed over the years to Ötting.

Whatever the origin of the name, this is one of the oldest pilgrimage centers in Bavaria, dating from the 15th century. More than half a million pilgrims yearly visit the **HEILIGE KAPELLE** (Holy Chapel), one of the oldest churches in Germany, to revere its famed *Black Madonna*.

In an arcade surrounding the chapel, hundreds of crutches, wheelchairs, pictures of accidents, letters, prayer petitions, and pious figurines have been left behind by pilgrims who, over the centuries, have claimed that they were miraculously cured by God when they prayed for healing in the chapel.

Two stories, or "wonders" as they are often called, are central to Altötting's fame. First, around 1489, a three-year-old boy is said to have fallen into a pond. Half an hour later he was pulled out of the water, dead. His mother took the child's body to the chapel and prayed before the Black Madonna. Friends and even visitors joined. The boy began to breathe and returned to life.

Later, in 1497, a farmer's son fell from his horse and was run over by a heavy wagon. He died from his severe injuries. The farmer made a vow and also prayed before Mary for divine intervention. The next day life returned to the boy and he was healed.

Today the stream of pilgrims flows uninterrupted. When Pope John Paul II, who is Polish, visited Altötting, he also

PALATINATE. Historically two areas of Germany were known as the Palatinate: the Lower Palatinate, which is roughly the same as the modern land, state, or province of Rhineland-Palatinate, and an area of northeast Bayern (Bavaria) surrounding Regensburg. They were traditionally ruled by the count of the Palatine, whose office goes back to Roman times.

ELECTORS are those princes, kings, and dukes who participated in the election of the Holy Roman Emperor who, by tradition, was crowned by the pope. The emperor was elected at Frankfurt am Main. Originally, all the princes of the empire took part in the election. But, over time, the number of electors was reduced to seven. But there was no agreement about who had the right to hold this important office. Emperor Karl IV (1316–78) issued his Golden Bull in 1356 to regulate this procedure by confirming the archbishops of Mainz, Trier, and Köln as electors along with the king of Bohemia, the count of the Palatinate, the duke of Saxony, and the margrave of Brandenburg. So important was this office that the secular rulers were eventually known as "elector" in preference to their other title.

knelt before the Madonna and asked God to "look after the future of the believers in this old Christian country, bear in mind the terrible distress of the last war, which inflicted, in particular on the people of Europe, deep scars ... look after the peace of the world." Two popes have visited Altötting: Pius VI in April 1782 and John Paul II in November 1980. From March to August 15, the feast day of the Ascension of Mary, the many pilgrims in Altötting give an impressive testimony of deep religiousness.

PLACES TO VISIT

KAPELLPLATZ (Chapel Square) is the beautifully maintained town square with many historic buildings and churches.

HEILIGE KAPELLE (Holy Chapel) or GNADENKAPELLE (Chapel of Grace) was built in the time of Charlemagne to an octagonal plan which resembles Aachen Dom. It was possibly a baptismal chapel

for a royal palace. Today the chapel is the center for pilgrimage.

At the high altar is the famed Black Madonna. The statue was carved from white linden wood, also known as basswood, and gets the name "black" from the fact that it was blackened by the smoke of millions of candles, which for centuries were placed in front of it when people prayed. In the 17th century the Madonna was placed in a richly ornamented glass case for protection.

Opposite the altar stand several urns containing the hearts of six Bavarian kings, two queens, two electors, and General Johann Tserclaes Tilly (1559–1632), who commanded the Catholic league in the Thirty Years' War. Behind this practice lies the belief that by burying their hearts in the chapel they are offering them to God.

STIFTSKIRCHE (Parish Church) is a wonderful Late Gothic church, built 1499–1511, to accommodate the growing number of pilgrims. It remained the site of the final services held after the completion of a pilgrimage until 1912, when a new neo-Baroque church, ST. ANNA-KIRCHE (St. Ann's Church), capable of holding 8,000 people, was opened.

In the crypt of the Stiftskirche's Tillykapelle (Tilly Chapel), you can gaze on the face and stare into the eyes of Tilly as he lies in his coffin. This unnerving experience makes one wonder about the motivations of this man who, educated by the Jesuits, lived the life of a monk and served as a soldier in the Roman Catholic cause.

A hero of the Catholic Counter-Reformation, Tilly was the devil incarnate to many Protestants who blamed him for the sack of Magdeburg (May 20–23, 1631), where at least thirty thousand people died. Although there is doubt about Tilly's role in this atrocity, there is no doubt that he ordered the garrison and male population of New Brandenburg to be put to the sword after storming the city (March 13, 1631). These acts make many wonder how faith can be combined with such barbarism. Protestants do well to remember that Roman Catholics ask the same question about the great English Puritan leader Oliver Cromwell's (1599–1658) actions in Ireland where he too executed the garrison of Drogheda.

Although Tilly originally saved Catholic armies from defeat by Protestants and reconquered much of Germany, he was beaten by Gustavus Adolphus (1594–

1632) and the Protestant Union at the battle of Breitenfeld near Leipzig (September 17, 1631). A few months later he met Adolphus again and was mortally wounded in a battle near Augsburg and Donauwörth. He died in Ingolsadt on April 17, 1632.

SCHATZKAMMER (Treasury) has many exquisite exhibits including a 1580 ivory crucifix of Flemish design, and the French Goldene Rößl (Golden Horse), a masterpiece of gold, silver, ebony, and jewels. It depicts the French king Karl VI, the Insane (1368–1422), kneeling before the Virgin Mary with his favorite horse close by.

ST. MAGDALENA KIRCHE (St. Magdalene's Church) is the only Baroque church in Altötting. Built in 1697, it is part of the local Jesuit theological college. The church has a magnificent pulpit with Italian stucco decorations.

In front of the ST. KONRAD-KIRCHE (St. Konrad's Church) is a water fountain where pilgrims drink the water and wash their eyes in an act of devotion. In the church itself, you can see the remains of Konrad of Parzham, a Capuchin, the gatekeeper at St. Anna-Kloster (Cloister of St. Anna) for 41 years. He was canonized by the pope in 1934.

WALLFAHRT-UND HEIMATMUSEUM (Pilgrimage and Local History Museum) contains a fascinating exhibition depicting the history of the pilgrimage to Altötting.

AUGSBURG

In 15 B.C., the Romans conquered the northern foothills of the Alps to the Danube, founding the military colony of Augusta Vindelicorum, modern Augsburg, named after their emperor and a local Celtic tribe. It served as a trading hub on the road via Claudia to Italy. After the fall of the Western Empire in 476, Augsburg became an Episcopal See. Under Bishop Ulrich (8th century), the city was fortified as an outpost against Hungarian invasions. The DOM ST. MARIA (Cathedral of St. Mary) is first mentioned in 10th-century documents and is the oldest church in the city.

In 1276, the city statutes gave the citizens a voice in the council, and in 1316, Augsburg became a Freistadt (free city), or autonomous city-state like Bremen, Hamburg, and Lübeck. Such cities were freed from feudal obligations except in respect to the emperor. After a further struggle against the bishop, the trades and merchants obtained their own guild constitution, giving them even more freedom. A prosperous Jewish community grew up in Augsburg that was protected by the city from the massacres associated with the First and Second Crusades. After the Black Death, Jews were slaughtered and expelled from the town until the beginning of the 19th century.

Consequently, many merchant families—the Paumgartners, Gossembrots, Welsers, and Fuggers—made the city the headquarters for their businesses. Jacob Fugger II (1489–1535) was a close friend of Emperor Maximilian I (r. 1493–1519). He used his wealth to help elect Karl V (1500–1558), who became the greatest of the Habsburgs and the most powerful ruler in Europe, the Holy Roman emperor (1516–56). All of these men were enthusiastic patrons of the arts, making Augsburg the leading Renaissance city in Germany.

In 1530, Karl V called a Diet (Parliament) in Augsburg to resolve the political, religious, and social problems created by the Reformation and minimize the discord which was sweeping German lands. The German princes, electors, and representatives of the free cities were all invited to attend and listen to one another "in love and unity" in order to arrive at Christian truth.

Because he had been declared a heretic, Martin Luther (1483–1546) was unable to attend the Diet. Instead he delegated his friend Philipp Melanchthon (1497–1560) to represent him. He was commissioned to present an expert opinion containing the essential beliefs of Protestants. Melanchthon wrote the final version, which was then forwarded to Luther for his comments and approval. The assembly resulted in the Peace of Augsburg and the Confessio Augustana (Augsburg Confession), which remains the Lutheran doctrinal standard. Luther prayed, "Christ our Lord, help the Augsburg Confession bear much and great fruit, as we hope and beg for. Amen."

The text of the Confession was read to the assembly, and Roman Catholic theologians prepared a refutation. But Melanchthon strove to reach a compromise. In his words: "We do not have dogma which deviates from the Church of Rome ... we are prepared willingly to obey the Church of Rome ... Moreover we revere the authority of the Roman pope and the entire leadership of the Church." But the papal legate, Lorenzo Campeggio (1472–1539), was uncompromising in his determination to refute Protestant beliefs which he labeled "false doctrine." The result was the Confutatio (Refutation), which was read to the representatives of the Free Cities, but not given to the Protestant theologians to allow a response. When the Protestants learned the contents of the Refutation, they said that it missed the point and did not refute their position.

Thus Karl V's valiant attempt to reach agreement failed. Nevertheless, he was able to use the assembly as a basis for the Peace of Augsburg (1555), which laid down the rule that each area was entitled to decide upon the religion of that area. This allowed bishops, cities, and princes to choose the religion which would be regarded as the state religion of their realms and secured Protestantism a secure and peaceful foothold in Germany until the outbreak of the Thirty Years' War almost 70 years later.

As a result of this war, Augsburg went into economic and political decline until the 19th century when the city faced bankruptcy. To avoid this fate, a group of Jewish bankers were invited to settle in Augsburg, but they failed and the city joined Bayern (Bavaria) in 1806. During the 19th century, the fortunes of the city improved, and Augsburg became a center for science and industry. Among the many inventions that brought a new prosperity was Rudolf Diesel's (1858–1913) combustion engine that was given its inventor's name, the diesel engine.

The Nazis began persecuting local Jews as early as 1924 when the cemetery was desecrated. Later, on Kristallnacht in 1938 (Night of Broken Glass), the synagogue was set on fire, causing extensive destruction. During World War II half of the city was destroyed by British bombing. After the war extensive rebuilding took place to restore the town's many ancient buildings.

The city crest shows a stylized pinecone which, in antiquity, was a sign of fertility. Augsburg is the birthplace of Bertolt Brecht (1898–1956) and the scene of his renowned play "Der Augsburger Kreidekreis" (The Augsburg Chalk Circle), which is also known as "Der kaukasische Kreidekreis" (Caucasian Chalk Circle), set in the Thirty Years' War.

PLACES TO VISIT

DOM OF ST. MARIA (St. Mary's Cathedral) was built in the 10th century on the spot of the first Roman settlement. This Romanesque and Gothic structure contains eleven chapels, seven of which are built outside the walls on the north side of the main altar. On the south of the altar is the stone Bischofsthron (Bishop's Throne), 11th century, which rests on two carved lions. South of the central nave are five stained-glass windows showing the prophets Jonah, Daniel, Hosea, Moses, and David. These are the earliest examples of stained-glass church windows in Europe.

In the south transept is a 15-meter tall painting of Saint Christopher dated 1491. There are also altar paintings by Hans Holbein the Elder (1465–1524) dated around 1493 which depict the life of Mary.

Opposite the Dom is the **Fronhof**, originally the bishop's palace, but now a government building. Here the Augsburg Confession was first presented by Melanchthon.

ST.-ANNA-KIRCHE (St. Anna's Church) is an unimposing church which contains an impressive marble sculpture *The Lamentations of Christ*. It is the oldest Renaissance building in Germany. The attached Fugger-Grabkapelle (Chapel of Fugger Graves) was donated in 1518 by Jacob and Ulrich Fugger. Albrecht Dürer designed the reliefs on the graves of the two brothers. In 1518, when Martin Luther was summoned to appear before the papal legate, he found temporary refuge here among the chapel's Carmelite monks. The LUTHERSTIEGE (Luther Museum), housed in the old monastery, contains the room where Luther lived and a rich collection of materials about the Reformation.

MÜNSTER ST. ULRICH UND ST. AFRA (Minster of St. Ulrich and St. Afra) is a former Benedictine abbey church built in 1500 on the site of an earlier church. According to legend, during the persecution of Christians by the Roman emperor Diocletian, a daughter of the king of Cyprus, Afra, had a dream in which she became the queen of Augsburg. Obedient to this omen, she moved to the city along with her mother and three other women, and they established a brothel. Some time later, the bishop of Gerona was forced into hiding and fled to Augsburg where, by mistake, he took up lodgings in the house of ill repute. One night Afra overheard the godly man's prayers. His strong faith caused her to repent and she became a Christian. Shortly afterwards she too became a victim of Diocletian and was burnt at the stake. Her mother, who was subsequently converted, built the first chapel in her honor.

An interesting aspect of this church is the fact that it adjoins a Protestant church of the same name. Such twin churches are common in Augsburg, where they demonstrate a genuine desire by the people to live in peace.

AUGSBURG SYNAGOGUE, Wintergasse, was originally built in 1858. A new building was consecrated in 1917 in the elaborate Art Nouveau style. After the fire of 1938, it fell into ruin but was restored in 1985 to create a very impressive building that is well worth visiting because it is the only surviving Art Nouveau synagogue in Germany. The style is a combination of Byzantine and Turkish elements with vivid colors and intricate artwork. There is also an excellent museum of Jewish history inside the main building.

B

FUGGEREI (Fugger Quarter) is the name of an area created by Jacob Fugger as an act of Christian charity to house the poor of the city. Modern cynics, of course, question his motives, but the reality of his deed speaks for itself. In addition to providing housing, he also left behind an endowment for the maintenance of the buildings and care of the people which still provides income today. This is a remarkable example of the way piety can provide for the well-being of generations. FUGGEREIMUSEUM (Fugger Quarter Museum) provides visitors with vivid insight into the development of this remarkable project over the centuries.

MOZARTHAUS (Mozart House) was the home of Leopold Mozart (1719–87), the composer's father. Although his son Wolfgang Amadeus Mozart (1756–91) wrote some fine church music, his work represents a turning from the Christian tradition of Johann Sebastian Bach (1685–1750) toward a new heroic art which culminates in Richard Wagner's (1813–83) aggressive paganism.

STAATSGALERIE IN DER KUNSTHALLE (State Art Gallery) contains further examples of the drift from a predominant Christian to the modern secular culture. Here you will find a fine collection of modern art, including Paul Klee's (1879–1940) *Dance of the Sad Child*.

NEUSCHWANSTEIN, near Fussen, makes a pleasant day trip from Augsburg. This neo-Baroque palace is the original Disneyland castle and therefore worth a visit by anyone who loves fantasy. It was built between 1869 and 1886 for King Ludwig II of Bavaria (1846–86), who was inspired by the operas of his friend Wagner. Theater designers, who deliberately mixed and matched styles to create the ultimate Romantic fantasy for their king, built the castle at great expense, almost bankrupting Bavaria. Ludwig was declared mad by doctors and deposed by his cabinet. Shortly afterwards, on June 13, 1886, he was found dead under mysterious circumstances. Apart from its connection to Wagner's neopaganism, the castle has little or no religious significance.

BAMBERG

B uilt on seven hills, Bamberg has often been called "the Rome of the North" and is a United Nations World Heritage Site. Scarcely scathed by World War II, Bamberg is rich in medieval and Baroque architecture, including many half-timbered houses which give it a fairy-tale character.

Founded in the 2nd century A.D. on a small island in the river Regnitz, the town divides into the western bishop's town and eastern burger's town.

Bamberg became a bishopric in 1007, when the Emperor Heinrich II (973–1024), who is the only German emperor to have been canonized, made it into an imperial residence and center for the evangelization of eastern Europe. Numerous crusading parties left from Bamberg to fight against Moslem invaders in lands to the south and east, including Hungary and Austria, as well as the better-known crusades in the Holy Land.

Dominating the town from its highest hill is the Dom (cathedral), built 1215–37, a magnificent example of German Romanesque architecture with Gothic and even Baroque additions. Restored in 1828–37, and again in 1969–74, the interior of the Dom is extraordinarily rich in Christian art. The exterior is a splendid sight with four imposing towers and exquisitely carved doorways.

PLACES TO VISIT

THE DOM is one of the great cathedrals of Europe. Built during the 13th century after fires destroyed two earlier buildings, today's dom contains both Romanesque and Gothic elements and is rich in sculptures and history.

Like Rhineland's imperial cathedrals, the dom has choirs at each end of the nave. The east chancel is dedicated to Saint George, the west chancel to Saint Peter. The symbolism here is of a pious knight, who represents the Holy Roman Empire, and the apostle Peter, who represents the papacy, because Roman Catholics believe Peter was the first pope and that all subsequent popes are his successors. This claim was disputed during the Reformation and is still not accepted by many Protestant historians. Thus the Dom's architecture displays the medieval mindset which saw Christendom as a dual realm ruled by God through both state and church.

The dom contains two very important tombs. The west choir contains that of Pope Clement II (d. 1047) and is the only papal tomb in Germany. He was the bishop of Bamberg before his election to the papacy. This is a marble monument with dates from 1450, decorated with carvings that show the four virtues and the pope's death.

In front of the east choir is the white limestone tomb of Heinrich II (973–1024) and his wife, Kunigunde. It took the sculptor Tilman Riemenschneider (1460–1531) 14 years to complete the carvings on the tomb which depict the death of Heinrich II, his judgment by God, and the miraculous healing of his wife Kunigunde by St. Benedict, who removed her gallstones. The carvings also show Kunigunde's just treatment of dishonest servants, and her ordeal by fire after she was falsely accused of adultery.

These sculptures remind us of a world we have lost, where miracles were part of daily life, justice was valued, and evidence in criminal cases was often sought directly from God. Today it is popular in New Age, and some Christian circles, to lament our loss and blame the rationality for the decline of faith in the miraculous. But we should never forget that alongside healings went grotesque tortures and grim ordeals without appeals to evidence. Thanks to the rational ways of thinking, which were encouraged by Thomas Aquinas (1224–74) and other Christian leaders, we no longer judge people by such barbaric methods as those suffered by the unfortunate Kunigunde.

Several other sculptures are a must. The most famous of all is the Bamberger Reiter (Bamberg Knight, 1240), or perhaps king, on horseback. This statue is unusual because it is the first known equestrian figure to have been produced since the end of the Western Roman Empire in the 5th century. The artist is unknown, although many scholars believe the statue is of French origin. Nineteenth-century Romantic artists speculated that the figure depicted a Hohenstaufen Emperor. During the Third Reich, the knight of Bamberg became a symbol of national pride and regeneration.

Near the southeast end of the nave is a statue of two women depicting the church triumphant and the synagogue defeated. A young, richly clad beauty represents the church, while a blindfolded, simply dressed woman holding a broken rod portrays the synagogue. Thus, for medieval Christians, this pair symbolized the triumph of the New Testament and Christianity over Judaism and the Old Testament. This graphic scene is flanked by statues of the apostles. Directly oppo-

site is a very delicate statue of Mary and her cousin Elizabeth. Here again Mary is represented as a beautiful young woman while Elizabeth is a tired old woman.

Originally, the statue of the synagogue defeated stood on a column outside the Dom on its north portal near the large sculpture of 12 apostles and 12 prophets, which is still there today. Note that below the place where the synagogue defeated once stood is a figure in a pointed cap, which in medieval art signified a Jew, with a little devil pulling his ears. This derogatory depiction of what was then a contemporary Jew is in marked contrast to the sculpture of the 12 apostles who are shown to stand on the shoulders of the 12 prophets. The contrast between these two works vividly displays the ambivalent attitude of many Christians towards Judaism. On the one hand, Jews were seen as a devilish people who rejected the church. On the other hand, Christians had to admit that without the Old Testament their religion was meaningless and the church was built on the foundation of Jewish religion, a fact that was exploited by Nazi apologists when they attacked both Christians and Jews as un-German.

Against the west wall of the south transept you find the Nativity Altar of Veit Stoss (1447–1533). This uncompleted work was commissioned by the artist's son, the prior of the Carmelite monastery in Nürnberg, when the artist was over 80. The altar was moved to Bamberg after the burgers of Nürnberg converted to Protestantism and drove the prior out of the city.

In the Chapel of the Blessed Sacrament, near the south aisle, is a painting of heaven within a rosary. This is attributed to Martin Luther's (1483–1546) friend and supporter Lucas Cranach (1472–1553).

DIÖZESANMUSEUM (Diocesan Museum), in the Dom, is rich in art and historical treasures. The extensive collection of ecclesiastical vestments and silver communion cups tell their own story about the development of Catholic piety. Even more interesting is a small fragment of wood and nail which medieval pilgrims believed came from the cross of Jesus. Today the church acknowledges that this is most unlikely. Yet they retain great historical value for anyone wishing to understand the events leading up to the Reformation.

NEUE RESIDENZ (New Bishop's Palace), adjoining the Dom, is a superb Baroque mansion which houses the Staatsbibliothek (State Library) with its magnificent collection of books and manuscripts. The palace also contains Bamberg's art gallery, which has many excellent medieval and Baroque paintings. In particular Hans Baldung Grien's (1484–1545) *Great Flood* and works by Lucas Cranach should not be missed.

The interior of the palace itself is unbelievably opulent, reminding visitors of the time before the Napoleonic Wars when many German principalities were ruled by prince bishops who united church and state under their control. The throne room with its elaborate frescoed ceiling provides unforgettable insight into the pomp and ceremony that once flourished in such courts.

NEUES RATHAUS (New Town Hall, 1733–36) was designed as a Catholic seminary by the Baroque architect Balthasar Neumann (1687–1753). It stands in the Maxplatz, a good starting point to explore the town. Nearby is the imposing Baroque church of **St. Martin,** designed for the Jesuits by the Baroque artists the Dientzenhofer brothers. It speaks of the power of the Counter-Reformation, which utilized art and artists to rebuff the advance of Protestantism.

E. T. A. HOFFMANN-HAUS, 26 Schillerplatz, is a museum devoted to the great German Romantic writer Ernst Theodor Amadeus Hoffmann (1776–1822). A native of Königsberg, now Kaliningrad, in East Prussia, Hoffmann was an unusually talented civil servant. He was an artist, composer, theater director, and critic. But his greatest talent and fame lay as an author of chilling tales of horror that inspired Offenbach's opera *The Tales of Hoffmann,* two ballets, Délibes's (1836–91) *Coppelia,* and Tchaikovsky's (1840–

B

93) beloved *Nutcracker.* He was also the author of *Mademoiselle de Scudéry,* which many regard as the first detective story.

Hoffmann's bizarre tales and preoccupation with horror appear to have been intended as a critique of spiritualism and similar occult movements such as mesmerism, which Hoffmann regarded as completely fraudulent. In his view, such phenomena were expressions of hysteria disguising sexual fantasies which often led to unbridled passions. Ironically, the unintended consequence of his work was to inspire the American authors Edgar Allan Poe (1809–49) and H. P. Lovecraft (1890–1937), whose own supernaturalism encouraged the superstitious fantasies that Hoffmann sought to expose.

BAUTZEN

This border area was part of Bohemia and was settled by a Slavic group known as the Sorbes, or Wends, in the 6th century. Today there is a revival of Sorb culture and a strong interest in its history among young people in the area, where Sorb is now taught in schools, although everyone speaks German. The Count of Meißen built a fortress in 1144 on the jagged rock that dominates the surrounding countryside and the river Spree. The town grew up around its castle at what became an intersection on important trade routes to the north and east. Severely damaged during the Thirty Years' War, the town regained its prosperity and escaped remarkably unscathed from World War II. Most of the damage you see today, and the extensive renovation projects you also see underway, date from 40 years of Communist misrule and deliberate neglect. Bautzen is a good place to visit on the way to Herrnhut.

PLACES TO VISIT

ORTENBURG (District Fortress). The romantic silhouette of this enchanting castle dominates the skyline as you approach Bautzen. The castle itself is well worth a visit and provides wonderful views of the surrounding countryside. The tower dates from 1486 when the area was for a short time, from 1469–90, ruled by Hungary. The bas relief on the wall is of the 16th-century Hungarian king, Matthias Curvinus.

ST. PETRIKIRCHE DOM (Cathedral of St. Peter). Built as a three-aisled hall church between 1213 and 1495, this Gothic church was built to bend from the middle section to represent the supposed position of Christ's body on the cross. The other highly unusual feature of the church is its ecumenical character, which goes back to the 16th century. When a significant group of local citizens converted to Protestantism, the townspeople wisely decided to divide their church between Protestants and Roman Catholics. Consequently, from 1524 the Protestants worshiped in the nave while the Catholics worshiped in the choir. These two areas are divided by a wrought iron screen and present a very interesting contrast. The Protestant nave is essentially simple and unadorned. The Catholic choir has an elaborate 18th-century high altar with a fine painting by Giovanni Antonio Pellegrini (1675–1741) that shows St.

Peter holding a set of keys. The reference, of course, is to Matthew 16:13–19, and is a not-too-subtle reminder to Catholic worshipers and any Protestant who looks on that the pope claims descent from Peter in direct apostolic succession. The other feature that strikes visitors is the huge *Crucifixion* by Balthasar Permoser (1651–1732), completed in 1714.

DOMSTIFT (Bishop's Palace), behind St. Peter's, is a fine Baroque palace that was actually used by the Roman Catholic bishop until recently. It houses the Dom's treasury, but you have to make an appointment to be allowed in by phoning 44102 in advance of your visit.

BERCHTESGADEN

The rather unusual name "Berchtesgaden" owes its origin to a figure of folklore Berchta, or in old high German *Perchta*. During the "Twelve Days of Christmas," Perchta flies through the air to scold or praise. Her entourage are good or bad Perchten/Berchten. In the Alps, it is a custom that masked figures run and jump (called Berchten-jumping) to bring about fertility of the fields. *Gaden* means a one-room house, shelter, or hall. The geographic feature of the horseshoelike mountainous region around the Königssee has been shaped by hundreds of years of salt and limestone mining. This led to the folk belief that the area

offered shelter to Berchta and her entourage, ergo: Berchtesgaden.

Today, tourism is the main industry of Berchtesgaden. Its location almost guarantees year-round visitors who can visit and/or view the Obersalzberg, a mountaintop where Hitler had his Berghof, a chalet equipped with bunkers, and his private retreat, the Eagle's Nest.

An Augustinian abbey was founded here around 1111 with the help of a diocesan donation by Count Berengar I of Sulzach. The abbey attracted laypeople and led to the development of a settlement. The salt mines at nearby Hallein and the salt trade provided employment for the whole region but also created

B

rivalry with Salzburg. Berchtesgaden was ruled by a provost from 1300 until 1491 when Emperor Maximilian I bestowed the title *Reichsfürst,* Prince of the Reich, upon the provost Ulrich Pernauer. In 1803 it was annexed to Austria. From 1810 to 1918 the area was part of Bavaria and Germany, as it is today.

PLACES TO VISIT

EHEMALIGE AUGUSTINERCHORHERREN-STIFTSKIRCHE ST. PETER UND ST. JOHANNES (former Augustinian Church of St. Peter and St. John). Originally bearing a Romanesque Augustinian foundation, the church was modified over the centuries to incorporate Gothic and 19th-century Romanesque elements. Its colorful facade is the result of the deliberate use of different colored stones to create a pleasing pattern. On the north side of the church is a painting, dated 1474, by Rueland Fruehauf the Elder, of God raising Christ from the dead. There is also a very interesting Baroque Madonna and high altar, which was designed by Bartholomäus Opstal.

FRAUENKIRCHE ST. MARIA AM ANGER (Church of Our Lady at the Meadow) is a pleasant 16th-century church containing a 15th-century copy of the Madonna found in Milan cathedral. There is also a good 17th-century carving of Christ in captivity.

ROMANISCHES KLOSTER (Roman-esque Cloisters) **AND GOTHISCHES Dormitorium MUSEUM** (Gothic Dormitory Museum) stand on the south side of the church. In the dormitory are woodcarvings by Erasmus Grasser (1450–1518), Veit Stoß (1447–1533), and Tilman Riemenschneider (1460–1531). There are also portraits of the ruling Wittelsbach dynasty and works by Lucas Cranach the Elder (1472–1553).

SCHLOSS (Palace) was formerly a royal palace of Bavaria's rulers. Today it is owned by the Wittelsbach Foundation and is open to the public. Inside is a rich collection of art, antique furniture, and weapons.

SALZBERGWERKMUSEUM (saltwork mining museum). Today it is easy to forget the value once placed on salt as a major commodity that brought riches to salt-mining districts. This museum is a must for anyone wanting to understand the social history of Europe and the importance of salt from Celtic times to the present.

MARIA-GERN (Mary the Beloved), built in 1709 to the north of Berchtesgaden, is a picturesque pilgrimage church.

Another 18th-century pilgrimage site is the **Kunterweg Church**, built 1731–33, to the west of Berchtesgaden.

BERLIN

During the 12th century, the Citadel Spandau was built by the margrave, or count, of Brandenburg as a frontier post against the Slavs. Soon two towns, Cölln and Berlin, grew up on the banks of the Spree. In 1307 the towns merged as Berlin-Cölln and joined the Hanseatic League. In 1415 Count Friedrich Hohenzollern (1372–1440) became the Kurfürst (elector) of Brandenburg. Fifty-five years later, Berlin became the official residence of the Hohenzollern dynasty, which was eventually to rule the whole of Germany. The elector Joachim II (1505–71) converted to Lutheranism (1539). A generation later Johann Sigismund converted to Calvinism (1613), although most of his subjects remained Lutherans, thus laying a foundation for religious tolerance. During the Thirty Years' War (1618–48), Berlin changed hands numerous times, suffering extensive damage, losing half of its population. In 1640 Friedrich Wilhelm (1620–88), known as the Great Elector, became the ruler. With the end of the Thirty Years' War, the city's economy slowly revived, and in 1675 Friedrich Wilhelm of Brandenburg defeated the Swedes at the battle of Fehrbellin, thus securing Prussia's independence. In 1685 the elector invited 6000 French Protestant refugees, known as Huguenots, to settle in Berlin, making almost a fifth of the population French. This wise act stimulated the economy and laid the foundation for Prussia's future greatness.

His son, Friedrich III, the elector of Brandenburg (1657–1713), proclaimed himself the first king in Prussia (1701), thus turning what had been a dukedom into a kingdom (after 1701 he was called Friedrich I, the king of Prussia, until he died in 1713). Eight years later he merged several small towns in the area to create his capital city, Berlin. A building boom followed during which such landmarks as Unter den Linden (Under the Linden Trees), the Brandenburg Gate, the Berlin Opera, and Tiergarten (Animal Park) were created.

MOSES MENDELSSOHN (1729–86) was the most popular German Jewish philosopher who defended the idea that it is possible to demonstrate both the existence of God and the immortality of the soul. He played a leading role in Jewish emancipation and German culture and the Enlightenment. He is often referred to as "the Third Moses." His grandchildren, including the composer Felix Mendelssohn-Bartholdy (1809–47), converted to Christianity.

B

He was succeeded by Friedrich II (1712–86), who made Berlin a thriving center of the European Enlightenment where philosophers like Moses Mendelssohn (1729–86), Gotthold Ephraim Lessing (1729–81), and Voltaire (1694–1778) encouraged a vigorous intellectual life. At the same time Friedrich effectively moved his residence to his summer palace Sanssouci (Without Worry), in nearby Potsdam.

Napoleon Bonaparte (1769–1821) conquered Berlin in 1806, but his rule had little impact on the city. In 1810, the Humboldt University was founded as the world's first modern university where professors were expected to publish the findings of their systematic research while students had to study hard and pass examinations. During the 19th century, Berlin grew as a center of industrialization and by the 1870s had a population of around 850,000. In 1871, Otto von Bismarck (1815–98), the German chancellor, succeeded in uniting Germany under Prussian rule, and Berlin became the capital of Germany. The city grew apace and by 1906 had two million inhabitants.

As a result of the British blockade of German ports, there were food shortages during the First World War and by the end of the war starvation. Things revived in the mid-1920s, and Berlin again became an artistic center. The Great Depression of 1929 saw unemployment rise steeply until 1 person in 3 was unemployed. The industrial east of the city was Socialist with strong Communist sympathies. Consequently, street battles with the Nazis soon erupted. The year 1933 saw Hitler (1889–1945) elected chancellor at the head of a Government of National Unity empowered to solve Germany's economic woes. On February 27, 1933, under mysterious circumstances, a fire broke out in the Reichstag (Parliament), giving the Nazis the excuse they needed to seize power through the notorious Enabling Act. Thousands of people—Communists, old style conservatives, monarchists, social democrats, and clergy—were arrested throughout Germany and sent to hastily constructed concentration camps for "reeducation." May 1933 saw an orgy of destruction when students burnt at least 20,000 books which they considered degenerate. Five years later, on November 9, 1938, the infamous Kristallnacht (Night of Broken Glass) saw a frenzy of destruction as Nazi mobs smashed the

OTTO EDUARD LEOPOLD VON BISMARCK (1815–98) was the greatest German politician of the 19th century. He was responsible for the unification of numerous German states into one united country. His wife was a devout Pietist, and Bismarck claimed to be a Christian, although historians argue about his actual beliefs. Bismarck was admired by the Dutch Christian statesman and philosopher Abraham Kuyper (1837–1920).

B

windows of Jewish shops and burnt businesses and synagogues.

At the beginning of World War II, Berlin was the capital of the Third Reich. Serious allied air raids began in 1944, reducing much of Berlin to rubble before the final Soviet assault in April 1945. Berlin was ringed with artillery approximately six feet apart, and shells rained down on the city. The final assault involved fierce street fighting.

After 1945, Berlin, like the rest of Germany, was divided into four military zones, and for a short while, the Allies strove to create a united Germany. Cooperation between the Allies broke down soon afterwards, and in 1948, the Russians reacted by imposing a road blockade and making numerous political and economic demands upon their former Allies. Instead of capitulating, General Clay (1897–1978), the American commander in Berlin, organized the largest airlift in history which lasted from June 26, 1948, until the Soviets lifted the blockade on May 14, 1949.

The next momentous event in Berlin's turbulent history was the revolt by East German workers on June 17, 1953 that was brutally crushed by Russian tanks. Then on August 13, 1961, the government of the DDR surprised the world by erecting a wall throughout the city to prevent its citizens from fleeing to the West. Thirteen feet high, over a 100 miles in length, the Berlin Wall became a symbol of the Cold War and Communist oppression. It was guarded by hundreds of troops, 293 sentry posts, dog patrols, and eventually mine fields and electrified fences. Seventy-eight people lost their lives attempting to cross the wall. In the early days, hundreds made daring escapes to the safety of West Berlin.

The year 1971 saw a treaty which restored telephone contact between East and West Berlin and allowed West Germans to visit the East. But tensions remained high for another 18 years until, against all expectations, public demonstrations which had begun in Leipzig escalated into mass rallies all over the DDR. At the same time Hungary lifted travel restrictions to the West. Over 175,000 East Germans fled to the West as refugees. Suddenly on November 9, 1989, the East German government lifted travel restrictions. Immediately over 50,000 people flooded into West Berlin, where there was dancing in the streets. The following day, schools were closed as East and West Germans celebrated and began tearing down the hated wall as East German troops and police looked on and even encouraged the demonstrators. Finally, on October 3, 1990, Germany was reunited, and on June 20, 1991, the Bundestag (Parliament) voted to make Berlin once more the capital of Germany, with most major ministries being transferred there by 2003.

B

PLACES TO VISIT

MUSEUMINSEL (Museum Island) is probably Germany's best-kept secret. Its museums rival, if not outshine, the Louvre and the British Museum.

KUPFERGRABEN (Pergamon Museum) houses a series of remarkable artifacts from the biblical world excavated by German archaeologists during the late 19th and early 20th centuries.

The Pergamon Altar, dedicated to the Greek gods Athena and Zeus, gives the museum its name. It was found at the site of the ancient city of Pergamon in what is now Turkey. Excavated by German archaeologists Humann and Conze in 1878–80, the altar was moved to Berlin "for protection" in 1902 and is probably the best surviving example of ancient Greek sculpture anywhere in the world.

Built in the 2nd century B.C., this masterpiece of art was one of the wonders of the ancient world. Viewing it transports the visitor back in time to the world of the New Testament. Around the walls of the room containing the altar are carved marble reliefs depicting the war of gods and humans from Greek mythology. Here you see the pathos of ancient Greek religion and the cruelty of both gods and humankind.

Another masterpiece from the world of the New Testament is the gateway to the Greek city of Miletus built around A.D. 120 by the Roman emperor Hadrian (76–138). The city was excavated between 1899–1913 by Theodor Wiegand (1864–1936) and the gate brought to Berlin in fragments before being restored to its original glory. Originally the gate stood on the route of a pilgrim's way leading to the shrine of the oracle of the Greek God Apollo in Didyma. Recently a number of important archaeological finds have been uncovered along this ancient pre-Christian pilgrimage route. A mosaic embedded in the center of the gateway room's floor depicts mythological creatures surrounding the god Orpheus, who was the center of a mystery cult that once rivaled Christianity.

Perhaps even more breathtaking is the Ishtar Gate and Processional Way, honoring the female deity Ishtar. It was built by Nebuchadnezzar II in Babylon during the 6th century B.C. and reconstructed by Waltar Andrae, who directed this section of the museum from 1928–51. Although parts of this structure are reconstructed, the exhibit contains original glazed bricks depicting mythical animals originally brought from Iran in the 1920s and 1930s.

These stunning exhibits are surrounded by literally hundreds of smaller ones, including an almost complete clay tablet containing a 12th century B.C. legal code from Assyria, statues of kings and gods, pottery, and numerous other items of interest to anyone who has read the Bible. Other galleries contain an almost intact statue of the goddess of love, Aphrodite, and the famed bust of the Greek lawgiver and general Pericles

KARL FRIEDRICH SCHINKEL (1781–1841) was the greatest German exponent of neoclassicalism in its early manifestation before the movement became increasingly militaristic. Schinkel is largely responsible for redefining the skyline of Berlin in the early 19th century with a series of graceful buildings. His many works include the Schauspielhaus (Concert Hall) (1818–21), and the Alte Museum (Old Museum). The fine lines and low profiles of his buildings continue to make Berlin a very liveable city designed for human use.

(490–429 B.C.), whose statesmanship led to the golden age of Athens. You will also see a bronze bust of Julius Caesar (100–44 B.C.), whose nephew and successor was the Caesar Augustus (63 B.C.–A.D. 14) mentioned in Luke 2.

Easily overlooked are various statues and grave stele (pillar) from the Greco-Roman period. These demonstrate that parental and marital love were just as important to the ancient world as they are today. Finally, the Pergamon houses an excellent collection of Islamic art which should not be missed.

ALTES MUSEUM (Old Museum), entrance Marx-Engels-Platz, is regarded by many as the greatest example of German neoclassical architecture. It was designed by Karl Friedrich Schinkel (1781–1841). Completed in 1830, it is Berlin's first public museum and one of the earliest museums in Europe reflecting the enthusiasm for history which gripped people at the time. Thus, even before entering the museum, visitors see an important architectural structure which tells a lot about the way 19th-century intellectuals looked back to

ancient Greek and Roman civilization for inspiration.

The central rotunda, based on the Pantheon in Rome, immediately impresses visitors, transporting their imagination to the glories of a past age. Since this museum is now used to house special exhibits, there is little else one can say.

BODEMUSEUM, on the Monbijou-brüke, houses a good Egyptian and papyrus collection. This covers the period from 5,000 B.C. to the 3rd century A.D. Look out for items relating to the Egyptian Cult of the Dead, as well as the various coffins from Thebes, which include a bronze coffin made for a sacred cat.

The early Christian and Byzantine collection provides fascinating insights into the development of Christian art. It includes the 6th-century Apse mosaic from the Church of San Michele in Ravenna, Italy, which depicts Jesus with an open Bible containing verses from John's gospel. The contrasts between Byzantine and Coptic icons are particularly interesting because they illustrate how common artistic themes

B

and interpretations of the gospel change with local cultures.

The painting collection contains Rubens' (1577–1640) *Christ Giving Peter the Keys of Heaven* and Vasari's (1511–74) *St. Paul and St. John Blessing the Poor*. In the sculpture collection you find *The Baptism of Christ* by the 17th-century artist Hans Krumper (1570–1634) and Nickolaus Gerhaert van Leiden's (1430–73) *St. Ann, the Virgin, and Child*. Finally, Donatello's (1336–1466) *Relief of the Madonna* should not be missed. For anyone interested in coins there is also a good numismatic collection.

UNTER DEN LINDEN AND SURROUNDING DISTRICTS

ALTE NATIONAL GALERIE (Old National Gallery), designed by Friedrich A. Stüler (1800–1865), a student of Schinkel, houses 19th-century works of art. Here the work of Adolf von Menzel (1815–1905) is important because many of his paintings show the spread of industrialization. This provides an indispensable background for anyone wishing to understand the popularity of modern philosophies from Hegel (1770–1831) to Marx (1818–83) and Nietzsche (1844–1900). Note the contrast between his *Flute Concert at Sanssouci,* which depicts the Enlightenment Rationalism of Friedrich II, the Great (1712–86), and *The Iron Works,* which captures the raw power of capitalist industry. The life of the poor is portrayed by Max Liebermann's (1847–1935) paintings. The shift from realism to Impressionism and modern art is captured in Edouard Manet's (1832–83) *The Winter Garden* and Claude Monet's (1840–1926) *St-*

GEORG WILHELM FRIEDRICH HEGEL (1770–1831) was a German philosopher whose system is commonly known as "Hegelianism." His complex idealist philosophy contains many elements the most influential of which are (1) the dialectic, which is generally interpreted to mean that all reasoning is dialectical proceeding from a concept to a new and contradictory concept which gives way to a third concept that transcends and synthesizes both earlier concepts. This is usually stated as thesis, antithesis, and synthesis; (2) the theory of self-realization by which the dialectical process in the individual leads to a determinate "self" which is "for itself"; (3) the theory of history which is a dialectical process leading to the manifestation of the absolute spirit and arguing that in every specific age the spirit manifests itself in the Zeitgeist or the "spirit of the age," which determines social and political life, knowledge, religion, and art. Hegel's work strongly influenced such people as Feuerbach and Marx. Critics, like Sir Karl Popper in his *The Open Society and Its Enemies* (1947), contend that it leads to totalitarianism and is so obscure as to bewitch the intellect.

Germain-l'Auxerrois. The work of German Romantics who wished to recapture the ethos of classical antiquity and eventually turned to Roman Catholicism for succor is also well represented.

BERLINER DOM (Berlin Cathedral), an imposing neo-Baroque structure built in the late 19th century, has been recently restored.

SOPHIENKIRCHE (St. Sophia's Church), Sophienstrasse. Built in 1712 and renovated in 1892 in neo-Baroque style, it is one of Berlin's most beautiful churches. In the cemetery are the graves of Leopold von Ranke (1795–1886), the great Christian historian and father of modern historical research, and the composer Karl Friedrich Zelter (1758–1832).

UNTER DEN LINDEN is the famous avenue of lime trees created in 1647 by the Great Elector. At one end is **ALEXANDERPLATZ,** named in honor of Tsar Alexander I (1777–1825) after his visit to Berlin in 1805. At the other end is the famous **BRANDENBURGER TOR** (Brandenburg Gate) erected in 1789, and the historic **REICHSTAG** (Parliament), the burning of which allowed the Nazis to pass the Enabling Act in 1933 and seize power.

MARIENKIRCHE (Church of Mary), Unter den Linden, is a 14th-century structure and one of Berlin's oldest churches.

PALAST DER REPUBLIK (Palace of the Republic) is a bronze glass modern monstrosity that was East Berlin's showplace as the Communist headquarters. The building is a health hazard due to asbestos pollution. The German government has decided to demolish and replace it with a replica of the original royal palace that stood on this site until the 1960s.

UNTER DEN LINDEN (German Historical Museum) contains exhibits depicting German history from the earliest times to the present. Here the exhibition "Germany in the Cold War" vividly illustrates the horrors brought about first by National Socialism and then Communism.

HUMBOLDT UNIVERSITY, on Unter den Linden, is where a galaxy of academic superstars strode the Berlin intellectual stage, including the philosophers Fichte (1762–1814) and Hegel (1770–1831), theologian Schleiermacher (1768–1834), church historian Neander (1789–1850), Old Testament scholar and defender of orthodoxy Ernst Wilhelm Hengstenberg (1802–69), and a host of others who helped create modern intellectual life. It is an impressive building flanked by two fine monuments of the Humboldt brothers, whose devotion to scholarship helped create the university.

STAATSOPER (State Opera House), Unter den Linden, was designed by Knobelsdorff (1699–1753) and opened in 1743. Largely destroyed in World War II, it was rebuilt in 1955, a tribute to the role of music in German life. In the center of Unter den Linden notice the equestrian statue known as Der Alte Fritz (Old Fritz), which celebrates the military powers of Friedrich II.

75

B

FAMOUS PROFESSORS AT HUMBOLDT UNIVERSITY

FRIEDRICH ERNST DANIEL SCHLEIERMACHER (1768–1834) was the most important German Protestant theologian of the 19th century, known as "the father of modern theology." He is the founder of modern liberal theology and, in many ways, religious studies. He rose to fame following the publication of his *Speeches on Religion to Its Cultural Despisers* (1799), where he defines religion as the "feeling" or "sense" of absolute dependence and separates the study of religion from science and other academic disciplines. His work set the tone for the rejection of natural theology and the development of nontraditional theological systems which reinterpreted Christianity in terms of the modern age, a project he began in *The Christian Faith* (1821–22).

JOHANN AUGUST WILHELM NEANDER (1789–1850) was born into a Jewish family as David Mendel. He converted to Christianity in 1806 and, after further study, became professor of church history at the University of Berlin in 1813. As a historian, Neander sought to illustrate the working of God in the lives of individuals by understanding the inner motives that motivated people. He inspired a generation of younger theologians and ministers with his deep piety and practical concerns. Neander was one of the founders of the Berlin Missionary Society in 1824.

ERNST WILHELM HENGSTENBERG (1802–69) was a colleague of Neander and Tholuck, and of Halle, with whom he helped form the Berlin Mission. He was a staunchly conservative Old Testament scholar who defended the integrity of the Bible and Christian orthodoxy against rationalist attacks. He founded and edited the *Evangelische Kirchen-Zeitung* (Evangelical Church Newspaper), to popularize orthodox teachings and apologetics. He also wrote numerous theological works.

ST. HEDWIGS-KATHEDRALE, behind the Opera House, is the 18th-century Roman Catholic cathedral modeled on the Pantheon in Rome. It has a very impressive dome that took years to complete because of its size. This church was built under the patronage of Friedrich II, who encouraged religious tolerance in the spirit of the Enlightenment. Until 1854 it was the only Roman Catholic church in the city.

NIKOLAIVIERTEL (Nikolai District) is a small, charming area reconstructed by the Communists in the 1980s to preserve

Berlin's medieval core. It contains Berlin's oldest church, the NIKOLAIKIRCHE, dating to 1230.

GENDARMENMARKT (Police Market) is one of Berlin's most beautiful squares. It gets its name from the fact that, in the 18th century, a troop of gendarmes was barracked here. Under the DDR, the name was changed to Platz der Akademie to commemorate the Academy of Sciences which had a building here. In 1992, the old name was restored. On one side of the square is the FRANZÖSISCHE DOM (French Cathedral); on the other is the DEUTSCHER DOM (German Cathedral). Set back between the two is the SCHAUSPIELHAUS (Theater).

FRANZÖSISCHER DOM (French Cathedral), which opened in 1705 as a church for French Protestants, was designed by two French refugees, Louis Cayard and Abraham Quesay, in Late Renaissance/Early Baroque style. It contains a small museum portraying the history of Berlin's Huguenot community. Although almost identical, the DEUTSCHER DOM (German Cathedral) was designed by an Italian architect, Giovanni Simonetti. It has recently been reconstructed to become an art gallery.

SCHAUSPIELHAUS (Theater), now known as the KONZERTHAUS, was built in 1819–21. Recently restored, it is one of Schinkel's masterpieces in neoclassical style. Anyone wishing to grasp the feel of 19th-century neoclassicism and the ethos of both the Enlightenment and Romanticism ought to attend one of the concerts staged by the Berlin Symphony Orchestra, which is based here.

TIERGARTEN (Animal Park): here you will find the Berlin KULTURFORUM, which includes the PHILHARMONIE (Berlin Philharmonic); the MUSIKINSTRUMENTEN MUSEUM, a fascinating museum of musical instruments; the superb STAATSBIBLIOTHEK (State Library); and the rather sterile NEUE NATIONALGALERIE (New National Gallery), which contains a fine collection of paintings with works by Paul Klee (1879–1940) and various German Expressionists.

The completely renovated KULTURFORUM houses an excellent collection of paintings, the Deutsche Sammlung (German Collection), which contains medieval and Renaissance paintings from the 13th–16th centuries. Here are works by Dürer (1471–1528), Lucas Cranach (1472–1553), and a variety of Reformation period artists as well as some excellent examples of pre-Reformation art, including the 14th-century *Madonna of Glatz* and Martin Schongauer's (1445–91) moving *The Birth of Christ*. Notice the way artistic techniques develop from the impressionistic *Passion Altar* created at the Ulm workshop of Hans Multscher (1400–67) to the refined skill of Lucas Cranach the Elder's somewhat cynical view of human nature in his *The Fountain of Youth*. In the 18th-century collection look out for Joshua Reynold's (1723–92) portrait of *Lady Sunderlin*. Notice the Turkish style of her clothing that provides yet another clue to the way Enlightenment artists looked beyond Europe for inspiration. The sculpture collection contains other works by Multscher and the more famous Tilman

Riemenschneider (1460–1531), whose *Münnerstädter Altar* (1490–91) and *The Four Evangelists* are superb. Here also you find the famed *Ravensburg Virgin with Mantle* and more modern 18th-century works such as Marin Zürn's (1590–1658) *St. Sebastian.* There are also some Italian works including Donatello's (1336–1466) *Pazzi Madonna.*

The Dutch collection contains works by Rubens (1577–1640), van Dyck (1599–1641), and Rembrandt (1606–69) among others. Here the transition from medieval Christian art to scenes based on stories from classical antiquity or ancient mythology, e.g., Rubens' *Andromeda Chained to the Rock,* and a growing interest in daily life, e.g., Vermeer's (1623–91) *Man and Woman Beside a Pitcher of Wine,* is noticeable. Works by Brueghel (1568–1625) and Hieronymus Bosch (1460–1516) crown the collection. Anyone wanting to understand the development of secularization could do no better than carefully study the work of these Dutch painters.

The French collection provides a good example of the growing fascination with peasant life in paintings like George de la Tour's (1583–1652) *Peasant Couple Eating,* and some excellent landscapes by Poussin (1613–75) and Claude Lorrain (1600–1682). The collection also contains some Italian works such as those by the Baroque artist Annibale Carracci (1540–1609).

THE NAZI ERA AND THE DDR

TOPOGRAPHIE DES TERROR (Topography of Terror Museum), Prinz-Albrecht-Gelände. This is situated on the site of the former State Secret Police and State Security Center of the Gestapo and SS. It contains graphic details about the fate of Germans who resisted the Nazi dictatorship. Here you will learn that, contrary to popular opinion, most of the opposition to the Nazis came from either Christians or conservatives. The Nazis prided themselves in being able to "turn" Communists and other left-wing opponents. But Christians stood firm against the tyranny.

GEDENKSTÄTTE DEUTSCHER WIDERSTAND (German Resistance Museum) contains a highly detailed record of the ill-fated July 20, 1944, plot to overthrow Hitler. Here again the presence of Christians among those executed is noticeable.

PLÖTZENSEE PRISON MEMORIAL, on the borders of Charlottenburg and Wedding, by the Gedenkstätte Plötzensee S Bahn, is where over 2,500 German political prisoners were executed between January and April 1945. Many of these people were Christians like Dietrich Bonhoeffer (1906–45), who were literally hung on huge meat hooks where they slowly bled or strangled to death.

DIETRICH BONHOEFFER-HAUS, Merienburger Allee 43, is a moving memorial to a great Christian theologian who died for his part in the July 20 plot to overthrow Hitler. Bonhoeffer's *Letters from Prison* are a modern spiritual classic. His other works are a fitting testimony to the engagement of a theologian in a specific situation and his attempt to apply biblical and theological under-standing to human evil.

KIRCHE MARIA REGINA MARTYRUM (Church of Mary Queen of the Martyrs) was designed by Hans Scäde as a memorial to victims of Nazi oppression. The church is entered through a courtyard representing the parade ground in a concentration camp, which symbolizes pain and suffering. The crypt is deliberately gloomy, but the upper church is illuminated by a gentle, natural light, and contains a large modern fresco by Georg Meistermann depicting the transformation of darkness into light, night to day, evil to goodness, through the redemption of Christ. Note the 14th-century madonna in the church and the modern sculpture *The Woman of the Apocalypse* by F. König in the courtyard.

HAUS DER WANNSEE-KONFERENZ (House of the Wansee Conference), where Nazi leaders planned the "final solution," is the next logical place to visit. It is located at 56–58 Am Grossen Wannsee, in Wannsee.

SACHSENHAUSEN concentration camp in Oranienburg at the end of the south Bahn line is a good place to visit next.

Here you can see the conditions under which political prisoners lived, including the famed theologian Martin Niemöller (1892–1984), who was held there "at Hitler's pleasure" for his bold criticisms during the Nazi regime. It is also important to realize that, after 1945, Sachsenhausen became an equally brutal prison for a number of years under Communist control. The full story of the Communist use of former concentration camps, where thousands of people died, has yet to be told.

A visit to the **NEUE SYNAGOGUE** (New Synagogue), Oranienburger Str. 30, near Museuminsel in the center of Berlin, is worthwhile. Completed in 1866, it was designed by the architects Eduard Knoblauch and Friedrich August Stüler (1800–1865) and built as an impressive example of Romantic architecture in Moorish style. Badly damaged in World War II, the church was reconstructed beginning in 1988. Attacked during Kristallnacht in 1938, this is now the main center for Berlin's Jewish community.

MARTIN-GROPIUS-BAU (Martin Gropius Building), Stresemannstrasse 110, contains the **Jewish Exhibit** of the Berlin

---

MARTIN NIEMÖLLER (1892–1984) was a First World War naval hero, pastor, and theologian who became the most important Protestant leader of the Christian opposition to the Nazis. He was imprisoned in Sachsenhausen and Dachau. Later Niemöller became the president of the Evangelical Church in Hessen and Nassau and president of the World Council of Churches from 1961–68. He was the author of many books, including *From the U-Boat to the Pulpit* (1934).

B

Museum, which documents the role played by Jews in the history of Berlin. The building also contains an excellent collection of modern art.

JÜDISCHER FRIEDHOF (Jewish cemetery), Grosse Hamburger Strasse, was founded in 1672 and is the oldest in Berlin. It once contained the grave of the philosopher Moses Mendelssohn (1729–86), the grandfather of the composer Felix Mendelssohn-Bartholdy, whose conversion to Christianity is commemorated in his great oratorio *Paulus (St. Paul)*. The graveyard was desecrated by the Gestapo in 1942. Now all you can see is a memorial plaque and bronze sculpture by Will Lambert dedicated to the 55,000 Berlin Jews who were deported to camps in the East.

JÜDISCHER FRIEDHOF (Jewish Cemetery), Senefelderplatz, Pankow, fared better than most and contains the graves of the composer Giacomo Meyerbeer (1791–1864), the historian Richard Moritz Meyer (1860–1914), and the painter Max Liebermann (1847–1935).

DOROTHEENSTÄDTISCHER FRIEDHOF (Dortheen Town Cemetery), Chaussesstrasse. In the cemetery are the graves of a legion of German intellectuals who decidedly shaped modern culture. Here you will find the philosopher Johann Gottlieb Fichte (1762–1814), the great theorist of nationalism whose writings planted the seeds of modern racism; Georg Wilhelm Friedrich Hegel (1770–1831), whose dialectic is seen by many as the distinguishing feature of modern thought; and

the architects Karl Friedrich Schinkel (1781–1841), Friedrich August Stüler (1800–1865), and Johann Gottfried Schadow (1764–1850). The composer Hanns Eisler (1898–1962) and the writers Heinrich Mann (1871–1950), Anna Seghers (1900–1983), Arnold Zweig (1887–1968), and Bertolt Brecht (1898–1956) are buried here.

BRECHT-HAUS, Chaussesstrasse, is where the Marxist avant-garde writer Bertolt Brecht lived from 1948 to his death in 1956. Brecht is best known for his *Threepenny Opera* (1928) and *Mother Courage and Her Children* (1939), which is a graphic account of life in the Thirty Years' War and an indictment of religious intolerance. One of the most gifted German writers, Brecht wrote plays and poetry, often drawing on the Bible for inspiration. He parodied great writers like Shakespeare, Schiller, and Goethe in various scenes in his plays.

In the KÄTHE-KOLLWITZ-MUSEUM, Fasanenstrasse 24, you will find an excellent collection of works by one of Germany's most famous women artists. Käthe Kollwitz (1867–1945) grew up in Pietist circles before becoming an agnostic. Note her moving series of prints *The Thirty Years' War,* which depict the terrible suffering of people during the 17th-century wars of religion, when in many areas of Germany two-thirds of the population died. More than anything else, the Thirty Years' War helps explain German attitudes to life and religion.

MUSEUM HAUS AM CHECKPOINT CHARLIE, Friedrichstrasse 44, recalls another type of horror—that of Communism and the DDR. Although very much a tourist attraction, this museum is worth visiting.

BERLIN WALL: Today this hated symbol of Communist dictatorship is hard to find, although there is a long section near the Reichstag building on Müherstraße called the "East Side Gallery." A new museum/monument incorporating a long section of the wall has also been created at Bernauer Straße/Adserstraße in Wedding to remind people of the horrors of this affront to humanity, but it is rather disappointing.

The new REICHSTAG, Germany's renovated Parliament building, was skillfully restored to preserve its 19th-century exterior while installing a state-of-the-art interior fitted to serve modern government and society.

KAISER-WILHELM-GEDÄCHTNIS-KIRCHE (Kaiser Wilhelm Memorial Church), Kurfürstendamm, is a neo-Romanesque structure completed in 1895 and reduced to rubble by air raids in 1945. Today there is a new concrete structure which, while unimpressive from the outside, contains some magnificent blue stained glass designed by Gabriel Loire (1904–96), the French Christian artist who almost single-handedly revived the art of stained-glass making in the 20th century. The stunning effect of the glass only becomes apparent from within the church.

Here there is also an active evangelical mission work organized by the Berlin City Mission. The original 19th-century bell tower has been preserved as a memorial to remind people of the horrors of war.

CHARLOTTENBURG DISTRICT

The horrors of the Nazi era and Communism seem unthinkable when you visit the museums near SCHLOSS CHARLOTTENBURG (Palace of Charlottenburg). The central feature is the Schloss, or palace, built 1695–99 as a country house for Queen Sophie Charlotte (d. 1705). The queen, who was a friend of the philosopher Leibniz (1646–1716), used it for cultural events. When she died, the surrounding district was named after her. Work on the palace was begun by the architect Johann Arnold Nering (1659–95) and was finally completed by Johann Friedrich von Göthe, who was responsible for the central dome, facade, and an orangery which was inspired by Versailles. The palace and extensive gardens are the embodiment of Enlightenment ideals. Extensively damaged during World War II, it has been meticulously restored to its former glory.

In front of the palace is an imposing bronze statue of the Enlightenment ruler Friedrich II, which was cast in one piece by the Baroque sculptor Andreas Schlüter (1664–1714). Regrettably, the main rooms in the old wing of the palace can be viewed only by joining a guided tour which is conducted in German. The guides do their very best

81

to accommodate English-speaking tourists, but you are advised to buy an inexpensive English guide booklet. In any case, the tour is highly recommended. In particular look out for the Porcelain Room, which provides vivid insight into the way Chinese civilization impressed Enlightenment thinkers. Originally Christian missionaries, like the Jesuit, P. Matteo Ricci (1552–1610), developed the technique of reflexivity as a means of understanding Chinese thought before preaching the gospel. Reflexivity is the technique that forms the basis of the modern study of anthropology. It involves attempting to understand a person's viewpoint from within that viewpoint itself. In other words, attempting to see the world as others see it by reflecting on one's own knowledge and experience as a way of finding common ground. Ricci's writings inspired Leibniz and other philosophers to create a cult of China that was used as a foil to criticize both Christianity and European civilization by suggesting the superiority of Chinese ways and beliefs.

The new wing of the palace, which needs no guide, was designed by Knobelsdorff (1699–1753) between 1740–46 in neoclassical style. Here the Napoleonic Room (Room 309) contains the French revolutionary artist Jacques Louis David's (1748–1825) masterpiece *Napoleon as Consul,* which emphasizes the importance of Rome for the Napoleonic age. It is also a tragic commentary on the disintegration of revolutionary ideals. There is also an interesting collection of the little-known Etruscan style of furnishing (Room 318) which again underlines the 18th- and early 19th-century quest for roots in classical, or as with the Etruscans, preclassical antiquity.

The Galerie der Romantik (Gallery of Romanticism), located in the Knobelsdorff Wing of the palace, is a rare gem. One room of this collection is devoted to biblical scenes. Look out for the portrait of *Karl Friedrich Schinkel* (1832), whose work made such an impression on the Berlin cityscape, by Carl Friedrich Ludwig Schmid (b. 1799).

Here you will find the world's best collection of works, 23 in all, by Caspar David Friedrich (1774–1840). His *Klosterruine Eldena (Ruin of Eldena Abbey)* (1824–25) along with Carl Blechen's (1798–1840) *Klosterruine Oybin (The Ruin of Oybin Abbey)* (1823) and Edward Gaertner's (1801–77) *Ansicht der Klosterruine Lehnin (A View of the Ruin of Lehnin Abbey)* (1863) capture the ongoing Romantic preoccupation with the spirituality of a lost past and the ruins of an age of faith.

Schinkel's *Mittelalterliche Stadt an einem Fluß (Medieval City on a River),* where a church dominates the cityscape, and Caspar David Friedrich's *Morgen im Riesengebirge (Morning in the Riesengebirge),* showing a crucifix towering over mountain tops, and his *Der Mönch am Meer (A Monk by the Sea),* capture the spiritual yearnings of Romanticism. Similarly, paintings like Blechen's (1798–1840) *Neustadt-Eberswalde (The New City of Eberswalde)* and Edward Gaertner's (1801–77) *Die Parochialstraße (The Parochial Street)* show a strong dissatisfaction with 19th-century life. Finally, note the gnarled trees, wild nature, and threatening clouds that characterize many of these paintings and the dissatisfaction of the artists with the confusion of this world.

Behind the main building is the Schlosspark laid out in rational geometric designs befitting Enlightenment sensibilities. At the rear of the park is a small MAUSOLEUM built like an ancient temple. It contains the tombs of Friedrich Wilhelm III, Queen Louise, Wilhelm I (1797–1888), and Queen Augusta (1811–90). There is also the beautiful SCHINKEL PAVILLION built in 1824 as the personal residence of Friedrich Wilhelm III. It was built in Pompeian style based on discoveries made during excavations, which began in 1748, at the Roman city of Pompeii.

ÄGYPTISCHES-MUSEUM (Egyptian Museum), opposite the palace, contains the world-famous, haunting bust of Königin Nofretete (Queen Nefertiti) of Egypt (1350 B.C.). Do not miss this. There is also the ancient Egyptian Kalabscha Gate and various other fascinating items from biblical times.

ANTIKEN-MUSEUM (Museum of Greek and Roman Antiquities), opposite the palace, contains an excellent collection of Roman treasures.

HEIMAT MUSEUM (Homeland Museum), at the side of the palace, depicts the history of the Charlottenburg area. Here you will learn something about the complexity of settlement in this part of Germany, which is an important issue when considering the spread of Christianity.

BRÖHAN-MUSEUM, opposite the Heimat Museum, which is almost directly opposite, contains an extensive collection of modern art, particularly Art Nouveau and Art Deco designs.

THE DAHLEM MUSEUMS

The best way to reach this superb museum complex is by taking the U Bahn (underground/metro) to the Dahlem station. On the way note that a number of the U Bahn stations have been restored to their original state. Thus the one at Wittenbergplatz, for example, has an authentic 1920s atmosphere complete with 1920s wall posters. In Dahlem follow the signs from the U Bahn to the museum complex.

ST. ANNEN-KIRCHE (St. Ann's Church), diagonally opposite the Dahlem U Bahn station, is an old stone building dating to the 13th century. In it you will find some 14th-century frescoes depicting the life of Christ. These were rediscovered in 1893. The carved altar and 17th-century pulpit are also interesting. More important is the fact that it was here that Martin Niemöller and his congregation opposed the Nazi tyranny as members of the Confessing

B

Church during the 1930s. In addition to holding a weekly prayer meeting, many members of the congregation were involved with various attempts to overthrow Hitler. Consequently, after the abortive July 20, 1944, assassination attempt on Hitler, a number of members of the congregation were arrested and executed. The 1960s student activist Rudi Dutschke (d. 1979), who began his political career as a Christian activist opposing Communism in the DDR, is buried in the cemetery along with the modern poet Volker von Törne (d. 1980).

MUSEUM FÜR VÖLKERKUNDE (Anthropological Museum) is one of the best in the world. Originating as a royal collection in 1829, the museum was founded in 1873 through the enthusiasm of the great German anthropologist Adolf Bastian (1826–1905). Walking around the galleries, you will begin to realize the appeal of now unpopular cultural diffusion theories. When artifacts are laid out in this manner, it is hard to avoid the thought that one group of peoples *must* have borrowed from another.

MUSEUM FÜR INDISCHE KUNST (Museum of Indian Art) contains a rich collection of Buddhist, Hindu, and Jain art as well as relics from the Mohenjo-Daro civilization. There is also a fine collection of Nepalese, Tibetan, and Thai works, most of which have religious significance. The museum is well supplied with very inexpensive guide

pamphlets in English. In the basement there is the rare opportunity to see an authentic reconstruction of a Buddhist Temple.

FRÜHCHRISTLICHE-BYZANTINISCHE SAMMLUNG (Early Christian and Byzantine Collection) is outstanding. Notice the 3rd-century marble sculpture depicting the Holy Spirit and the ivory relief of Christ's triumphal entrance into Jerusalem.

GERMAN FOLK MUSEUM, outside the main complex, concentrates on popular culture and contains some interesting examples of peasant superstitions and practices from folk religion.

CONTEMPORARY CHRISTIANITY

BERLINER MISSIONSWERK UND BERLINER GESELLSCHAFT FÜR MISSIONS-GESCHICHTE (Berlin Missionary Society and the Berlin Society for Mission History), Georgenkirchstr 70, is one of the oldest missionary societies in Germany. It is unique in that it combined Calvinist and Lutheran elements within one society. Founded in 1824 by Neander and Tholuck among others, it arose out of an evangelical revival that swept through eastern areas of Germany. Today the society, like most German churches, is essentially liberal in its theology. It maintains a good bookstore and an excellent mission archive for scholars. The Berlin Society for Mission History was formed in 1994 through the initiative of a young former East German scholar, Dr. Ulrich van der Heyden, who was concerned that in the rush to reunify and modernize, the priceless archives of this and other missions might disappear through neglect. An excellent scholarly society devoted to the study of mission, it holds regular conferences.

GOßNER MISSION, Handjerystr 19–20, is another smaller Berlin mission that broke away from the Berlin Missionary Society in 1836 because of policy differences. Led by Johannes Evangelista Goßner (1773–1858), it developed as a faith mission. In 1845 it sent missionaries to work among German immigrants in the U.S., and it still supports an active mission program throughout the world.

EVANGELISCHES JOHANNESSTIFT, Schönwalder Allee 26, Spandau, was founded in 1858 by Johann Heinrich Wichern (1808–81) as part of an evangelical awakening in the Protestant Church. This is a most remarkable venture by this Christian community, which runs a hospital, various therapy units, and numerous programs aimed at helping the needy. If you read German, you will find a good Christian bookshop here with an excellent secondhand section where you can often find real classics.

GEMEINDE AUF DEM WEG (Church on the Way), Babelsbergerstraße 40 (030-8541-833), has a membership of over 2000 people, the largest congregation in Germany. Two other churches, one in Bielefeld and the other in Espelkamp, are slightly larger, but they are immigrant Mennonite congregations and not indigenous German churches. The Gemeinde auf dem Weg is a charismatic church that developed out of a Baptist youth work over 20 years ago. Its leader is a psychologist, Dr. Wolfard Margies, who is an excellent preacher. Here you will find lots of people who are welcoming and speak English. Simultaneous translation is also provided for visitors.

BÜCHER FÜR CHRISTEN (Books for Christians), Rembrandstr 11, Friedenau, is a small Christian bookshop run by members of the Plymouth Brethren. They carry a number of English titles and even have a Web site: http://www.christshop.com/bfe

CHRISTLICHES ZENTRUM BERLIN (Berlin Christian Center), Herwarthstraße 5, Südstern, was founded by Peter Dipple and is another charismatic church where you will find simultaneous translation and people who speak English.

CHRISTLICHES JUNGENDZENTRUM ORANIENBURG (Christian Youth Center, Oranienburg) is one of the most exciting and possibly the most innovative Christian venture in Germany. But we are not giving you the address because too many casual visitors will interfere with the ministry. Therefore, you should only visit here if you are deeply involved in youth work or are looking for a Christian mission that deserves financial support. Oranienburg has a population of over 30,000 and most of its workers had good jobs with the DDR. Today unemployment is over 20 percent and most people who are employed work at low-paying jobs. No wonder alcoholism is rife, family violence rampant, sexual abuse common, and teen suicide high in the area. Since only five churches survived the atheistic propaganda of the DDR, the town is a spiritual wilderness with no more than 400 people attending church. "That's what makes it such a great place for ministry," says Herbert Weimar, a former Marxist Youth who was converted to Christ at the cost of a promising career in the Party in the early 1980s. After the fall of the Berlin Wall, Herbert and a former East German Baptist pastor, Winfried Müller, founded the Oranienburg Christian Youth Center, which opened in 1991. They also run a church that attracts over 150 new converts to its services. The center is a renovated old government building that was transformed through hard work and constant prayer into an attractive youth club and coffee bar, a refuge teens could call their own. This work is remarkable.

KLOSTER CHORIN (Chorin Monastery), 58 kilometers northeast, is a former Cistercian cloister built in the 13th century that is preserved as an impressive example of Gothic brickwork. It is well worth a visit by anyone wanting to leave the city to see the beautiful Brandenburg countryside.

BINGEN

Bingen was originally a Celtic settlement fortified by the Romans, who called it Bingium. Across from Bingen, on the north side of the Rhine on the Rochusberg (Mount Rochus), stands the Rochuskapelle (St. Rochus Chapel). St. Rochus was the patron saint of pestilence and its victims. During the French Revolution the chapel was destroyed, but in 1814 a typhoid epidemic swept Bingen, resulting in the rebuilding of the chapel. The opening was attended by the poet Johann Wolfgang von Goethe (1749–1832), who describes the events in his *Aus einer Reise an Rhein, Main und Neckar 1814 und 1815* (*A Trip Along the Rhine, Main, and Neckar in 1814 and 1815*).

Bingen is important to Christians because it was the home of the famed medieval mystic Hildegard von Bingen (1098–1179). Until recently there was really nothing much to see of a Christian nature in Bingen. But feminist theologians and even some neopagans have awakened an interest in the work of Hildegard because she was such an important woman in medieval society. The old abbey is being renovated and a museum created to illustrate her contribution to Christian thought.

HILDEGARD VON BINGEN (1098–1179) was born into local nobility at Bokelheim in 1098 or 1099. At the age of eight she was sent to be educated at the convent of Disibodenberg by a recluse named Jutta. At the age of fifteen she became a nun. She succeeded Jutta as abbess of the Diessenberg convent in 1136 and later founded a new convent in Rupertsberg near Bingen. Like her contemporary Bernard of Clairvaux (1090–1153), she was a Benedictine. A mystic, seer, poet, and composer, whose beautiful songs have recently been issued on several CDs, she also studied nature, describing various plants and seeds. Her *Causae et Curae (Causes and Treatment of Illness)* is a classic of both medieval and herbal medicine. Her medical writings are thus an important source for information about the knowledge of nature in Europe during the Middle Ages. They also remind us that the use of herbs and herbal cures is not something invented by modern New Age mystics. Rather, a knowledge of herbs and their use is deeply rooted in the Christian tradition of healing.

Her visions about the meritorious Christian life were written for simple people to inspire faith and godly works. For her the life of humans was a mirror of divine love. This vision is expressed in such books as *Scivias (Know the Ways of the Lord)*, where she discusses ethics and dogma. These works were approved as orthodox by the powerful archbishop of Mainz and later Pope Eugenius III (d. 1153). Her famed piety led the emperor, various kings, and the pope to correspond with her, and many of her letters and other writings have survived. She fought to remove abuses and create a reformed church centered on piety. Her "political meddling" irritated some members of the establishment, but she was loved by common people who appreciated her spiritual advice and preaching. She died in 1179 at the age of 82.

Because people reported miracles which they attributed to her prayers and later attributed to visits to her tomb, various attempts were made to have Hildegard canonized during the 13th and 14th century. But it was not until the 15th century that this happened. Her feast day is September 17.

PLACES TO VISIT

BINGENBRÜCK HILDEGARDIS-GEDÄCHTNISKIRCHE (Bingen Bridge Hildegard Memorial Church) contains a statue of Hildegard of Bingen.

ST. MARTIN KIRCHE (St. Martin's Church), Eibingen, 4 kilometers north-west of Geisenheim. On the 750th anniversary of Hildegard's death in 1929, Pope Pius XI elevated this church to the status of "basilica minor."

DRUSUS BRÜCKEN KAPELLE (Drusus Bridge Chapel) is the oldest bridge chapel in Germany built on a Romanesque

B

bridge over the river Nahe. Now very rare, bridge chapels were once common throughout Europe (a fine example is to be found in Derby, England). They were used by travelers who prayed for protection as they left the safety of the city walls or customs post. This particular chapel was constructed in 989 by Archbishop Willigis. The chapel was reconsecrated in 1677 after plague had devastated the area in 1666, resulting in an increase in local banditry and danger to travelers.

BINGER MÄUSETURM (Bingen Mouse Tower) is set in the middle of the Rhine on a small outcrop of rock. This fortification served as a customs house from 1208–20. The legend is that here an evil bishop, Hatto of Mainz, was eaten alive by mice.

BONN

Anyone who loves spy stories knows Bonn from John le Carré's *A Small Town in Germany* (1968). Bonn was founded by the Romans on the site of a Celtic settlement conquered in A.D. 44. The city lay on a key route from Koblenze in the south to outposts in the north. In 1238, Bonn became the residence of the archbishop of Köln, who continued to live in Bonn until 1794. The university was founded in 1815. The great Roman Catholic biblical scholar Johannes Martin Augustinus Scholz (1794–1852) was on the faculty and for a short while the dean. A student of Hug, he responded to rationalist attacks on the Bible by traveling widely in the Middle East in search of early New Testament manuscripts. He succeeded in finding 616 original texts. From 1949–90 Bonn was the undisputed capital of West Germany. Now the city is in transition as the seat of government slowly moves back to Berlin.

PLACES TO VISIT

BONN MÜNSTER (Bonn Cathedral), built in 1239, is a good example of late Rhineland Romanesque, although most of the interior has been renovated in the Baroque style. The well-preserved cloisters are Romanesque.

BEETHOVENHAUS (Beethoven House), 20 Bonngasse, is the birthplace of the composer Ludwig van Beethoven (1770–1827) and a must-see for music lovers.

The composer Robert Schumann (1810–56) and his wife Clara Wieck (1816–96) are buried in the **old cemetery** near the main railway station. Schumann's music along with that of Beethoven led into the Romantic age of German culture. Although they were cosmopolitan artists, their work set the stage for the great Nationalist pseudo-religious movements of the 19th century that found expression in the music of Richard Wagner (1813–83).

In the cemetery you will also find a small Teutonic knights chapel built in 1250 and moved to its present site in 1846.

HAUS DER GESCHICHTE DER BUNDES-REPUBLIK DEUTSCHLAND (House of the History of the Federal Republic of Germany), Adenauerallee 250. For anyone uninterested in music, the main attraction of Bonn is the excellent museum which was the brainchild of Chancellor Helmut Kohl (1932–). Here is a superb exhibit of 20th-century German history that begins with the Nazi dictatorship and includes the defeat of the Nazi regime, post-war reconstruction, the Cold War, and eventual reunification. Anyone wishing to understand our times ought to visit this impressive museum. When entering, don't fail to watch the video exhibits of wartime destruction, refugees, and the pathetic clips of children, large and small, appearing on movie news programs to say where they were "found" in an attempt to find their parents. The unspoken message of these films says more about modern German uncertainty and reactions to religion than entire books.

RHEINISCHES LANDESMUSEUM (Rhineland Museum). This excellent collection contains the famed Roman masterpiece, the sun god mosaic, from around 250. There is also the altar to mothers, which was part of the family cult in the Roman army stationed on the Rhine. Numerous other Roman statues and other items can be seen here. The medieval collection contains a good section on the Franks, depicting life before and after the age of Charlemagne (742–814). Other exhibits include Gothic paintings as well as works by later masters.

COBURG

Coburg is first documented in 1056 when the town belonged to Emperor Otto II. Martin Luther, based in Wittenberg, decided to attend the Saxon Reform Congregation scheduled for April 25, 1518, in Heidelberg. On April 5, accompanied by two friends, Luther set off on foot, arriving in Coburg ten days later, tired, but in good spirits. This was his first visit to Coburg. Twelve years later, in 1530, Luther found refuge in Coburg Castle during the debates of the Augsburg Parliament which created the Augsburg Confession. Luther reached Coburg on Good Friday, April 15, 1530, and preached on Easter Day. Then during the night of April 23–24, he was secretly taken to Coburg Castle, where he lived incognito, for fear of arrest by Imperial troops, in the Fürstenhaus (Prince's Lodgings) until October.

During his stay Luther had Psalm 1:6 ("For the Lord knows the way of the

C

righteous, but the way of the wicked will perish"), Psalm 118:17 ("I shall not die, but I shall live, and recount the deeds of the Lord"), and Psalm 74:21 ("Let not the downtrodden be put to shame; let the poor and needy praise thy name") painted on the walls of his rooms for encouragement.

While in hiding, Luther suffered a long illness from which he slowly recovered. He also learned of the death of his father, Hans Luther, on June 5.

Because of its location on a direct trade route from the Alps via Augsburg and Nürnberg to the port of Hamburg, Coburg was a rich, strategically placed duchy. In 1532, the town and castle, which were Protestant, withstood a siege by the Imperial Catholic armies of Wallenstein. But Coburg is perhaps best known as the birthplace of Queen Victoria's husband, Prince Albrecht (Albert), of the House of Sachsen-Coburg-Gotha, which excelled in arranging dynastic marriages with the royal houses of Europe. Prince Albrecht is credited with introducing Christmas trees into the Anglo-Saxon world.

PLACES TO VISIT

SCHLOß EHRENBURG (Castle Ehrenburg), the official residence of the Duke of Coburg from 1547–1918, was named in honor of Emperor Karl V upon his visit in 1547. Here one finds the richly decorated Queen Victoria's apartments that convey the sense of high imperialism associated with her reign. Anyone wishing to understand the 19th-century missionary movement needs to appreciate the way the ideology of imperialism competed with Christianity as a motive for spreading the gospel.

The Schloß chapel is a stunning example of Lutheran Baroque architecture with luxurious stucco decorations.

Work was begun on VESTE COBURG (Coburg Castle) around 1050 and it was added to over the centuries. Today it is the best-preserved large medieval fortress in Germany with three defensive zwinger (wall rings) enclosing several inner courts. The FÜRSTENBAU (Duke's Quarter) contains well-preserved Martin Luther rooms plus a rich collection of artworks by Reformation artists like Lucas Cranach the Elder (1472–1553) and Albrecht Dürer (1471–1528), as well as works by the Dutch artist Rembrandt van Rijn (1606–69) and other great painters.

PFARRKIRCHE ST. MORITZ (Parish Church of St. Moritz), close to the impressive MARKTPLATZ (Marketplace), which is rich in Renaissance buildings, is well worth a visit. The oldest surviving building in the town itself, this fine 12th-century Gothic church has two very different towers with helmetlike caps.

COLOGNE- SEE KÖLN

DRESDEN

Around A.D. 600, Sorbe tribes from the steppes moved into the region because it was a flood-free stretch of the Elbe valley; they pushed the indigenous Germanic tribes to the west. In old Sorbic, Dresden is *drezd'ane*. The area was part of the bishopric of Meißen from 968. Dresden was first mentioned in documents in 1004, when the area was called *Nisa*. The city was founded about 1200 and first described as a city in 1216. In Slavic the name means "Swamp in the Forest." After defeating the Saxons, Charlemagne turned east to subdue the Sorbes and protect the borders of his realm.

Despite this, the general area was far less Christian than other parts of Germany with only one percent of the population, a low figure for the Middle Ages, in religious orders. In 1450, Dresden boasted a population of 6000. Unfortunately by 1501 a series of epidemics had reduced the population to a mere 2,500. In response to the problems created by these plagues, various churches donated funds to build numerous bathhouses. The poor and destitute were then required to take regular baths on predetermined days. Gradually, as the 16th century advanced, the town prospered through trade in grain, local tin mines, the manufacture of pewter, and the brewing of beer.

During the Reformation, the strong-willed ruler Georg (ruled 1500–39) remained a Roman Catholic until his death. Only then did new times begin, with far-reaching political, intellectual, and social effects on life in Dresden. Martin Luther (1483–1546) visited Dresden in 1516 and 1518 when he was invited to a friendly supper. This meeting turned into an interrogation about his new theology during which one of his sermons was strongly criticized. Following Luther's break with Rome, there were many hostile encounters and even the beheading of a Protestant in Dresden. Luther's books, brought by traveling booksellers, were banned. The books were burnt and the booksellers imprisoned. During this time of unrest, Dresden became a center of anti-Protestant propaganda led by the printer Wolfgang Stöcke, a highly educated artisan who had originally printed both Protestant and Catholic polemics in his native Bavaria. At first the Augustinian monks in Dresden were open to the Reformation. But later they supported the Catholic cause.

The first Protestant rulers, Heinrich der Fromme (Heinrich the Pious) (ruled 1539–41), and sons Moritz (ruled 1541–53) and August (1553–86) faced staggering odds and only gradually transformed their land into a Protestant

D

area. Nevertheless, with the conversion of Heinrich the Pious, all the people in his domain officially became Protestants according to the principle of *cuius regio eius religio* (whoever rules may establish the religion of the land). From then on, with the exception of the rule of August der Starke (August the Strong) (1670–1733), Saxony has remained Protestant.

August the Strong gained his name because he is supposed to have broken an iron horseshoe with his bare hands, and because of his unrestrained sexual adventures and numerous mistresses, one of whom was the abbess of Quedlinburg. He converted to Catholicism in 1697 to gain the Polish crown. A particularly vile ruler, he wreaked havoc in his newly acquired kingdom of Poland, destroying both its economy and military power until he was deposed in 1706. His throne was restored by the Russians in 1710, making him a puppet ruler for the next 23 years.

During this time, the Saxon economy was also devastated as August raised funds to turn Dresden into the Florence of the Elbe. His grandiose building program impoverished his people, but created an amazingly beau-

tiful Baroque city, the glory of which was the Zwinger (Outer Courtyard). August the Strong's life and outrageous actions so angered his Protestant subjects that it took another century before the ruler August III dared build a Roman Catholic church in Dresden, called the Hofkirch (Court Church). *Hamlet* was first staged in Dresden in 1626, and Italian opera arrived in 1672 but only flourished in the mid-18th century. Through the Peace of Dresden in 1745, the State of Prussia was granted the Austrian Province of Selesia, and in 1814 the Saxon Bible Association was formed.

The famed Dresden Boys Choir was founded around 1200 during a religious revival which saw the construction of many new churches. A choir was formed at the Court in 1548, which eventually developed into the Saxon State Orchestra and Saxon State Opera Company, both of which are still first class. During the 16th century, Heinrich Schütz (1585–1672) was the choirmaster. During the 19th century, Carl Maria von Weber (1786–1826) made Dresden a center of both the new German opera and Romanticism. Deeply Catholic, he wrote secular operas

HEINRICH SCHÜTZ (1585–1672) is generally considered the father of German music. He is the first composer to write in the German language; earlier works were composed in Latin. A forerunner of Johann Sebastian Bach (1685–1750), his church music is among the best Christian music. He developed what became the Baroque style of music and made the court in Dresden a center of European musical culture.

and pious church music. He was succeeded in the German musical canon by Richard Wagner (1813–83), who at times toyed with Catholic imagery while developing his essentially pagan works. Wagner's operas *Tannhäuser* and *Lohengrin* were written in Dresden. The composer Robert Schumann (1810–56) was also very productive during his stay in this highly cultural city, as was Richard Strauss (1864–1949), who premiered nine of his operas in Dresden.

Perhaps the greatest Allied blunder of World War II was the bombing of Dresden at Stalin's request. On the night of February 13–14, 1945, in the closing weeks of the war, Allied bombers completely destroyed the inner city, which was packed with refugees and a large number of Allied prisoners of war. Kurt Vonnegut vividly recaptures the events of that night in his surrealist science fiction novel *Slaughterhouse Five* (1969). He survived as an American prisoner of war working in an old slaughterhouse deep underground. Later he was forced to clear the rubble and bury the dead. In all, over 50 historic churches were destroyed in the raid and between 30,000 and 250,000 people killed.

PLACES TO VISIT

Long a symbol of the Reformation, the **FRAUENKIRCHE** (Church of Our Lady) was built in 1726 by Georg Bähr (1666–1738). Its vast sandstone dome was a wonder of 18th-century architecture that produced magnificent acoustics. J. S. Bach was one of the first people to play on the Silberman organ in an Advent recital following the opening of the church. Before the church stood an imposing statue of Martin Luther. The bronze statue remains, but the church is in ruins due to the collapse of the dome after the British bombing destroyed Dresden on February 14, 1945. Today, the area around the church is a vast construction site as it is rebuilt using the original plans and, as far as possible, original materials. The effort taken to rebuild this impressive church is a moving experience that speaks of the futility of war and the nature of faith. The new church is due to open in the year 2006.

The Roman Catholic **KATHEDRALE TRINITATIS** (Cathedral of the Trinity) is a well-restored Baroque sanctuary built between 1738 and 1755 and is the largest church in Saxony. Over the high altar is a painting of the Ascension by Raphael Megs.

MORMON-GEMEINDEHAUS (Mormon Temple) was opened in 1988 in the Strehlen area adjacent to the Großer Garten (Great Park). Unlike many Protestant denominations, the Mormons quickly recognized the collapse of Communism and speedily established their presence in former East Germany.

Restored by the Communists in the the 1970s, the **ZWINGER** was built by Matthäus Daniel Pöppelmann (1662–1736) with sculptures by Balthasar Permoser (1651–1732) and is regarded as the jewel in the crown of German Baroque. The decadent ethos, sensual love of pleasure, and lack of social concern, reflects the wealth of a small ruling class. It helps explain the popularity of Pietism and the strong reaction of contemporary German Pietists and English Methodists against the arts,

D

KARL MAY (1842–1912) is beyond doubt the favorite author of Germans and by far the best-selling writer Germany has produced. Yet his place in German life is highly ambiguous possibly because of his very success, which makes him an anathema to most intellectuals.

May's best-loved character is the Apache chief Winnetou, whose adventures have thrilled generations of readers. Unlike so many writers of his time, May's work is remarkable for its lack of racism. He genuinely appreciated other cultures and often promoted the value of interracial marriage in his stories. Africans, Arabs, the English, French, Russians—all figure in May's works as good and evil characters with a complete disregard for nationalism or racial origins. Men are good or bad as men, not because they belong to a particular race or creed.

A serious intent and deeply spiritual motivation inspires all of May's writings. Beyond doubt his early writings, including his Winnetou series and related novels, fall in the category of Christian fiction at its best. But May's tolerant spirit annoyed many Roman Catholics, while his refusal to convert to Protestantism alienated Protestants. Consequently, May was rejected by more conservative Christians who often treated him very shamefully. In turn, he gradually rejected them and moved away from orthodoxy, at least in his novels.

By the end of his life, May was writing highly philosophical novels which speculated about religious pluralism and clearly reflect the influence of Ludwig Andreas Feuerbach (1804–72). Thus, his later novels move from Christian novels to something approaching the type of theosophical speculation that became popular in the New Age movement. May's work influenced generations of readers from Albert Einstein (1879–1955) to the anthropologists Robert Löwie (1883–1957) and B. Malinowski (1884–1942) and theologian Albert Schweitzer (1875–1965). But his popular style alienated him from the literary elite who looked down on the optimism and positive outlook of his adventure stories. In spite of his continued popularity in the German-speaking world, very few of his books are available in English, although his most popular work *Winnetou* was translated in 1977.

including the theater, which were seen as wasting valuable resources that could be better used to help the poor.

GEMÄLDERGALERIE ALTER MEISTER (Old Masters Collection), northeast side of the Zwinger, was first assembled by August the Strong and contains numerous artistic masterpieces including works by Rubens (1577–1640), van Dyck (1599–1641), Raphael (1483–1520), Titian (d. 1576), Brueghel (1568–1625), Hals (1580–1666), Rembrandt (1606–69), and numerous other artists plus German works by men like Hans Baldung Grien (1484–1545), Lucas Cranach (1472–1553), Albrecht Altdorfer (1480–1538) and Albrecht Dürer (1471–1528), and many others. Anyone interested in art history must visit this outstanding collection of art.

GEMÄLDERGALERIE NEUER MEISTER (New Masters Collection), Albertinum, is housed in a converted arsenal and was established in 1884. It contains works by Caspar David Friedrich (1774–1840), Adolf von Menzel (1815–1905), Max Liebermann (1847–1935), and many other Romantic and modern artists. In particular, look out for the work of the evangelical Christian artist Adrian Ludwig Richter (1803–84), who was one of the very few evangelical Christians to gain recognition as a great artist during the 19th century. His success in blending Christian faith with artistic creativity in a semi-Romantic style speaks for itself.

KARL MAY MUSEUM, Karl May Strasse 5, Radebeul. This fascinating museum in the suburb of Radebeul should not be overlooked. Here you will discover the life and work of Karl May (1842–1912), Germany's all-time best-selling author whose works have influenced generations. The museum is well laid out with books, manuscripts, and numerous items related to May's work. Of particular interest is his collection of materials related to North American Native culture, which May loved and popularized in Germany.

EICHSTÄTT

Located in the Altmühl (Oldmill Valley), Eichstätt was known in Celtic as *Alcmona,* meaning "holy" or "quiet river." The town is often referred to as a "Spiritual City," the center of which is the cathedral, a Benedictine cloister (abbey), and the new Catholic University, which was founded in 1980. The town grew up around the monastery founded by the English missionary St. Willibald (700–786), who first evangelized Muslims before being sent to join St. Boniface's (680–754) German mission. He began to evangelize the Eichstätt area, where he founded a monastery on the site of the present cathedral (which was founded in the 14th century). The bishopric was created by St. Boniface in 720. In these efforts he was supported by his brother, St. Winnebald, and sister, St. Walburga. All three were born in the South of England and were relatives (through their mother) to St. Boniface, whom they joined as pioneer missionaries to Germany.

St. Willibald (700–786) was born in the Christian kingdom of Wessex, England. After becoming a monk, he traveled widely, visiting Rome, Cyprus, Syria, and Palestine, where he went on a pilgrimage to various sites associated with Christ and visited numerous Christian communities. His travels were written about in what is probably the first Western European travel book, the *Hodoeporicon* (728). Following visits to Constantinople and Rome, he was assigned to the monastery of Monte Cassino, where he carried out extensive reforms and revitalized its spiritual life. At the request of St. Boniface (680–754), he went to Germany as a missionary. There he was ordained priest and later, in 724, bishop of Eichstätt. He founded several monasteries, including a large double (i.e., for men and women) monastery at Heidenheim. His monasteries were based on the practices of Monte Cassino, where his brother Winnebald (d. 761) was the abbot and his sister, Walburga (d. 779), the abbess. He was a bishop for 45 years and died in Eichstätt.

St. Walburga (710–79), abbess of Heidenheim, was born in the English kingdom of Wessex, where she entered the abbey of Wimborne. At the request of Boniface, she joined his mission to Germany, where she worked closely with her brothers, Willibald and Winnebald (d. 761), who were also missionaries. After Winnebald's death in 761, she became the head of the double monastery of Heidenheim.

Eichstätt is associated with the pious Pappenheim family, whose son, Count Gottfried Heinrich Pappenheim (1594–1632), became a field marshal of the Holy Roman Empire and a leading military figure in the armies of the Catholic Counter-Reformation. In 1634 the town was almost totally destroyed by fire. Rebuilt in the Baroque style, the inner city (which is surrounded by the old city wall) has character and charm.

PLACES TO VISIT

DOM (Cathedral) reflects a variety of architectural styles—Romanesque, Gothic, and Baroque. It also contains the relics of St. Walburga. The Pappenheim altar, donated in 1489, is a 30-feet high masterpiece of Late Gothic carving by the Nürnberg artist Steinmetz von Wirsberger.

The lifelike statue to St. Willibald, the first bishop, by the German sculptor Loy Hering is a fine example of Renaissance style which is rare in Germany. Hering also carved the Wolfstein altar and the Crucifix in the SAKRAMENTSKAPELLE (Chapel of the Holy Sacrament).

MORTUARIUM (mortuary), a funeral chapel built in the late 15th century, contains four fine stained-glass windows by

Hans Holbein the Elder (1465–1524). The roof vaulting is also carefully crafted.

DIÖZESANMUSEUM (Diocesan Museum) contains various artworks along with a very interesting 12th-century vestment, known as St. Willibald's chasuble, which is of Byzantine origin.

RESIDENZPLATZ (Bishop's Place of Residence) adjoining the cathedral has a fountain with a 59-foot column containing a gilded statue of the Virgin Mary.

The Jesuit church, **SCHUTZEN-GELKIRCHE** (Guardian Angel Church), is located in the Leonrodplatz (Leonrod Place).

CONVENT OF ST. WALBURGA, named after the sister of St. Willibald and St. Winnebald, is a 17th-century Benedictine monastery church and convent. A popular pilgrimage center, it contains the saint's tomb.

EISENACH

Founded in the 11th century under the protection of the Wartburg Fortress, Eisenach, like many medieval towns, grew on an important trade route. During the Middle Ages Eisenach was a great cultural and jousting center. Here troubadours and knights competed in the annual contests that inspired Richard Wagner's (1813–83) opera *Tannhäuser*. Here too Martin Luther (1483–1546) lived as a young student and later took refuge, from May 4, 1521–March 6, 1522, in the Wartburg Fortress after he was declared a heretic at the Diet of Worms (1521). During this time Luther, who was disguised as Junker Jörg (Gentleman George), translated the New Testament into German. Professor Ernst Abbe, who founded the world-famous Zeiss optical works, was born here in 1840.

PLACES TO VISIT

LUTHER STATUE in front of the **NICKOLAIKIRCHE** (Church of St. Nicholas)

has a series of bronze plaques on its base depicting key episodes in Luther's life. The Romanesque church was founded in 1200.

GEORGENKIRCHE (Church of St. George), originally built between 1180–88, was remodeled in Gothic style in the early 16th century.

Inside the church is a statue of Bach. It was created in 1939 and commemorates the Bach family's close ties with this church. Johann Sebastian Bach moved away from Eisenach to live with his brother, Johan Christoph, in Ohrdruf after his parents died in 1695.

On the north wall is a large painting commissioned to commemorate the centenary of the Reformation. It depicts Luther and Huss as well as the presentation of the Augsburg Confession to Emperor Karl V. In 1989 the congregation played an important role in organizing demonstrations against Communism in the closing days of the DDR.

LUTHERHAUS (Luther's House) was once the residence of the Cotta family,

E

RICHARD WAGNER (1813–83) was the author of numerous stirring musical compositions, marches, and operas. Wagner was deeply affected by the philosophies of his time and the widespread rejection of Christianity by the educated elite, including Feuerbach and later Nietzsche (1844–1900), with whom Wagner was close friends for a number of years. His rabid anti-Semitism, revolutionary commitments, and great talent as a musician made him a powerful propagandist for the growing German National movement of the 19th century. His son-in-law, Houston Steward Chaimberlain (1855–1927), played a major role in inspiring the Nazi movement through his many books. The most important of these was *The Foundations of the 19th Century* (1911). Chaimberlain is one of the few people to whom Adolf Hitler (1889–1945) openly acknowledged an intellectual debt.

with whom Luther is supposed to have lived as a young student. It is an interesting 15th-century half-timber house that houses a museum devoted to the life and times of Luther.

BACHHAUS (Bach's House), the birthplace of the great composer, houses a fascinating collection of original musical instruments from Bach's lifetime.

FRITZ REUTER AND RICHARD WAGNER MUSEUM, Reuterweg, is a must for opera lovers. This was the home of a famous 19th-century German Nationalist, poet Fritz Reuter (1810–74), who was a close friend of Richard Wagner (1813–83).

WARTBURG CASTLE is the main reason most people visit Eisenach. This impressive fortress is perched on a high cliff with a magnificent view of the surrounding countryside. The castle became a museum at the suggestion of Goethe (1749–1832), and during the

19th century, it became a major symbol of German Nationalism.

Built by Count Ludwig I in 1067 as a defense against Saxon invasion, it became a major medieval court. You have to join a German-speaking guided tour to enter the castle itself. Although the guides are very helpful, it is worth obtaining an English text before the tour begins. Despite these minor inconveniences, the tour should not be missed.

On the tour you will visit the **KNIGHTS HALL,** the **CHAPEL,** built in the 13th century, the **HALL OF SONGS** which inspired Wagner, the **LANDGRAVE'S HALL,** and the **FESTIVAL HALL.** Each site is rich in history and legend. Notice the mural in the Festival Hall, actually a 19th-century creation depicting the triumph of Christianity over paganism. The tour ends with the MUSEUM which contains paintings by Luther's friend Lucas

Cranach, including portraits of Luther's parents.

Finally don't miss the **LUTHERSTIEGE** (Luther's Room). This is not part of the main tour but should be a must for visitors. Here you can see where Luther labored to translate the New Testament into German. It has period furnishings, some of which Luther probably used, and an original copy of Luther's translation of the Bible. On the back wall, you can see where the plaster has been chipped away. This is where Luther is said to have flung his inkpot when the Devil appeared to tempt him. The inkspot itself was removed by souvenir hunters.

EISLEBEN
(LUTHERSTADT-EISLEBEN)

Founded due to a mining boom in the foothills of the Harz mountains during the late Middle Ages, Eisleben became a prosperous industrial center. Martin Luther's father owned mines in the area. Martin Luther (1483–1546) was born, received his early education, and died here.

PLACES TO VISIT

One of the few blessings of 50 years of Communist rule is that Eisleben is off the main tourist routes. Slightly out of the way, although actually very easy to reach, it doesn't even appear in many guide books and hasn't a Web site of its own. But don't let these things put you off. Eisleben is well worth a visit. In the town you will see many somewhat run-down medieval houses.

LUTHER GEBURTSHAUS (the house where Luther was born), Lutherstraße 16, is now a well-constructed museum depicting the life of the Reformer. It is said that Luther was born shortly before midnight on November 10, 1483. But no one was really sure of the exact time. So he could have been born on the 11th, and even his mother admitted she didn't know the exact year. These confusions don't bother historians, who give his date of birth as November 10, 1483. Knowing the confusion about Luther's real birthday helps us remember that the world in which he lived was very different from our own.

Christians often worry about the exact date of Christ's birth and are troubled about apparent inconsistencies in biblical chronology. The fact is that in the past people viewed time and dates quite differently. The chronology of Luther's life is actually very difficult to reconstruct despite a wealth of documents, and historians are quite open about the fact that they do not understand many things related to Luther's life. Therefore, in the absence of alternate evidence, they usually accept traditional accounts.

The frank admission of historians that many events in Luther's life are hard to reconstruct makes us realize that the "assured" results of biblical criticism, such as those put forward by the so-called Jesus Seminar, are not as certain as many people want to believe. We have far more evidence about the life and times of Luther than we do about the life and times of Jesus. Yet theologians speak with seemingly complete certainty about Jesus, telling us that many of the events in his life are fictitious, whereas historians refrain from commenting on similar events in the life of men like Luther. This ought to teach us all to be more humble when we approach any historical event and not to believe those who tell us that "such-and-such a thing never happened in the way the New Testament tells its story." The fact is, we simply do not know the answer to many questions about the life of Jesus. Therefore, as with the life of Luther, it is always wise to follow the traditional account.

The best modern biography is Martin Brett's three-volume *Luther*. Brett suggests that 1482 is probably the true year of Luther's birth. Another sidelight which Brett throws on Luther's life is his comment that "because of the uncertainty over the date of his birth, Luther later had little concern for astrology or horoscopes. For him the course of his life was one of miraculous leading."

LUTHER STERBEHAUS (the house where Luther died), Andreaskirchplatz 7. In this interesting house you can still see the bed where Luther died. In the rear, there is also a fascinating mining museum reminding visitors of Luther's origins. Actually, Luther was proud of his peasant origins and spoke of himself as a farmer's son. In reality, his father was a moderately successful businessman who owned copper mines. His father could not inherit the family farm near Möhra because under Thuringian law it was the younger son who inherited the family estate.

Once again, we are reminded that when dealing with another age and society, we cannot assume that our own view of the world is the same as the one we are seeking to understand. To the modern mind, Luther's claim to be a "farmer's son" is technically incorrect just as the genealogies of Jesus found in the New Testament are often said to be "incorrect" because they omit entire generations. But, in fact, this is the way people thought in the past, as do many people today who still live in peasant communities. To Luther, he was the son of a farmer just as Jesus was the son of David.

For Luther and many of his contemporaries, the importance of his peasant origins lay in the fact that someone from such a lowly background could succeed in becoming a professor of theology. This was unthinkable social mobility and a proof of God's providence.

MARKTKIRCHE ST. ANDREAS (Market Church of St. Andrew) is where Luther often preached when he visited the town, as he did shortly before his final illness. This is a Late Gothic hall church with an interesting winged altar. There are three other small churches in the town, all of which are moderately interesting.

HEIMATMUSEUM (Local History Museum), Andreaskircheplatz 7, has an interesting collection of mining tools from Luther's time.

ERFURT

In 742, St. Boniface established Erfurt on a ford in the river Gera as a bishopric and center of regional evangelism. The town prospered during the Middle Ages because the region was rich in woad plants, the main source of blue dye before the introduction of indigo in the 16th century. It was also on the main trade route to Russia. The town was fortified in 1168 and its university, where Luther studied from 1507–11, was founded in 1392. The university was closed when Erfurt came under Prussian rule in 1816, but has recently been reopened as a Catholic university.

The growth of Leipzig and decline of the woad trade, which has been revived in the last few years as an organic source of dye, led to the town's decline in the 16th century. In the 18th century, the town became the center of a rich horticultural region and seed trade. It was badly damaged during the Napoleonic wars, although many fine medieval buildings can still be found here. Napoleon Bonaparte met the famous German philosopher Goethe here on October 2, 1808. Today Erfurt is the capital of Thüringen and one of the most dynamic towns in the former DDR. Its Altstadt (Old City) escaped destruction in World War II.

PLACES TO VISIT

Erfurt is rich in religious history and was a center of spiritual ferment during the 16th century. Therefore there are many churches and former monasteries scattered around the town.

DOMBERG (Cathedral Hill) is the site of two magnificent churches and various 16th-century houses.

MARIENDOM (Cathedral of Mary) was built in 1154 to replace Boniface's earlier wooden building and has been enlarged over the centuries. This large building conveys an amazing impression of lightness. The final product is a fine example of Gothic architecture. In the central tower is one of the largest bells in Europe, the Maria Gloriosa, which miraculously escaped destruction when the Nazis began melting down church bells to make munitions.

E

Look out for the carvings of the wise and foolish virgins on the north doors. Here too are the twin statues of the church triumphant and the synagogue defeated. Notice the distorted way the woman who portrays the synagogue is standing. On closer inspection, you will see that she is desperately trying to hide a lamb behind her back. The symbolism refers to the burnt offerings of the Old Testament and the failure of Jews to recognize Christ as the Lamb of God. Inside the dom you can also find a Judensau on the side of the choir stalls. Here a Jew, recognized by his pointed hat, is riding a sow in a tournament with a Christian knight on horseback. The fish, carried by the knight, and the initials IXOYC (the Greek name of Jesus written in the Latin alphabet) emphasize the point that he is not an ordinary knight but a true Christian. In light of the destruction of Germany's Jewish community during the Third Reich, such symbols now call Christians to repentance for the tragedy of Jewish history in Europe.

The Romanesque altar of the Virgin (1160) is a rare masterpiece. The stained-glass windows, which help give the building its feeling of lightness, depict both biblical scenes and everyday life in the Middle Ages.

The triple-spired SEVERIKIRCHE, also on the Domberg, was built between 1278–1360. It is the earliest example of Gothic architecture in Erfurt. It is dedicated to St. Severus of Ravenna in Italy.

The high altar is an elaborate Baroque creation built in the late 17th century. The church contains the richly decorated sarcophagus of St. Severus.

PETERSBURG is an area behind the dom that formed the core of the medieval town. In the Middle Ages, it was also the core of the city's spiritual life, which centered on the Benedictine monastery of St. Peter. The former monastery was turned into a fortress by the archbishop of Mainz in the 17th century and was later used as a powder magazine by Prussian troops in the early 19th century. Today it is largely in ruins.

AUGUSTINERKIRCHE AND KLOSTER (Church of St. Augustine and monastery), Augustinerstraße 10, was founded in the 13th century. Like many places in Germany, it is closed on Mondays and can only be seen inside by joining a guided tour. This is where Luther lived and studied as an Augustinian monk. One of the monk's cells is said to be Luther's. Coming here helps the visitor understand the piety and religious devotion of the great Reformer and the spiritual influences that shaped his life. Here you will find some exquisite stained glass, including a window depicting St. Augustine of Hippo (354–430), after whom the order of monks that Luther joined was named.

Close to St. Augustine's, near the Krämerbrücke, is the SCHOTTENKIRCHE (Scottish Church), which has a misleading Baroque facade that hides a pure

Romanesque structure of great simplicity. The church's name reminds visitors of the international nature of medieval Christianity and the fact that many of the monks who studied in Erfurt were from Britain.

MICHAELISKIRCHE (Church of St. Michael), Michaelisstrasse, is an Early Gothic church that was originally the University Chapel. Here Luther would have worshiped as a student. It has a fine Renaissance altar, good glasswork, and a restful courtyard.

COLLEGIUM MAJUS (Main College) is the only part of the old university to survive the bombing of World War II and is located opposite the Michaeliskirche. The building contains an excellent collection of ancient manuscripts in its Amploniana archive, many of which are on display to the public.

KRÄMERBRÜKE (Bridge of Shops) is unique in Germany and indeed northern Europe as an example of a medieval bridge that contains houses still in use as people's homes, most of which were actually built or rebuilt in the 17th century. As in Luther's time, the bridge still

has a number of shops. At the end of the bridge is a **BRIDGE CHAPEL**. Such places were common in the Middle Ages, when they were used by travelers to pray for safety before leaving the security of a town. Today this small Gothic structure is a Methodist church.

KAUFMANNSKIRCHE (Merchant's Church), Johannesstrasse. This is Erfurt's oldest church and the place where Johann Sebastian Bach's parents were married. It is a Romanesque structure decorated with paintings by local artists.

ANGERMUSEUM (Anger Museum), Bahnofstrasse. The name of this area has nothing to do with the English word *anger*. Rather, it takes its name from the German word for *meadow* and is now a popular shopping district. The museum is housed in a Baroque mansion that was once the home of the local governor. It contains some excellent medieval art, including *The Crucifixion* and *St. Michael* by the Master of St. Severus (late 15th/early 16th century). There are also works by the Cranachs (16th century) and Hans Baldung called Grien (1484–1545).

ERLANGEN

Located at the confluence of the Schwabach and Regnitz rivers, Erlangen was founded in the 9th century and is mentioned as early as 1002. It became the property of the bishop of Bamberg in 1017, when it was transferred from the bishopric of Würzburg. Emperor Karl IV (1316–78) acquired the area and built the Altstadt (Old City). Later, in 1686, after Louis

XIV of France (1638–1715) revoked the Edict of Nantes in 1685, French Huguenots were given refuge here by the farsighted ruler Margrave Christian Ernst of Kulmbach-Bayreuth. The arrival of the Huguenots brought new industries, prosperity, and education to the town.

The palace of the Markgraf (margrave), or duke, is now the main building of the Friedrich-Alexander University, founded as a Protestant institution by Margrave Friedrich in 1743 in nearby Bayreuth. It was moved to Erlangen in 1748 to become one of the outstanding educational centers in Germany. The physicist Georg Simon Ohm (1787–1854), famed for his "Ohm's Law" of electrical resistance, was born in Erlangen.

PLACES TO VISIT

The main attraction of Erlangen is its NEUSTADT (New Town), built on a rectangular grid pattern in exquisite Baroque style to accommodate French Huguenot refugees. The plan was very carefully conceived, making it one of Europe's first planned communities. Today many Baroque houses have survived to give the visitor an insight into Protestant Baroque culture and Huguenot society.

The unusual HUGENOTTENBRUNNEN (Huguenots Fountain) stands in the English garden behind the Schloss. It was given as a gesture of thanks to the Margrave of Bayreuth in 1706 by the French refugees and is a good place to begin your visit to Erlangen. It reminds us of the suffering of Christians in the 17th and 18th centuries through what today we would call "ethnic cleansing." The Huguenot contribution to those countries that gave them refuge was considerable. Today towns like Erlangen stand as a memorial to their culture and endurance.

SCHLOSS, Schlossplatz, is now the MAIN UNIVERSITY BUILDING in front of which stands a statue of its founder. The philosopher Johann Gottlieb Fichte (1762–1814), a disciple of Kant (1724–1804), taught here from 1805–6, during which time he wrote *The Characteristics of the Present Age* (1806) advocating a theory of history based on the progress of reason. He played an important role in the creation of modern nationalist ideology. Friedrich Schelling (1775–1854), a leading German Romantic philosopher, and Ludwig Feuerbach (1804–72) also taught at Erlangen. During the 19th century, the Pietist Erlangen School developed as a result of a revival movement in the church. It was led by Johann Christian Konrad von Hofmann (1810–77). Today the university has one of the more conservative theological faculties in Germany and maintains a strong interest in missions.

FAMOUS PROFESSORS AT THE FRIEDRICH-ALEXANDER UNIVERSITY

FRIEDRICH WILHELM VON SCHELLING (1775–1854) was a leading German Romantic philosopher who as a young man was a disciple of Fichte, and who in turn influenced Hegel. He lectured at Erlangen from 1820–27, where he advocated a pantheist philosophy that contributed to the rise of German neopaganism.

LUDWIG FEUERBACH (1804–72), the son of a lawyer and legal philosopher, was born in Landshut. He obtained his doctorate from the university of Erlangen in 1828, where he taught until 1832 when the scandal associated with the publication of his *Thought on Death and Immortality* (1830), a vicious attack on Christianity, caused his dismissal from the faculty. Feuerbach went on to write *The Essence of Christianity* (1804–72) and various other works that developed his criticisms of religion. Feuerbach was a systematic materialist philosopher. He studied under Hegel, whose idealism he rejected in favor of his own thoroughgoing materialism. Subsequently, he strongly attacked religious beliefs, especially those of Protestant Christianity as represented by Schleiermacher (1768–1834), by arguing that the idea of God is an outward projection of man's inner nature. Thus the idea of the Holy Family reflects the inadequacies of actual human families and subconsciously compensates for them in the imagination of the believer. His work is usually thought about in terms of the profound influence it had on Karl Marx (1818–83), who accepted and developed his basic criticisms of religion. Therefore, he is usually described as a "left-wing philosopher." This interpretation of Feuerbach's influence overlooks the fact that he also deeply affected many right-wing thinkers like Paul de Lagaard (1827–91), thus contributing to the 19th-century revival of German neopaganism.

JOHANN CHRISTIAN KONRAD VON HOFMANN (1810–77) converted to Christianity as a student at Erlangen. He studied with Hengstenberg in Berlin before returning to Erlangen as professor of theology, where he became the leader of the "Erlangen School." He developed the idea of *Heilsgeschichtliche Theologie* (a theology of redemption), which originally sought to counter the prevailing rationalism by an emphasis on both scholarship and a personal experience of Christ.

TRINITY CHURCH on the Martin-Luther-Platz (Martin Luther Place) is a hall church with elevated seating around its walls.

ST. PETER UND ST. PAUL (Church of St. Peter and St. Paul) is a Baroque structure with an imposing painted ceiling.

HUGENOTTENKIRCHE (Huguenot Church), Bahnhofplatz, built between 1686 and 1693, has unusual wooden galleries that create the impression that the church is a round building. It stands as a testimony to the simplicity and communal spirit of the Huguenot community.

ESSEN

Evidence exists that the region around Essen was settled before A.D. 800. A stone blade tool found near Düsseldorf, south of the city, in 1865, suggests human settlement more than 100,000 years ago. Bone fragments from this period have also been unearthed in nearby Bottrop. The origin of the name *Essen* is unknown. Some think it developed out of *asnidhi,* the name for the personal property of Altfrid of Hildesheim's parents.

The town was founded by the Frisian missionary Luidger (742–809) who, after he was ordained in Köln, lived for two years as a monk in the Italian monastery of Montecassino before returning to Germany. Charlemagne made him responsible for mission work in his realm and in 794 entrusted him with the founding of a new bishopric. Thus the city of Essen grew up around the Münster (church) and stift (convent) founded by Luidger to provide education for the daughters of Saxon aristocrats.

In 796 Luidger founded the nearby abbey of Werden, where he is buried, as a Benedictine monastery. Later it became an imperial abbey and center of culture during the Middle Ages. The town of Werden became part of Essen in 1929.

The 6th-century Codex Argenteus (Gothic Bible), the work of Wulfila, Ulfila, or "Little Wolf" (310/313–381/383), was once housed here in the library. Likewise, parts of the *Heliand Song (Holy Hymn),* which marks the beginning of German literature, are said to have been composed in Werden around 830. The first abbess of the convent was Altfrid's sister, Gerwida. Daughters of the Imperial House of Saxony also attended the monastery, which contains some impressive art treasures in its minster.

Today, Essen is best known because of its industrial and commercial importance as the home of Krupp Iron Works. Because of the industrial importance of Essen, the city was almost totally destroyed by British bombers during World War II.

PLACES TO VISIT

MÜNSTER (Cathedral), Burgplatz. The west chancel is a 10th-century Romanesque structure modeled on the Aachen Dom, but the nave itself is a Gothic construction from the 13th century. In the *Ottonian Crypt* is the famed *Golden Madonna,* a priceless artwork that is the oldest known statue of Mary in Western Europe. A 10th-century seven-armed candelabra is also on display.

DOMSCHATZKAMMER (Cathedral Treasury) contains a wealth of ecclesiastical art, processional crosses, swords, and early German copies of the gospels.

MUSEUM FOLKWANG, Bismarckstrasse, houses a superb collection of 19th-century and 20th-century paintings, sculpture, and photography, including works by the German Romantics Carl Gustav Carus (1789–1869), Caspar David Friedrich (1774–1840), and Joseph Anton Koch (1768–1839), and the realists Arnold Böcklin (1894–1966), Anselm Feuerbach (1829–80), and Wilhelm Lebl (1844–1900). Works by Picasso (1881–1973) and Salvador Dali (1904–89) are also found here. Anyone wishing to understand the intellectual climate of the 20th century ought to view the works on display here after reading Hans Rookmaaker's *Modern Art and the Death of a Culture* (1967) or Hans Sedlmayr's *Art in Crisis* (1957).

Few places capture the creation of modern society as well as **Villa Hügel,** Haraldstraße, which was once the private residence of the Krupp family and is now open to the public. The *Krupp Collection,* which is kept in a separate location near the main house, provides unique insights into the development of modern industry and industrial capitalism.

EXTERNSTEINE

Some writers believe the area is named after Irmingard (832–66), the daughter of Queen Hemma, the wife of Ludwig der Deutsche (Ludwig the German) (843–76). From her father, she received the cloister Buchau, on the Federsee 60 kilometers southwest of Ulm close to Bad Buchau, and an income through her position in the church. She became abbess of Frauenchiemsee, an island in the Chiemsee, 100 kilometers southeast of Munich, Bavaria. During the Middle Ages, Externsteine was a place of Christian pilgrimage. Around 1115 monks created hermitages here in the caves and made rock carvings. The most remarkable of these is the five-meter tall

Kreuzabnahme (Descent from the Cross) with the bent (Irmin Column), which Bishop Heinrich II of Paderborn had carved in the rock between 1115 and 1127. In the 19th century, Romantic writers influenced by the Grimm Brothers and cult of antiquity argued that this was really an ancient pagan shrine. This idea was developed by members of the Völkische Movement in the late 19th and early 20th century. Later it was promoted by Nazi ideologues seeking a "pure Gemanic religion." According to them it was a pagan

shrine destroyed by the Christian Franks after they defeated the Saxons. They then identified the name of the area with ancient star and sun worship and the "true religion" of the Germans. Because all the existing archaeological remains are clearly Christian, these Nazi neopagan writers had to argue that earlier pagan carvings were destroyed by Charlemagne and his followers during the Saxon wars. Today it is the best-preserved sanctuary of its kind in Germany and a center for Nordic neopaganism.

FRANKFURT AM MAIN

Originally a Bronze Age settlement taken over by the Romans and later occupied by the Franks, Frankfurt grew at the site of a ford across the Rhine. It is first mentioned in documents in the 8th century. Charlemagne (742–814) gave the citizens the right to hold fairs; this right was reconfirmed by Karl IV in 1356, and the city prospered through trade. It became a free imperial city in 1372 and accepted Protestantism in 1530. Philipp Jacob Spener (1635–1705) began the Pietist movement in Frankfurt am Main with the publication of his *Pia Desideria* in 1675 and the foundation of his *Collegia Pietatis;* however, his enthusiasm for Christian piety offended many

people, and in 1686 he was encouraged to accept a call to Dresden.

From the election in 1152 of Emperor Friedrich I, called Barbarossa because of his red hair, Holy Roman emperors were chosen here. It was the site of Imperial coronations from 1562 until Napoleon dissolved the Empire in 1806. At that time he destroyed the city's fortifications and turned the area into a park, the Anlagen, which even today partially encircles the city.

A stock exchange was established here in 1595, and the Rothschilds opened their first bank here in 1798. Long before that, however, Frankfurt attracted a large Jewish community, which played an important role in the city's development. Anne Frank, for example, was born here in 1929 (1929–1945). Frankfurt's most famous son is the German statesman, writer, and poet Wolfgang Goethe (1749–1832). A center of German liberalism, it was the site of the ill-fated 1848 German Parliament. Paul Tillich (1886–1965) was a professor at the university here until he was fired by the Nazis in 1933. During World War II, much of the city, including 2000 medieval houses, was reduced to rubble.

PLACES TO VISIT

ST. BARHOLOMÄUS DOM (St. Bartholemew's Cathedral) is where Holy Roman emperors were elected from 1356 and where, after 1562, they were crowned. The church was originally built in 852 and renovated in 1882. It was badly damaged during World War II and restored in 1950. Murals, in the choir, by the Köln school (1225), depict the legend of St. Bartholemew, who according to the early church historian Eusebius, reached India in the 2nd century. There he preached the gospel before going to Armenia, where he was flayed alive.

The north chapel contains the Maria-Schlaf Altar (Altar of the Sleeping Virgin), created around 1435, portraying the 12 apostles gathered around Mary's deathbed. This is the only altar to have survived the war in its original state. Close by is the tomb of Günter von Schwarzburg, who made an unsuccessful bid for the Imperial throne against Karl IV in the 14th century. The adjacent door leads to the Wahlkapelle (Voting Chamber), where for centuries the electors chose the Holy Roman emperor.

F

PAUL TILLICH (1886–1965). Many evangelical and Roman Catholic Christians rightly object to the heretical aspects of Tillich's theology, which he developed at Union Seminary in New York. Most critics do not realize that Tillich, who was the son of a pastor, was a devout defender of Christian orthodoxy until he served in the trenches during World War I. The slaughter he observed, followed by the betrayal of his fiancée, who became pregnant by his best friend while he was at the front, led to a complete mental breakdown and loss of his earlier simple faith. After completing his theological studies, Tillich became a professor at Marburg before eventually settling in Frankfurt. He emigrated to America in 1933 following the Nazi seizure of power. To his great credit, Tillich was one of the very few Christians who saw through Nazi propaganda and consistently opposed them from the very beginning. His recognition of the evils of Nazism was closely connected with his understanding of the biblical meaning of idolatory and the importance of making God the Lord of all. This is an aspect of his theological system that is of great value.

On the west wall of the north chancel is Anthony van Dyck's (1599–1641) *Descent from the Cross* (1627). A sculpture of the *Crucifixion* (1509) by Mainz sculptor Hans Backofen (1470–1519) is nearby.

PAULSKIRCHE (Church of St. Paul), Römerplatz, was originally a preaching hall for German Pietists within the Lutheran Church. Its main importance is as the meeting place of the abortive German Parliament of 1848. This gathering of liberal and radical politicians from all over the German-speaking world attempted to create a unified Germany. At the urging of Austria, it was brought to an abrupt end by the king of Prussia, who used his army to crush the fledgling democratic movement. Following the failure of this reform movement, many German evangelicals emigrated to America in search of greater religious and political freedom. Although many evangelicals looked to this Assembly in the hope that its reforms would grant them greater religious freedom, many of the Parliament's members were strongly committed to secularism and Romantic forms of Germanic neopaganism, according to Professor Frank Eyck, one of the leading authorities on this movement. The church now houses an important historical exhibition depicting these tragic events which cast a long shadow over future German history.

JÜDISCHES MUSEUM (Jewish Museum), Untermainkai 14–15, is housed in what was once the Rothschild mansion. The origins of Frankfurt's once thriving Jewish community are unknown. What is certain is that they were well established in 1074 and until 1460 lived throughout the city. In that year they were forced to move into a ghetto, which the Jews called "New Egypt." Restricted in space and limited to four stories in height, the houses, which were intended to house 200 people, soon supported a population of well over 3000. So cramped was the living space that the home of the Rothschild family was only 30 feet wide. Yet, in this small four-story house, over 60 people lived in tiny apartments. It was from this virtual prison that the Rothschilds launched their banking empire. After the Napoleonic reforms in the early 19th century, the walls around the ghetto were demolished, and Jews were allowed to move into other areas of the city. A center of Jewish intellectual and religious life, the Frankfurt community gave birth to Reformed Judaism and several other revitalization movements that deeply affected Jewish history. Although many Frankfurt Jews escaped overseas during the Nazi years, a large number were deported to concentration camps, and over 700 others committed suicide before leaving Frankfurt. The museum documents this fascinating and tragic history with documents and numerous religious objects.

No one visiting Frankfurt should leave without seeing the **GOETHE HAUS UND MUSEUM** (Goethe House and Museum), in Grossen Hirschgraben. Although completely destroyed in

World War II, the original furniture was preserved. The house was lovingly reconstructed in the 1950s. The adjoining museum contains a wealth of documents and other artifacts related to Goethe's life.

Anyone wishing to understand the development of German intellectual life and through it modern theology must grapple with the immense intellect of Goethe, whose work placed his personal stamp on an age. Both the liberal theologian Schleiermacher (1768–1834) and the conservative Neander (1789–1850) stand in Goethe's shadow, as does almost every other German thinker throughout the 19th century. His aphorisms, plays, and poetry did for modern German and Germany what Luther and his Bible did for the 16th and 17th centuries.

FRANKFURT AN DER ODER

Founded in 1225 at a ford in the river Oder, Frankfurt an der Oder flourished from East-West trade and joined the Hanseatic League in 1365. During the Thirty Years' War, Swedish troops captured the town from the Catholic League. The town was declared a fortress by Adolf Hitler in January 1945. It became the site of a battle in the last days of the war, and most of the town was destroyed in the fire which followed. Rebuilt by the Communist DDR, it became a center of the East German computer industry. A university was founded in 1506, but closed in 1811, and reopened in 1992. Among its distinguished graduates were Alexander von Humboldt (1769–1859). The writer and poet Heinrich von Kleist (1777–1811) was born here.

PLACES TO VISIT

The once impressive **MARIENKIRCHE** (Church of Mary) is now an imposing ruin. It was here that the composer Michael Praetorius (1571–1621) played the organ until he moved away at the age of 15. Its main altar, created by a member of the Nürnberg School of artists, is now in the **ST. GERTRAUDKIRCHE**, which has a large collection of medieval furnishings and other items salvaged from the Marienkirche. Among the church's treasures is a 1471 edition of the works of St. Thomas Aquinas (1224–74). There is also a large gilt 14th-century candlestick with intricately carved biblical scenes on its stem. There is a rare bronze Gothic font by the Master Arnold (d. 1376). It boasts 44 panels depicting scenes from the Old and New Testaments.

KLEISTHAUS MUSEUM (Kleist House Museum) is dedicated to the great German Romantic writer Heinrich von Kleist (1777–1811). Profoundly influenced by the philosophy of Kant (1724–1804), the young von Kleist came

111

to believe that we live in a world without ultimate meaning where we cannot know reality. His Romantic novelette *Michael Kohlhass* (1810) vividly illustrates this philosophy. After making a superhuman attempt to establish justice, the hero is eventually condemned by the very laws he sought to uphold. Thus, like Kierkegaard (1813–55) after him, von Kleist seeks to expose the absurdity of life and the paradoxical nature of human choice. Reason and feelings are in stark contrast as the troubled novelist attempts to grasp the meaning of a reality without God.

From Frankfurt Oder a visit to nearby EISENHÜTTENSTADT, about 28 kilometers to the southwest, makes an interesting diversion on the way to the monastery NEUZELLE, which lies just beyond the town itself. Eisenhüttenstadt is a dismal modern town founded in 1951. What makes a visit worthwhile is the knowledge that the town was designed as an ideal Communist community. Only young Communists, often wartime orphans, were allowed to live there as workers for what was then the largest steelworks in East Germany. Today the steelworks employ a fraction of its former workers and unemployment runs at a record high. Intended to

be a model community, the town had no churches until the early 1990s.

A few kilometers south of Eisenhüttenstadt is KLOSTER NEUZELLE. Founded in 1280 on a hill overlooking the Oder river valley, the monastery was a center of Roman Catholicism in a predominantly Protestant area following the Thirty Years' War. The present church was built in the 18th century, when it experienced a golden age. It became the last great Cistercian monastery in Northern Germany to be secularized when the area became part of Prussia in 1817. Under the Communist government of the DDR, it was turned into a boarding school. But since the Wende (the fall of East Germany), it has been returned to the Catholic Church and extensively restored to its former glory as a Baroque church. The care with which this church has been restored is an indication of the seriousness with which German Catholics take the evangelization of former Communist lands. Sadly, the mainline German Protestant Church has not made a similar commitment to the East.

Inside the church you will find some excellent frescoes depicting biblical scenes by the Italian artist Johannes Vanet. At the east end of the church is Georg Neunherz's *Decree of Redemption,* which is a joyful painting to the praise of God.

FREIBURG IM BREISGAU

Founded in 1091 as a stronghold by Duke Berthold II of Zähringen (d. 1120), Freiburg im Breisgau was developed by his brother Duke Konrad on an oval plan. Walls were added around 1200 when work began on its cathedral. From 1368–1805, when Napoleon gave the area to the State of Baden, the picturesque university town was regarded as part of the Habsburg Empire. Close to the Black Forest, it is the center of a resort area. Located on an important trade route and close to silver mines, Freiburg prospered during the Middle Ages. The Habsburgs acquired Freiburg in 1368 through an agreement with the citizens, who bought the right to be a free city from the local feudal lord and entered into a protective agreement with the Habsburgs.

The city was stormed by peasants during a revolt in 1515. They established a short-lived tyranny, but were soon defeated by Imperial forces. Later in 1564, a large proportion of the population, over 2000 people, died of the plague. During the Thirty Years' War, the city was stormed by the Swedes in 1632 and 1638, but with relatively little damage to its beautiful buildings. From 1677–97, the French ruled Freiburg.

They strengthened its defenses to make it one of the strongest fortress cities in Germany. In 1713 and again in 1744, the French recaptured the city, which had been returned to Austrian rule. During their last occupation, they systematically destroyed its fortifications and dismantled the city walls. The German air force attacked Freiburg by mistake in 1940, killing 57 people. Later, on November 27, 1944, a massive British air raid destroyed large parts of the old city, killing 3,000 people. Miraculously, the cathedral was scarcely touched by the bombing, although nearby houses were completely destroyed.

From 1254–57, Albrecht the Great (1206–80), the Christian philosopher and teacher of Thomas Aquinas (1224–74), was provincial of the Dominican order in Germany based in Freiburg. The university was founded in 1457 by Archduke Albrecht VI of Austria. The first book containing a map which called the New World "America" was published here by Martin Waldseemüller (1480–1521) in 1507. During the 19th century, the great Roman Catholic biblical scholar Johann Leonhard Hug (1763–1846) taught here. More recently its most famous professor was Martin Heidegger (1884–1976).

F

FAMOUS PROFESSORS AT THE UNIVERSITY OF FREIBURG

JOHANN LEONHARD HUG (1763–1846) was one of the great 19th-century biblical scholars. Hug responded to rationalist criticisms of the Bible by arguing that writers like D. F. Strauss were poor historians who failed to understand the historical method. Historians, Hug argued, had to evaluate claims about miracles and supernatural events in terms of the historical evidence, not philosophical presuppositions that automatically ruled them out. He also attacked Strauss's understanding of myth, claiming that by the time the New Testament was written the Romans had developed a historical consciousness that made Strauss's theories impossible. Finally, he pointed out that Strauss failed to do justice to the evidence of the Old Testament. Hug's other work involved the dating of biblical texts and a strong defense of traditional views of authorship based on sound scholarship.

MARTIN HEIDEGGER (1884–1976) was the father of postmodernism and a major influence on radical theology. He accepted the chair of philosophy in 1928 and became rector of the university for a short time from May 1933 to April 1934. Supporters have long argued that Heidegger's resignation proved his disapproval of Nazism. But Hugo Ott's biography *Martin Heidegger: A Political Life* (1994) finally showed this claim to be false by revealing the full extent of Heidegger's Nazism.

More recently, Reinhard May has shown in his *Heidegger's Hidden Sources* (1996) that the most important passages in Heidegger's main work *Being and Time* (1927) were the result of "creative appropriation," which is a polite name for plagiarism. Apparently Heidegger copied large sections of Asian classics, including translations made by the Jewish philosopher Martin Buber (1878–1965). The extent and impact of his fraud have still not penetrated the academic community in North America, where many careers have been built on the interpretation of Heidegger's "insights."

PLACES TO VISIT

FREIBURGER MÜNSTER (Cathedral of the Beloved Virgin) is one of the great churches of Germany. Begun in 1170 and not completed until the 17th century, this is a masterpiece of Christian art. The original design was for a late Romanesque church of which only the transepts and two small towers remain. Early in the 12th century, the masons and architects began to build in the new Gothic style, effecting a remarkable transformation of the existing building through the imposition of a Gothic superstructure. The nave itself is pure Gothic. Finally in the 17th century some Baroque elements were added.

Today the transepts and early towers are almost impossible to find on the ground plan and not even easily recognized by the casual visitor. Look carefully, though, and you will see the small towers rising from what on the outside looks like part of the nave. Inside there are some 12th-century frescoes in the transept areas. The imposing spire is one of the oldest in Germany. It contains 16 bells, including one cast in 1258. The carvings in the West Porch depict the Madonna and Child and other scenes from the New Testament. Many regard these as the most important carvings of the time to have survived intact in Germany. The high altar by Hans Baldung Grien (1484–1545) dates from 1516 and shows the Coronation of the Virgin with the apostles in the wings. In the **UNIVERSITÄTSKAPELLE** (University Chapel), located off the ambulatory, the altarpiece has two side panels of the Nativity and Adoration of the Magi by Hans Holbein the Younger (1488–1543). A beautiful Romanesque silver crucifix stands in the Villinger-Böcklin chapel; there is also an exquisite carved altarpiece in the Locherer chapel dated from 1521.

MÜNSTERPLATZ (Minster Square), which faces the south side of the cathedral, was heavily bombed during World War II. It has been restored in its original late medieval style. Look out for the 15th-century **Kornhalle** (Grainhall), which is now a monastery for nuns of the Benedictine Order.

AUGUSTINERMUSEUM (Augustinian Museum), Augsutinerplatz, is situated in a former Augustinian monastery founded in 1278. It contains some interesting artworks from the medieval period, plus Renaissance paintings, including Grünewald's (1480–1528) altarpiece *The Miracle of the Snows* and an impressive 14th-century crucifix.

FULDA

Founded in 744 by the Bavarian missionary Sturmius (715–79), who worked in St. Boniface's (680–754) mission to German-speaking peoples, Fulda is one of the great Christian sites in Germany. Although it receives scant attention in most secular guidebooks, here the 8th-century mission to northern Europe began. Boniface founded a monastic mission outpost as his main base from which to train and send out missionaries throughout northern Europe. Many of the people who supported this effort were English Christians who came to the continent to evangelize pagans to whom they were often related through family ties.

During the 9th century, the monastery became a leading educational center. It produced copies of the Bible and beautiful illustrated manuscripts, including the oldest German book, *The Lay of Hildebrand*.

F

BONIFACE (680–754) was born in Crediton in Devon and entered a small monastery in Exeter as a child. Later he studied at a Benedictine house near Southampton. After composing a Latin grammar and various other prose works, he was eventually ordained at the age of 30 and taught in the monastic school for a number of years.

His initial interest in missions seems to have been provoked by Wilfrid of York and Hexham (634–709), who spent a winter (678–79) in Frisia, the Netherlands, making several converts. Wilfrid's work led Willibrord of Northumbria (658–739) to embark on a mission to the Frisians in 690. He was joined by Wynfrith (Boniface) in 716, who went on to visit Rome, where he received papal authority to evangelize the Germans. He began his own mission in 719 with a very successful preaching campaign in Bavaria and Thuringia, where he converted many Hessians. Pope Gregory II (669–731) recalled him to Rome, where he was consecrated bishop on St. Andrew's Day, 722, when according to tradition he changed his name to Boniface.

Calling upon friends and relatives in Britain, Boniface brought a large number of English missionaries to Germany, including a sizeable group of very able women. This group embarked on a major missionary campaign during which time they founded many churches, abbeys, and monasteries, including their main base of operations, Fulda. The abbey in Fritzlar, which was headed by Wigbert (d. 747), a monk from Glastonbury, in Somerset, and the bishoprics of Würzburg and Erfurt were also part of the missionary campaign.

Boniface was martyred by pagan Frisians in 754. One of the remarkable facts of history is that many of Boniface's letters to the pope and other people have survived, showing him to be a man of deep piety who placed great reliance on intercessory prayer. He was also a man of great courage who did not hesitate to chop down the sacred oak tree in Geismar, lower Hessia, to prove the futility of worshiping idols. Nor did he hesitate to criticize the growing paganism among Christians, to the extent that he even rebuked Pope Acharias (d. 752) for permitting superstition in Rome itself. In German, Boniface is known as *Bonifatius*.

PLACES TO VISIT

FULDA DOM (Fulda Cathedral), Kastanienallee, is an imposing Italian-style Baroque church designed by Johann Dientzenhoffer in 1704 as a pilgrimage center. Both the church and its forecourt are modeled on St. Peter's in Rome and are dedicated to Saints Salvador and Boniface.

Behind the high altar is the crypt with the imposing tomb of St. Boniface, who is depicted leaving his grave at the resurrection.

DOMMUSEUM (Dom Museum), behind the dom itself, contains a remarkable collection of Christian art and information about Boniface and his mission. On the way into the main collection, you pass a highly ornate, gilded reliquary, the center of which are ecclesiastical vestments, a miter (bishop's hat), and Boniface's sword.

If you are Protestant, be prepared for a real shock when you realize that the miter is sitting on the skull of Boniface. At first this seems too grotesque for words. Certainly, it is very un-Protestant. Then, slowly, a strange sense of awe may overtake you as you realize that you are looking at the skull of one of the greatest evangelists of all time. Boniface was martyred by pagan Frisians in 754 at age 74. Few things have the power to bring about an awareness of the reality of history and continuity of the church as this very strange site. Once you have seen it, you may begin to understand why for centuries it was the center of pilgrimage.

Inside the museum proper is the actual mutilated manuscript of the Gospels that Boniface was carrying at the time of his death. Once again, this brings a sense of how close we are to such events.

While viewing the museum, look out for the sculptured nativity scenes in which one of the three kings is depicted as a medieval knight in full armor. Then look again and note that he is a black African. Such statues are common throughout the continent, reflecting the legend that indeed one of the kings who paid homage to Christ was an Ethiopian. This gem of medieval art shows the lack of racism in traditional Christianity. It is a timely reminder that until the Enlightenment in the 18th century, blacks were regarded as highly civilized, spiritual people.

Alongside the Dom is one of Germany's oldest surviving churches, the MICHAELSKIRCHE (Church of St. Michael), built in the early 9th century by a monk named Racholf. Its simple style is modeled on the Church of the Holy Sepulchre in Jerusalem. Although it has a Baroque roof, the inside of the church, particularly its crypt, retains the original Romanesque style.

The town of **Fulda** was reconstructed in the 18th century in Baroque style and still contains many fine examples of Baroque houses. There is also a **Schloss** (palace) and several smaller churches which may be visited.

HALLE

Until recently, Halle was a grim East German industrial town. Today, Halle is rapidly becoming a pleasant city that should not be overlooked by anyone interested in the history of evangelical Christianity or music. Archaeologists say that the area around Halle was developed as a center for salt mining during the Iron Age. The first recorded mention of the town and its fortress was in 806. Otto I (912–73) gave the town to the Magdeburg Monastery of St. Moritz in 961. In the 16th century, Cardinal Albrecht von Brandenburg initiated an extensive building program when he made Halle his residence and built a new cathedral. In the next couple of centuries, Halle became a center for scientific discovery and the Industrial Revolution. The University, which played an important role in the history of both Pietism and Rationalism, was established in 1694, and in 1878, the German Academy of Natural Scientists, the Liopoldina, was founded here.

The town has a long musical tradition starting in the 13th century with the founding of the Musicians Brotherhood. One of Germany's first opera houses was built here in 1654 by Duke August. The great musician George Friederic Handel (1685–1759),

known throughout the English-speaking world for his oratorio *The Messiah,* was born here in 1685. He was the cathedral organist for a short time and composed some of his early music here before traveling to Italy and eventually settling in England in 1710. Johann Sebastian Bach (1685–1750) tried, and failed, to obtain an appointment in Halle. But his son Friedmann was more successful in 1743, when he became the organist at the Marktkirche (Market Church).

Most important for Christians is the influence of Halle Pietism, which became an immensely influential movement in the 17th century and early 18th century. As a reaction against an arid religious orthodoxy tinged with rationalism that began to dominate the church following the Reformation, a spiritual revival movement developed in Germany during the 17th century. Pietists drew on the writings of Johann Arndt (1555–1621), who sought to recall people to a devout lifestyle through the publication of his *Books on True Christianity,* which were translated into English as *True Christianity* in 1712. Arndt's simple devotional orthodoxy inspired Philipp Jacob Spener (1635–1705), August Hermann Francke (1663–1727), and a number of other great Christian leaders including

Count Nikolaus Ludwig von Zinzendorf (1700–1760), who in turn influenced both Methodism and the Great Awakening. Spener's *Pia Desideria* (1675) became the major text in this remarkable revival.

The success of Pietism led to a flurry of hymn writing, an outpouring of missionary activity, and numerous philanthropic and scholarly works. Orphanages, like the famous *Francke Stiftung* in Halle, and schools were founded, biblical scholarship received a boost through careful study of the text, and Christian art, like the music of Bach, flourished. Within the various German churches Pietists were both welcomed and attacked. In Prussia, Pietism received support from some kings and certain members of the aristocracy.

However, the Enlightenment ruler, Friedrich II, the Great, hated Pietism and threw the state's support behind its many enemies. Thus he initiated a long period of decline due to constant state-sanctioned harassment. Part of Friedrich II's campaign against the Pietists involved the promotion of rationalist professors to university chairs, thus undermining their intellectual base in universities like Halle.

During the 19th century, the famous theologian Albrecht Ritschl (1822–89) virtually buried Pietism intellectually through his highly distorted, but very influential, *History of Pietism* (1880–83). Ritschl claimed that Pietism was an anti-intellectual, obscurantist movement which hindered the growth of a vibrant Christianity. Recently, Ritschl's assessment has been shown to be false as a result of the publication of Martin Brecht's multivolume *Geschichte des Pietismus (History of Pietism)* (1993).

PLACES TO VISIT

Marktkirche Unser Lieben Frauen (Market Church of Our Dear Ladies) is on the Marktplaz (Market Place), a huge square with its 19th-century statue of Handel. This is a triple-aisled 16th-century Gothic church which incorporated the towers of two former Romanesque churches, St. Marien (1141) and St. Gertruden (1121). The new church was built by the Roman Catholic archbishop of Magdeburg, Albrecht, who wanted to make Halle a bastion of Catholicism in a spreading sea of Lutheranism. Later, when Halle succumbed to the Reformation, it became a Protestant church. The high altar was painted in 1529 by one of Lucas Cranach's pupils, the Master of Annaberg, and shows Archbishop Albrecht accompanied by Saint John and the Virgin Mary.

Moritzkirche (Church of St. Moritz), on the Hallorenring, contains some exquisite Gothic star vaulting and powerful, realistic, stone sculptures by Konrad von Einbeck completed in 1412. Look for his moving *Man of Sorrows*. The altarpiece depicts *Mary at the Crucifixion* by G. J. Hener from Orslamüde and was installed in 1511.

LEADERS OF THE HALLE REVIVAL

PHILIPP JACOB SPENER (1635–1705). Born in Rappoltsweiler (Ribeauville), Alsace, of devout parents, Spener studied at the University of Strassburg (1651–53) before visiting Switzerland, where he encountered Jean de Labadie (1610–74). This ex-Jesuit had converted to Calvinism and founded a small movement devoted to personal piety and the creation of a Christian community. Under de Labadie's influence, Spener experienced an evangelical conversion and developed a strong interest in Christian devotional classics like *The Imitation of Christ*. He returned to Germany, where he served as a minister first in Strassburg (1663) and then in Frankfurt am Main (1666). While ministering in Frankfurt am Main, Spener founded the *Collegia Pietatis* to encourage Christian piety among ministers and laity alike. He also published *Pia Desideria* (1677), which was intended to reawaken the church after the disillusionment created among clergy and laity alike by the Thirty Years' War. Spener's activities quickly created heated opposition, and in 1686 he gladly accepted a call to become the court preacher in Dresden. For a short time it seemed as though Saxony was about to become the center of a great Christian revival. But the enthusiasm which Spener's work generated in both Dresden and Leipzig caused government officials to panic, and they expelled him and his followers from Saxony. Spener was given refuge in Berlin, where he died a few years later. Members of the University of Leipzig's faculty and other clergy who were deprived of their living moved to Brandenburg, where they helped establish the University of Halle in 1694. Thus, Pietism flourished at Halle and throughout Prussia until suppressed by rationalist critics who gained favor during the reign of Friedrich II.

AUGUST HERMANN FRANCKE (1663–1727). Born in Lübeck, Francke studied theology and ancient languages at the universities of Erfurt, Kiel, and Leipzig, and for a short time lectured at Leipzig. He founded the *Collegium philobiblicum* in 1686 with his friend Paul Anton (1661–1730) to encourage Bible reading and Christian piety. He worked with the father of Pietism, Philip Jacob Spener (1635–1705), in Dresden before returning to Leipzig in 1689, where his lectures provoked a strong anti-evangelical reaction. From there he accepted a call to Erfurt, but once again his biblical teaching and insistence on pious living provoked opponents, and he was deprived of his church in 1691. Eventually, with Spener's help he moved to Glaucha, which was close to Halle. From 1692 to his death, he combined pastoral duties with the creation of the University of Halle as a Christian institution. He also founded an orphanage, trained clergy, established foreign missions, and wrote devotional literature. His main works are *Rules for the Protection of Conscience and Good Order in Conversation or in Society* (1689), *On Christian Perfection* (1690), and his *Autobiography* (1692).

STAATLICHE GALERIE MORITZBURG (Moritzburg State Gallery) is housed in a restored fortress that was once the residence of the archbishop of Magdeburg. It was destroyed in the Thirty Years' War but later restored and made into a museum. It contains an excellent collection of German art, including important Romantic paintings by Caspar David Friedrich (1774–1840) and Hans von Marees (1837–87), and modern works by Kandinsky (1866–1944) and the Brüke Group.

TECHNISCHES HALLOREN- UND SALINENMUSEUM (Salt Mining Museum), Mansfelder Straße 52. This fascinating museum, located on an island in the river on the site of an old salt works, provides a graphic history of the Halle region and insights into the social developments which led to the Reformation. As you view the exhibits, remember that Martin Luther's father was a miner, although not a salt miner, and that it was the newly emerging industrial class which grew up in Saxony around industrial centers like Halle that eventually became firm supporters of Protestant preachers.

HÄNDEL-HAUS (Handel's house) is the birthplace of the great composer who set so many scriptural passages to unforgettable

CONSERVATIVE PROFESSORS AT MARTIN LUTHER UNIVERSITY, HALLE-WITTENBERG

FRIEDRICH AUGUST GOTTREU THOLUCK (1799–1877). Born in Breslau, which is now part of Poland, Tholuck came from a very poor background. Following an evangelical conversion, he struggled to gain an education and proved himself a highly gifted linguist. After completing his degrees, he became professor of theology at Halle, where initially he faced considerable opposition from rationalists on the faculty, who resented his piety. For years, he prayed that God would move him to another university, but instead a revival broke out among his students, and slowly the atmosphere in Halle became more conducive to evangelical theology. Tholuck was a founding member of the Berlin Missionary Society in 1824 and was admired as an evangelical leader by such figures as Charles Hodge (1798–1878) and Augustus Strong (1836–1921).

MARTIN KÄHLER (1835–1912). Born near Königsberg in east Prussia, now part of Russia, he was appointed professor of theology at the University of Halle in 1860. Strongly influenced by Tholuck and other orthodox theologians, Kähler vigorously opposed the so-called "quest for the historical Jesus" that drove a wedge between the "historical Jesus" and "the Christ of faith." He also made a significant contribution to the study of the history of 19th-century theology.

music. It is now a museum dedicated to his life and work and contains many valuable period instruments.

HALLE DOM (Halle Cathedral), am Domplatz, is a 14th-century church that was transformed in 1520–23 by Archbishop Albrecht into a Gothic cathedral with three naves. Following the Reformation, it was again remodeled as a Baroque church. Its greatest treasure is a collection of 17 large stone statues by Peter Schroh depicting the apostles and various saints. Handel once played here.

FRANCKESCHE STIFTUNGEN (Francke Foundation), Franckeplatz, B 3, is a historic library containing a rich collection of historic Christian literature and valuable manuscripts. It is now part of the **MARTIN-LUTHER UNIVERSITY** in Halle. Francke moved to the new university in 1692 and was appointed professor of theology in 1698. Under his influence, a revival swept away the formalistic spirituality of a dead Lutheranism. Students flocked to Halle to study with him.

MARTIN-LUTHER-UNIVERSITÄT (Martin Luther University), on the Moritzburg Ring, is a fascinating place to visit. It is the first modern university. Under August Hermann Francke's influence (1663–1727), the faculty abandoned the use of Latin in favor of German as the language of instruction. American, British, and other German universities slowly followed Martin-Luther-Universität's lead, some more than a century later. The main building is an elegant neoclassical style and was built 1832–34. During the 19th century, Friedrich August Gottreu Tholuck (1799–1877), a staunch defender of orthodoxy and a founder of the Berlin Mission, taught here for 51 years. More recently, Martin Kähler (1835–1912) served on the faculty. The university houses a superb mission archive.

FRANCKESCHES WAISENHAUS (Francke Orphanage), on the Moritzburg Ring, is a large Baroque institution and was arguably the first modern orphanage in Europe. Founded by Francke in 1695 as a refuge for abandoned children and school for the poor, it grew into a large and highly successful enterprise. Francke's example was followed by other Christians throughout Europe and was a source of inspiration for a generation.

HAMBURG

Charlemagne founded a mission here in 810 and built a fortified church to help convert the northern tribes. In 831, Louis the Pious created a bishopric and in 834 built a cas- tle, Hammaburg, but in 835 the church, castle, and surrounding town were plundered by Viking raiders. After they were rebuilt, a period of peace followed until the Vikings pillaged the area again in

983. Archbishop Unwan, who held the bishopric from 1013–29, rebuilt the town. Important trading concessions were granted the city by Emperor Friedrich I Barbarossa in 1189, ensuring the town's prosperity. In 1241 Hamburg formed an alliance with Lübeck that formed the basis for the Hanseatic League. The city became Protestant in 1529, and Germany's first stock exchange was founded here in 1558. It was granted the status of a free imperial city in 1618. Skillful diplomacy maintained the city's neutrality throughout the Thirty Years' War, thus avoiding the destruction which reduced formerly prosperous cities like Magdeburg to ruin. During the 15th century, Hamburg came under Danish control for a short time. In the early 19th century, Hamburg was ruled by the French. In 1815 it joined the German Federation and later the German Empire in 1871. Nevertheless, until the end of the Weimar Republic the city retained its special status as an independent state within Germany, ruled by its own senate. Today Hamburg is a separate land, or state, within Germany.

A fire devastated the city's medieval buildings in 1842, leading to extensive rebuilding. On July 28, 1943, Hamburg was the first German city subjected to a British firestorm. In that raid, over 42,000 civilians, more than all the British civilian casualties in World War II, were killed when high explosives and incendiary bombs turned eight square miles of the city into an inferno. During this raid the city's ancient churches were destroyed. Although some have been rebuilt, most were not reconstructed according to the original designs. In the closing days of the war, the SS commander of Hamburg wisely chose to surrender the city to the British rather than see its total destruction as Hitler had commanded.

Hamburg is the birthplace of Johannes Brahms (1833–97) and Felix Mendelssohn-Bartholdy (1809–47). C. P. E. Bach (1714–88) died here in 1778. The writers Gotthold Ephraim Lessing (1729–81), Friedrich Gottlieb Klopstock (1724–1803), and Heinrich Heine (1797–1856) all worked here during important periods of their lives. It is also the birthplace of Johann Gerhard Oncken (1800–1884), the founder of the German Baptist Church.

PLACES TO VISIT

ST. JAKOBIKIRCHE (St. Jacobs Church), Mohlenhofstrasse. Not very impressive as a building, this church contains the 17th-century musical masterpiece Arp Schnitger organ, which is still in use.

ST. MICHAELIS (St. Michaels), Ost-West-Strasse, was built by Ernst Georg Sonnin and Leonhard Prey, 1751–77, and fully restored after World War II. This church is a northern Baroque masterpiece. Its lantern turreted tower has become an emblem of the city. George Philipp Telemann was the musical director here from 1721–67, Carl Philipp Emanuel

TWO FAMOUS GERMAN POETS

MATTHIAS CLAUDIUS (1740–1815) was born near Lübeck (a town near Hamburg), the son of a pastor. His real name was Asmus. He worked as a tutor and journalist before becoming one of the best-loved poets in the German language. Through his deeply spiritual poetry and other writings, Claudius sought to defend traditional orthodoxy in an age of rationalism and pantheistic mysticism.

HEINRICH HEINE (1797–1856) was a German-Jewish poet who maintained a love-hate relationship with Germany, Romanticism, and Christianity. He converted to Protestantism, but became disillusioned and moved to Paris, where he eventually joined the Roman Catholic Church. His *History of German Religion and Philosophy* is a penetrating and prophetic analysis of the impact of pantheism on German society.

Bach is buried in the crypt, and Johannes Brahms was baptized here. There is a daily free organ concert that begins at noon. The theologian, preacher, and professor Helmut Thielicke (1908–85) was the minister here from June 1954 until his death in 1985. Thielecke was well-known for his resistance to the Nazis and for his many books, including *The Evangelical Faith*.

KUNSTHALLE (Fine Art Museum) alone makes a trip to Hamburg worthwhile. Here one finds the Grabow altarpiece constructed in 1379 for St. Petri Church by Master Bertram (1340–1414) of Minden. Painted in 24 separate panels that illustrate the drama of man's creation, fall, and redemption, it is one of the largest medieval altarpieces in Germany. Note the panel depicting the creation of the animals with the lynx attacking a sheep. In the next room you will find the St. Thomas à Becket altar-

piece commissioned by Hamburg merchants who traded with England in the Middle Ages. It was painted by Master Francke (1380–1430), who belonged to Bertram's workshop. Finally, in the medieval section don't miss Lucas Cranach's (1472–1553) *Three Electors of Saxony,* which depicts three key figures in the life of Luther and the Reformation.

The FLEMISH GALLERY contains some excellent 17th-century works including van Dyck's (1599–1641) *The Adoration of the Shepherds* and Rembrandt van Rijn's (1606–69) *Presentation in the Temple.*

The 17TH- AND 18TH-CENTURY GALLERY has a number of works by a variety of well-known European painters including Goya's (1746–1828) *Don Tomas Perz Estaha* and *The Creation of Eve.*

In the 19TH- AND 20TH-CENTURY GALLERY one finds Caspar David Friedrich's (1774–1840) haunting *Wan-*

derer Above the Mists, which captures the spirit of 19th-century Romanticism as no other work can. Also note his *Eismeer,* which depicts a ship struck by an iceberg. Based on a true story, the painting symbolizes the fate of democracy after the failure of the Frankfurt Parliament of 1848. Modern painters such as Max Liebermann (1847–1935) and Lovis Corinth (1858–1925) are well represented. There are also works by Edvard Munch (1863–1944) and Paul Klee (1879–1940).

HAFENRUNDFAHRT (Harbor Boat Tour). Until Bismarck convinced the city fathers of Hamburg to join the German Empire, the city enjoyed the status of a duty-free port. As a compromise, Bismarck negotiated a special status for traders whose warehouses were located in the network of canals that formed the harbor. These 19th-century buildings and the complex waterways form a central part of any harbor boat tour that can be the highlight of a trip to Hamburg. While visiting the harbor remember that Hamburg was the major port of departure for Germans and other Europeans who emigrated to America in the 19th century. After the failure of the 1848 Revolution, many Christians, particularly Baptists and Pietists, left Germany because their hopes that they would be granted freedom of religion were dashed. Therefore, they sought refuge in America, where they made a major contribution to the founding of such institutions as Wheaton College in Wheaton, Illinois.

HEIDELBERG

Heidelberg is said to be founded at the foot of a mountain which was sacred in Celtic mythology. It was occupied by the Romans in 1 B.C., who built a temple dedicated to their gods Mithras and Mercury. In the 3rd century the Alemanni conquered the Roman settlers and destroyed the town. In the early 11th century the bishop of Worms built a castle here, which became a royal residence in 1155, when the town became the capital of the Rhineland palatinate. During the Reformation the local rulers embraced Protestantism. At first the rulers embraced Lutheranism, but soon they turned to Calvinism, which is the reason the town gave its name to one of the most important Calvinist statements of faith, the Heidelberg Catechism of 1563.

The fate of the townspeople was decisively affected by the marriage of Elizabeth Stuart (1597–62) to the Count of the Palatinate, Friedrich V (1592–1632) in 1613. After foolishly accepting the crown of Bohemia, Friedrich and his bride moved to Prague, where they set up court in defiance of the emperor. Within a year they were vanquished by Roman Catholic forces loyal to the emperor, hence their pitiful titles "the Winter King and Queen." These actions were the spark needed to begin the Thirty Years' War, during which Heidelberg was sacked by Catholic forces under Tilly on September 16, 1622 after a siege of 11 weeks.

Prosperity returned in the next few decades only to be swept away by another dynastic marriage, that of the duke's daughter, Elizabeth Charlotte, to the duke of Orleans in 1671. This meant that when the male line of Palatine rulers died out, the French claimed Heidelberg and enforced their claim by conquering the area. This action eventually led to the destruction of the magnificent Schloss (castle) by retreating French troops in 1689. The next few centuries were kinder to Heidelberg, which came through World War II virtually unscathed.

Richard Thorpe's film *The Student Prince* (1954) about a prince who studied incognito at Heidelberg University in the 19th century, catapulted Heidelberg into American consciousness. With many popular tunes like "Deep in My Heart, Dear" and "Golden Days," the musical was a great hit, and Heidelberg was established as the favorite tourist destination of Americans.

The university was founded in 1386 and is one of the oldest in Germany. During the 19th century it was a center of German Romanticism that produced such important poets as Clemens Brentano (1778–1842), Joseph von Eichendorf (1788–1857), and Achim von Arnim (1781–1831).

PLACES TO VISIT

SCHLOSS (Castle), first built in 1155, was turned into a palace in the 17th century and then destroyed in 1671. This is a magnificent ruin, which was preserved by a 19th-century French count. Today it is a fascinating place to visit as it still maintains a sense of grandeur. Here the divines, who wrote the *Heidelberg Catechism* in 1562, deliberated with princes. Fifty years later, in the 17th century, the events that triggered the fateful Thirty Years' War were planned by Friedrich V of the Palatinate and his advisors. Many historians believe that he was encouraged by his wife to accept the Bohemian crown regardless of the fact that this action threatened to provoke a war. They also speculate that had he refused to rule Bohemia, the war might well have been avoided.

DEUTSCHES APOTHEKEN-MUSEUM (German Pharmaceutical Museum) is in the basement of the *Otto-Heinrich Wing* of the schloss. Here you are given a glimpse into the history of medicine and the development of healing which today we often take for granted. The museum contains some very interesting instruments and a reconstructed alchemist's laboratory.

BUCHAUSSTELLUNG DER UNIVERSITÄTS-BIBLIOTHEK (University Library's Book Exhibition), Plöckstrasse, has numerous early German manuscripts and priceless books.

KURPFÄLZISCHES MUSEUM (Palatinate Local History Museum). Among the many important exhibits is the jawbone of the "Heidelberg man," which is one of the oldest human remains, dated 500,000 B.C. There is also Tilman Riemenschneider's (1460–1531) wonderful *Altar of the Twelve Apostles* and various Romantic works.

HEILIG-GEIST-KIRCHE (Church of the Holy Spirit), Unterestrasse, is a fine example of Late Gothic.

JESUITENKIRCHE (Jesuit Church) is a good example of Baroque architecture with a very interesting art museum attached.

HERRNHUT

Y ou won't find Herrnhut in other tourist guides, and you will even have difficulty finding this small community on the map. But if you follow the A6 east from Dresden to Bauzen and then the A178 towards the Czech border, Herrnhut lies 14 kilometers northwest of Zittau. A group of Moravian refugees fleeing from religious persecution in Bohemia began work establishing a community here on June 17, 1722, when their carpenter, Christian David, felled the first tree on what was then the estate of Count Nikolaus Ludwig von Zinzendorf (1700–1760). Five years later, in the nearby Bethelsdorf Church on Zinzendorf's estate, the Herrnhuter Brüdergemeine (Herrnhut Brotherhood) was founded. In 1732, exactly 60 years before the publication of Wilhelm Carey's *An Enquiry into the Obligations of Christians to Use Means for the Conversion of the Heathen* (1792), this evangelical and strongly pietistic community sent out its first missionaries. This event marks the beginning of the modern Protestant missionary movement. Today there are Herrnhut missionaries worldwide.

It was through the life and preaching of Moravians that eventually on May 24, 1738, a young English preacher, John Wesley (1703–91), one of the main founders of Methodism, felt his "heart strangely warmed." Wesley's conversion, which was directly linked to the work of Zinzendorf, changed both American and English society. For this reason, if no other, Herrnhut deserves to be visited by anyone interested in church history.

PLACES TO VISIT

GEMEINDENHAUS (Congregational Building) was built in 1756 and badly damaged at the end of World War II. This important historical building was recently restored.

FRIEDHOF (graveyard) is where you will find the grave of Count Zinzendorf and numerous other Christian leaders.

VÖLKERKUNDEMUSEUM (Ethnographic Museum), Goethestraße 1, is

127

where you can discover the history of Moravian missions through a fascinating collection of material from all over the world.

HEIMATMUSEUM (Local History Museum). The history of Herrnhut and its faithful community is preserved in this simple but impressive collection.

INGOLSTADT

During the middle of the 6th century, Ingolstadt was founded as a settlement in the wide plain of the Danube. Located on both sides of the Danube, Ingolstadt is first mentioned in 806 when it was referred to as Ingoldestat in a contemporary document. Ingolstadt was a Frankish court estate in the 8th century, when the Carolingian rulers regarded the town as their personal fief. In 841 a large part of Ingolstadt was given to the Cloister Niederaltaich, which is located on the Danube 80 kilometers SE of Regensburg. Later, the Magyaren, who were driven out of southern Russia into Hungary, advanced further west and destroyed Ingolstadt. The town was rebuilt in the 11th century. The inner city, with its clear geometric arrangement, was constructed in the 13th century and protected by the Altes Schloss (Old Castle). This is also referred to as the Herzogskasten (Duke's Box), because of its straight, almost boxlike design. Later the town was fortified by Ludwig IX (1423–83) in 1425.

During the Thirty Years' War, Protestant forces under Gustavus Adolphus faced Tilly's Catholic army near Nordheim on the Danube. During the night of April 3, 1632, Finnish troops crossed the river to erect a pontoon bridge. The main Swedish army followed, and a decisive battle took place on April 5, during which Tilly was mortally wounded. That evening his followers carried the dying general to Ingolstadt, where attended by Gustavus's personal physician, he died 14 days later. On April 18, Adolphus laid siege to the heavily defended city only to abandon his assault on May 4 due to its impressive fortifications. Thus Ingolstadt remained in Catholic hands.

Its famous university was founded in 1472. Martin Luther's antagonist, John Eck (1486–1543), taught theology here. And in 1776 one of the professors, Adam Weishaupt, founded a secret society, the Illuminati, which appears to have died out after a few years. Nevertheless, the idea of the Illuminati and the occult ideas Weishaupt propagated live on in numerous conspiracy theories and the New Age movement.

During the 19th century, the university was moved to Landshut and the many monasteries were secularized by Napoleon. The town was fortified again in 1828 in neoclassical style by King Ludwig I of Bavaria (1786–1868), who was more interested in the aesthetics of fortifications than their military value. During World War II, one-fifth of the town was destroyed only to be lovingly rebuilt in the 1950s and 1960s.

PLACES TO VISIT

ST. MORITZ (St. Mauritius), the oldest church in the city, was consecrated in 1234.

HEILIG-GEIST-SPITAL (Holy Ghost Hospital) was founded by Emperor Ludwig, the Bavarian, in 1319. Its church is one of the jewels of the city with impressive vaulted ceilings in the inner chapels. A Franciscan basilica was built in 1275 by members of a Bettelorden (mendicant friars). It stands out because of its austerity, its numerous epitaphs, and its tombs and their inscriptions, in particular the "Esterreicher" epitaph.

DAS LIEBFRAUEN MÜNSTER UNSERER LIEBEN FRAU (Church of Our Lady). This impressive church was commissioned by Duke Ludwig the Bearded in 1425 and took over 100 years to complete. The vaulted ceiling was finally completed in 1503–4. It was named after a valuable relief of St. Mary, who is also the patron saint of Bavaria. This relief is of Parisian origin and was donated to the church together with many pieces of jewelry by Duke Ludwig the Bearded, who in his youth had been a nobleman at the court of his sister Isabeau de Bavière in Paris.

The high altar (1560–72), with its magnificent paintings by Hans Mielich

and his students, is an outstanding masterpiece of altar architecture from the time of the Counter-Reformation. A painting on the back of this altar depicts the Ingolstadt-Bavarian academic world. It was created for the university's 100th birthday in 1572.

The stark, simple oratory of the religious society of secular priests of the AKADEMISCHE MARIANISCHE KONGREGATION (Marian Student Congregation) was decorated by the Asam Brothers. The roof fresco by Cosmas Damian Asam (1686–1739) is the most famous part; its theme is the theology of Christ's incarnation and his message of salvation offered to humankind.

The rococo church of MARIA-DE-VICTORIA-KIRCHE (Chapel of Maria-de-Victoria), 1732–35, also referred to as Asam-Kirche (Asam Church), was designed and built by the gifted Asam brothers Cosmas Damian (1686–1739) and Egid Quirin (1692–1750). Its most impressive feature is the "trompe" ceiling fresco that covers an area of 490 square meters (approximately 5,000 square feet) and depicts the spreading of Christianity by Mary. The main altar (1763) created by J. M. Fischer (1692–1766) is adorned by four statues representing Law, Medicine, Philosophy, and Theology. In the sacristy of the church is the famous *Lepanto monstrance*, which is also called *Türkenmonstranz (Turk Monstrance)*, and is named after Lepanto, in the Gulf of Corinth, where in 1571 European armies defeated Turkey. It was a receptacle for the consecrated host and was crafted by the goldsmith Johannes Zeckl in 1708. This impressive hand-crafted sculpture reminds visitors that for centuries Islam, usually associated with "the Turks," threatened Europe with invasion to such an extent that Europeans developed a phobia about the threat of Muslim invasion.

BAYRISCHES ARMEEMUSEUM (Bavarian Military Museum) houses a huge collection of military equipment and model soldiers which vividly illustrates the role of armies in society from the pre-Reformation, through the Reformation and Thirty Years' War, to the present. Anyone wanting to understand the social context of theology ought to visit this collection, which is housed in a magnificent 15th-century fortress, the **HERZOGSCHLOß**.

CITY FORTIFICATIONS, built 1368–1434, with three rings of walls, remain essentially intact, helping the visitor understand why even Gustavus Adolphus found this city too difficult to conquer.

JENA

Once a major cultural and educational center, Jena is now struggling to regain its former glory. First mentioned in written records in the 9th century, Jena flourished as a medieval market town in a hilly area where the mild climate allows vines to grow. From 1331–1485, the town was ruled by the Wettin dynasty. They were succeeded by the dukes of Ernestine. The university was founded in 1558 as part of Melanchthon's (1497–1560) efforts to spread evangelical doctrine through sound education. As today, the university was continually seeking funding and is probably unique in having founded its own brewery during the 18th century. During the 18th century, when Jena was ruled from nearby Weimar, the great German intellectual and statesman Goethe (1749–1832) took pains to make the university one of the best, and second largest, in Germany.

The pious Johannes Gerhard (1582–1637) taught at the university when it was still orthodox. Later philosophers like Gottlieb Fichte (1726–1814) and Georg Wilhelm Friedrich Hegel (1770–1831) made it a center of rationalism. Carl Schlegel (1772–1829), Friedrich Schelling (1775–1854), and the dramatist and poet Friedrich Schiller (1759–1805) were also on its faculty. Karl Marx (1818–83) wrote his doctoral thesis, which was a vigorous defense of atheism, *The Differences Between the Democritean and Epicurean Philosophy of Nature,* here in 1841.

The Battle of Jena, where Napoleon defeated the combined armies of Saxony and Prussia, was fought on October 14, 1806, to the north of the town. Carl

Zeiss (1816–88) began the manufacture of microscopes here in 1846. In 1884, Zeiss partnered with Professors Ernst Abbe (1840–1905) and Otto Schott (1851–1935) to found his famous optical company. Jena is the home of three important museums which reflect central strands in modern thought.

PLACES TO VISIT

JENAER KUNSTSAMMLUNG UND GEDENKSTÄTTE DER DEUTSCHEN FRÜH-ROMANTIK (Jena Cultural Collection and Memorial to the Early German Romantic Movement), Untern Markt 12a. This was the home of the philosopher Johann Gottlieb Fichte from

FAMOUS PROFESSORS AT THE UNIVERSITY OF JENA

JOHANNES GERHARD (1582–1637). Lutheran theologian and professor of theology at Jena who wrote various theological and devotional books, including systematic exposition of Lutheran theology that was for many years the standard work on the subject.

GOTTLIEB FICHTE (1726–1814) was a disciple of Kant. He became famous after moving to Berlin for his 1808–09 *Address to the German Nation,* which is generally regarded as the source of modern Nationalism. Prior to this work, Fichte, who was influenced by the skepticism of Lessing (1729–81), published anonymously his *Critique of All Revelation* (1794–95), which applied Kantian thought to questions of biblical theology. Fichte's system of metaphysical monism practically dispensed with God by substituting moral insight for religious consciousness. He is one of the key figures in shaping modern religious and political thought in an anti-Christian direction.

FRIEDRICH SCHILLER (1759–1805). Influenced by Kant, he was one of the leaders of the *Sturm und Drang* period of German culture. *Sturm und Drang* is usually translated "Storm and Stress." But this is very misleading. A far better translation would be "Storm and Surge" or "the time of striving."

Many of Schiller's works have theological themes. His *History of the Thirty Years' War* (1791–93) is a masterpiece of early scientific history, while his *Wallenstein* (1799) treats the same theme in a highly poetic play. Today literary critics tend to mock what is probably Schiller's best-known poem, *Das Lied von der Glocke* (Bell's Song). But the hasty dismissal has probably more to do with political correctness and a lack of sympathy for its clearly pious tone than anything else. Anyone visiting Jena should at least read this poem in a good translation.

1795–99. The house is now the home of a valuable collection of materials relating to early Romanticism.

SCHILLER GEDENKSTÄTTE (Schiller Museum), Schillergäßchen 2. This house was the home of the great German classical poet and dramatist Friedrich Schiller. The garden has been preserved in 18th-century style to show Schiller's favorite workplace. His bookcase, writing desk, and other items are to be found in the house.

GOETHE-GEDENKSTÄTTE (Goethe Museum). Here Goethe wrote his epic poem *Hermann and Dorothea*. The house contains various items of interest reflecting the life and work of the poet, who embraced a form of cosmic pantheism.

ERNST-HAECKEL-HAUS (Ernst Haeckel House), Berggasse, contains an interesting collection related to the life of Ernst Haeckel (1834–1919). Haeckel was an artist, one of Germany's leading scientists during the late 19th century, and the main spokesman for Darwinian evolution in Germany. He was the founder of the explicitly anti-Christian Monist League. Haeckel's influence, through books like *The Riddle of the Universe* (tr. 1908), continues through the current New Age movement, which has adopted many of his ideas even though few people today recognize his name. He is famous for the saying, "The devil, if there is one, can take my soul, if I have one." Haeckel did more to shape modern thought and anti-Christian sentiment than most people

realize. A visit here is like entering the lions' den, and is very instructive for anyone wanting to understand modern ideas.

STADTKIRCHE ST. MICHAEL (Parish Church of St. Michael), behind the Market Square, is a good example of classic Gothic. The church also houses the original tombstone of Martin Luther, designed by Cranach, which was brought here when Catholic armies threatened Wittenberg during the Thirty Years' War.

OPTISCHES MUSEUM (Optical Museum) on Carl-Zeiss Platz, was created by the Carl-Zeiss Foundation. Here you can find a fascinating collection of glasses and optical instruments.

HOTEL SCHWARZER BÄR (Black Bear Hotel), 2 Lutherplatz. Anyone who wants to say that they have slept in the same house as Martin Luther might want to book themselves in here. This is where Luther stayed for one night while returning to Wittenberg from his stay in the Wartburg.

COLLEGIUM JENENSE (Jenense College), Kollegien, is a fine Baroque building which is now a UNESCO listed building. Originally founded as a Dominican monastery, it was closed during the Reformation and then turned into the University of Jena. It was here that Karl Marx obtained his doctorate in 1841 on *The Difference Between the Democritean and Epicurean Philosophy of Nature*. This short work of a mere 75 pages was a strident attack on the idea of God.

JERICHOW

Situated in a tiny village is the ancient missionary center of Jerichow named not after the biblical city but a pre-Christian Slavic settlement. The magnificent red brick Romanesque Abbey was built in 1114 as a center from which northeast Europe could be evangelized. Used as a barn, brewery, and for numerous other secular purposes, the church was restored beginning in 1980. Today it is preserved as a UNESCO World Heritage site. The twin Gothic-style towers were added in the 14th century. The former cloisters have been turned into a very interesting museum which depicts the progress of the gospel in northern Europe.

PLACES TO VISIT

KLOSTERKIRCHE JERICHOW (Jerichow Monastery Church and Museum). The interior of this plain, simple, yet monumental building evokes a sense of awe and is well worth visiting. The museum reminds the visitor how very recently much of Europe was pagan and the great efforts made by numerous unremembered missionaries to convert their neighbors.

KÖLN
(COLOGNE)

Like Aachen, Köln is one of the great historic cities of Germany. Founded in 38 B.C. as the Roman administrative center for their German conquests, it was called *Oppidum Ubiorum*. The name was changed to *Colonia Claudia Ara Agrippinensium* in A.D. 50. The city was elevated to the status of a Roman Colony, giving the population special privileges, to honor the fact that it was the birthplace of Agrippina, the third wife of the Emperor Claudius. He is known to most people by the popular TV series *I Claudius* based on the novels of Robert Graves, while Agrippina is remembered as the mother of the infamous Nero. For the next 500 years, the heavily fortified city flourished and became a center for Christian mission and an archbishopric. St. Ursula, a 2nd-century Christian princess, and her 11,000 virgin companions were, according to legend, martyred in Köln, making the city a pilgrimage center. Numerous churches were built to commemorate the martyrs.

After a period of decline brought about by barbarian invasions, Köln's fortunes revived in the 8th century when Charlemagne made his court chaplain Hildebord the Archbishop in 795. In 881 Köln was looted by the Vikings and only slowly recovered. During the next few centuries, 150 Romanesque churches were built, often replacing older structures on alleged sites of martyrs' tombs. New defensive walls were built in 1180. These walls protected the city. Subsequently, it became one of the richest in Europe and with Lübeck formed the Hanseatic League in 1250 to unite merchant cities for mutual defense and the promotion of trade. Unfortunately, the walls were torn down in a frenzy of modernization in 1881.

Köln became a free imperial city in 1475. During the Reformation the citizens, who had a long history of disputes with the archbishop, surprisingly supported the Roman Catholic cause. Luther's works were publicly burnt in front of the cathedral in 1570 by members of the university's theology faculty. In 1794 the French stormed the city, starting a long association between the Rhineland and France. The arrival of French Revolutionary forces led to a liberalization of the city's religious policies. Thus, Jews and Protestants were allowed to settle in Köln for the first time since the Reformation. Following Napoleon's defeat in 1814, Köln became part of Prussia.

A Jewish community existed in Köln during Roman times but seems to have disappeared after the Viking raid of 881. The Jews slowly returned afterwards, and a thriving Jewish community existed in the city in 1096 when over 1000 were massacred by members of the First Crusade. The archbishop of Köln protected the Jews during the Second Crusade by allowing them to find refuge in Wolkenburg castle between 1146 and 1147. But with the arrival of the Black Death in 1372, even the archbishop was unable to protect Jews, and they were once more massacred. The community was reestablished after these tragic events only to be expelled in 1424. Jews returned to Köln during the 19th century, and the city became a place of refuge from Nazi persecution in the 1920s and early 1930s due to the policies of Konrad Adenauer (1876–1967), who was mayor of Köln from 1917–33. He was dismissed by the Nazis for opposing their policies. After he was sacked, persecution of Jews was encouraged, and just under half the Jewish population emigrated. Nevertheless, in 1941 over 11,000 were sent to concentration camps, where most of them died.

World War II saw the total devastation of Köln by British night bombers, with 90 percent of the buildings being destroyed. In 1945, Konrad Adenauer once more became mayor and began the rebirth of the city. Adenauer was then appointed the first German Federal Chancellor, a post he held from 1949–61. Köln is also the birthplace of the modern German writer and novelist Heinrich Böll (1917–85) and the setting for many of his stories. In *The Train Was on Time* (1949; translated 1956), he provides a penetrating analysis of Nazi Germany. Many of his other stories deal with German guilt and the trauma of war.

PLACES TO VISIT

KÖLNER DOM (Cologne Cathedral), dedicated to St. Peter and St. Mary, was for centuries the tallest building in Europe. Construction began in 1248 and continued to 1559 when it abruptly stopped. Then, by popular demand, it was begun again and completed between 1824 and 1880. Amazingly, the 19th-century builders followed the original 13th-century plans to complete one of the most beautiful churches in Europe. Built in Gothic style, the twin-towered dom was modeled on the cathedrals of Amiens, Paris, and Rheims.

The dom was built to house the relics of the Magi, which are housed in the Dreikönigsschrein (Shrine of the Three Kings), an elaborate reliquary behind the high altar. This shrine was designed by the famous medieval goldsmith, Nicolas of Verdun (1181–1205), who began work on it in 1181. It has elaborate gold sculptures of the prophets and apostles, and scenes from the life of Christ. Work was completed in 1220 and it immediately became a major pilgrimage site. Indeed, the ambulatory, or walkway behind the high altar, was

extra wide to accommodate the vast crowds which used to flock to the shrine for healing and spiritual nourishment.

Stained-glass windows in the north aisle (1507–8) depict the lives of the dom's patron saints. The windows in the south aisle were made in 1848. The choir windows (1315–30) tell the story of the adoration of the Magi and were intended to show that even earthly rulers bow to Christ. In the south transept is a stone Madonna (1420). In the north transept stands a statue of St. Ursula and her followers (early 16th century) and a statue of St. Christopher by Tilman van der Burch (1470). The high altar was the gift of Archbishop Wilhelm von Gennep (1348–62). On the north side of the altar is simply carved a 9th-century crucifix, the *Cross of Gero*.

The Marienkapelle (Mary Chapel) contains a modern altar by Willy Weyres (1956) and Stefan Lochner's (1410–51) magnificent *Adoration of the Magi* altarpiece (1440). Lochner was the greatest of the late medieval Köln school of painters. Other chapels which make up the dom complex contain the graves of various notables. For example, Archbishop Philipp von Heinsberg's (d. 1191) grave is to be found in the St. Maternus chapel. As the sculptures on his tomb suggest, he ordered the construction of Köln's medieval walls. Queen Richeza of Poland (d. 1059) is buried in the St. Johannes chapel alongside the Dom's founder, Archbishop

Konrad von Hochstaden (d. 1261). His tomb, however, wasn't constructed until 1320. Notice the 13th-century All Saints window and 14th-century carvings on its walls. In the Chapel of the Magi, which originally housed the relics, there is another 13th-century window and a plaque near the entrance which marks the resting place of Maria de Medici's heart.

SCHATZKAMMER (Cathedral Treasury) contains a wonderful Byzantine cross from the 13th century, and a staff which is supposed to have belonged to St. Peter and was the object of medieval devotion. Two carvings by Lochner, the prominent *Madonna of the Violets* and less conspicuous *Nativity,* should not be missed. Also look out for the 6th-century Syrian silk illustrating a hunt and another Byzantine woven cloth showing lions.

WALLRAF-RICHARTZ MUSEUM/ MUSEUM LUDWIG is a cultural complex which also houses the Philharmonic Orchestra. In the Wallraf-Richartz museum on the first floor are paintings by great masters from the 14th to 19th century. The medieval *Köln School* collection is particularly important. It contains early works by the *Master of Veronica* (1395– 1415), including two very different crucifixions and late works by Stefan Lochner, including his *Last Judgment* and *Madonna in a Rose Garden.* Note also the works by the *Master of the Glorification of the Virgin* (1460–90) and *Master of St. Bartholomew* (1440–1515). Other prized works include Dürer's (1471–1528) *Fifer and Drummer* and Lucas Cranach the Elder's (1472–1553) *Virgin and Child.* There are various Italian works and a great collection of Dutch and Flemish art, including Rubens' (1577–1640) *The Holy Family* and the *Stigmata of St. Francis.* There are also works by Frans Hals (1580–1666) and the well-known Rembrandt (1606– 69) *Self Portrait,* where the artist is wearing a turban in his old age.

On the second floor is the MUSEUM LUDWIG containing a fine collection of modern art. Here you will discover that the Dada school was born in Köln shortly before the First World War. The deliberate absurdity of Dada captures the ethos of the consciously dying civilization discussed in Hans Rookmaaker's *Modern Art and the Death of a Culture* (1967) and Hans Sedlmayr's *Art in Crisis* (1957). Anyone wishing to understand the intellectual climate of the 20th century needs to visit this unique exhibition. Another exhibit not to be missed is the RUSSIAN AVANT-GARDE ART, which contains pre-Stalinist art. Here you see the heroic nature of early Soviet Communism and begin to understand how this philosophy which caused so many deaths could capture the hearts of so many people. A good video film to see after visiting this exhibition is the award-winning French-Russian film *Burnt by the Sun* directed by Nikita Mikhalkow (1994).

KÖLNISCHES STADTMUSEUM (Köln City Museum), Zeughausstraße, contains some interesting exhibits detailing the city's history, plus a permanent exhibition of Jewish religious and household objects preserved by Germans who hid them for Jewish friends.

GERMANIA JUDAICBIBLIOTHEK (German-Jewish Library), Joseph-Haubrich-Hof, contains the largest collection of Jewish books in Germany and is found on the third floor of the city's Central Library.

JESUITENKIRCHE ST. MARIAE HIMMELFAHRT (Jesuit Church of the Ascension of Mary), Marzellenstraße, was designed by Christoph Wamser in 1618. It is Köln's only imposing Baroque church and quite unusual for the Rhineland in its ornate interior decoration, which is a dramatic contrast to the simplicity of the Romanesque. Badly damaged in the war, it was restored in 1956.

MINORITENKIRCHE MARIAE EMP-FÄNGNIS (Minority Church of Mary's Conception) was originally a university church for foreign students and faculty. If you were ever called a "dunce" in school, this is the place to visit, because it is the last resting place of the great medieval Franciscan Scottish theologian Duns Scotus (1264–1308). His work attempted to combine Augustinian and Aristotelian philosophy to emphasize the primacy of love over reason. A forerunner of the Reformation, he was ridiculed; hence the word *dunce* was coined by later Catholic theologians. Outside the church is a statue of Father Schall von Bell, one of the earliest Christian missionaries to China.

RÖMISCH-GERMANISCHES MUSEUM, Roncalliplatz 4. Anyone visiting a city where so many Christian churches are built over Roman temples or Christian Roman graveyards cannot help being curious about the Roman settlement of Köln. This excellent museum contains the Dionysos mosaic, discovered in 1941, which is the finest surviving Roman mosaic in northern Europe and dates from the 3rd century. Another feature is the tomb of a Roman settler, Lucius Poblicius, a veteran of the Fifth Legion, who was buried around A.D. 45. You should also take a close look at the philosophers' mosaic that depicts seven Greek philosophers.

MUSEUM FÜR OSTASIATISCHE KUNST (Far Eastern Art Museum), Universitätstraße 100, houses an excellent collection of Chinese, Japanese, and Korean art much of which is religious in nature. The building itself was designed by Kunio Mayekawa (1905–86), and its Japanese garden by Masayuke Nagare (b. 1823).

The **BUDDHIST ART** collection is particularly good for anyone wanting to understand the ethos of a religion which increasingly appeals to Americans.

KÄTHE-KOLLWITZ-MUSEUM, Neumarkt 18, contains a few sculptures and numerous prints by the Königsberg artist Käthe Kollwitz (1867–1945), whose work movingly presents a powerful

K

denunciation of the futility of war. In particular, look out for the series on the *Thirty Years' War*, when Roman Catholic and Protestant armies devastated Germany, killing up to two-thirds of the civilian population in some areas. Anyone wanting to understand the development of German theology in the 18th century and early 19th century should visit this museum.

COLOGNE'S 12 APOSTLES. This is the name given to the 12 Romanesque churches which survived World War II. And even then many of these churches have been painstakingly reconstructed using original materials. The churches are:

1. ST. ANDREAS, Komödienstraße, a 10th-century structure containing the shrine of one of the leading medieval philosophers ST. ALBRECHT THE GREAT (1206–80), who was the teacher of St. Thomas Aquinas (1224–74). This tomb reminds us of the major role Köln played in European intellectual history as a center of Christian and Catholic thought. Through the work of Albrecht, the newly recovered philosophy of Aristotle (384–322 B.C.), which was being used by Muslim apologists in Spain to attack Christianity, was reinterpreted in a Christian manner. Although not all Christians agree with the apologetics his pupil Thomas Aquinas pro-

duced, all acknowledge that both men were two of the greatest thinkers of Christian history.

2. ST. APOSTELN, Neumarkt, is important as an example of pure Rhineland Romanesque. Its construction began in 1030. The church was restored after the war as a concert hall with an attached prayer chapel. It contains 13th-century statues of Christ and a 19th-century painting of the *Archangel Michael* by Friedrich Overbeck (1789–1869). This church is worth seeing because its present fate reminds the visitor that in Germany even functioning churches often double as concert halls and are rarely full except when there is a concert.

3. ST. CÄCILIEN, Cäcilienstraße, is today the SCHNÜTGEN MUSEUM, which houses a fine collection of sacred art from the 6th century to the 19th century. If churches are to be turned into museums, this is certainly one of the better options. Originally a college for women founded in 881, it became a college church in the 10th century and today houses some remarkable examples of Christian art, including a collection of medieval ivory carvings. Much of the art was made by craftsmen in Byzantium.

4. **GROß ST. MARTIN,** Am Fischmarkt, once dominated the Köln skyline with its splendid towers. A former monastery, it was built between 1185–1220, opposite the old Roman port of Köln on an island which is now part of the city.

5. **ST. GEORG,** Georgesstraße, is an 11th-century church with 16-feet-thick defensive walls on the west side. It was built between 1059–67 over the ruin of an earlier Roman church. The *Gabelkreuz* (V-shaped cross) was a creation of Christian mysticism around 1380 reminding us that Thomas à Kempis (1380–1471), the author of the influential *Imitation of Christ,* was born in the outskirts of Köln and influenced by Rhineland mysticism before becoming a monk in the Netherlands.

6. **ST. GEREON,** Gereon/Christopherstraße, has a unique elliptical design and houses the remains of St. Gereon and numerous martyrs from the Christian Therbian Legion of the Roman army, who were slaughtered en masse for refusing to sacrifice to pagan gods. On the floor of the crypt are 11th-century mosaics. The church, built between 1219–27, also contains some 13th-century frescoes and a 17th-century bas relief of the Last Supper.

7. **ST. KUNIBET,** Konrad-Adenauer-Ufer, once the last church along the river before travelers left Köln, survived the war remarkably well. It has a life-size group of statues of the Annunciation (1439) and some fascinating murals of the Virgin Mary. Construction on this church began a year before the dom was built in 1247.

8. **MARIA IM KAPITOL,** Pipinstraße/Lichthof, was built on the site of a Roman temple to the gods Jupiter, Juno, and Minerva. In the 8th century, a nunnery was founded by the grandmother of Charlemagne; construction began in 1065. It is another fortresslike church, which once faced the river. Very badly damaged in the war, the church is a remarkable example of dedicated restoration work. The carved wooden doors are of 12th-century origin and illustrate the life of Jesus.

9. **ST. MARIA LYSKIRCHEN,** Am Leystapel, is a three-aisled church overlooking Köln's Rhine port. Built around 1250, it came through the war virtually intact. It contains some excellent 13th-century frescoes depicting biblical scenes.

10. **ST. PANTALEON,** Mittelstraße, was originally a 7th-century

Benedictine monastery. Built in the 10th century, the church contains the remains of Archishop Bruno. It has an interesting *roodskreen* and 16th-century stained-glass windows.

11. ST. SEVERIN, Severinkirchplatzt, is the oldest surviving Romanesque church in Köln. Built in 1230–37, its crypt dates back to 1043 and is built over the site of a 4th-century Christian cemetery and earlier church from the Roman city. It has a fine Gothic nave. In the church is a painting of *St. Severinus* (d. 482), whose tomb is in the crypt. There is an elaborate 19th-century reliquary behind the high altar.

12. ST. URSULA, Ursalaplatz, was built around 1287 to commemorate the martyrdom of St. Ursula who, according to legend, was an English princess martyred with 11,000 virgins. It is also on the site of a 4th-century Roman Christian cemetery and earlier church constructed by a Roman believer, Clemantius, who built his church over the saint's tomb. The church contains the reliquary of St. Ursula and St. Etherius (c. 1170). Another 120 small relics remind the visitor of the power of relics in Christian devotion from the 2nd to at least the 16th century.

THOMAS À KEMPIS (1380–1471) was a medieval German Christian writer whose real name was Thomas Hemerken, i.e., the hammer, from the small town of Kempen close to Köln. He was educated by the Brethren of the Common Life before entering the monastery of St. Agnes near Zwolle in what is now the Netherlands. His book *The Imitation of Christ* is one of the great classics of Christian spirituality which continues to inspire many Christians to piety and devotion. It contains many unforgettable sayings such as, "Without the Way, there is no going; without the Truth there is no knowing; without the Life there is no living" and "Vanity it is, to wish to live long, and to be careless to live well."

LEIPZIG

Rich in history and proud of its cultural heritage, Leipzig became the center of resistance to Communist rule. Mass demonstrations began in September 1989 which quickly spread throughout the DDR, leading to the fall of the Berlin Wall. At the heart of these demonstrations was the pastor and congregation of Leipzig's historic Nikolaikirche.

Originally a fishing village populated by the Slavic Wends, the town, Libzk, is first mentioned by Bishop Thietmar of Merseburg when he reported the death of the bishop of Meissen in his *Chronicle* of 1015. The Wends fortified the town and built a castle which eventually came under German control through Otto the Rich, Margrave of Meissen, in 1160. He prohibited fairs within a five-mile radius, thus consolidating Leipzig as the center of local commerce. By the mid-15th century, the name of the town had developed into Leypezik, which later became Leipzig.

Given its favorable location on major trade routes between western and eastern Europe, Leipzig flourished as a trading and commercial center. In 1409 ethnic riots in Prague caused German-speaking students and faculty to flee to Leipzig, where they founded its famous university. In 1507 Emperor Maximilian I (1459–1519) granted the town special trading privileges, thus securing its future prosperity.

Martin Luther debated his old friend and future enemy, John Eck, at the invitation of the university and under the protection of Elector George the Bearded (1471–1539) in three sessions, June 27–28, June 30–July 3, and July 4–13, 1519. At first Duke George welcomed Luther's teachings, but eventually he moved over to the Catholic side to become a fierce opponent of the Reformation. Following the Duke's death, Leipzig became Protestant in 1539.

Leipzig was stormed five times during the Thirty Years' War and extensively destroyed. Economic recovery followed the Peace of Westphalia in 1648, and the 18th century saw a period of great prosperity that made Leipzig the center of German culture. For 27 years, Johann Sebastian Bach (1685–1750) was the "cantor," or choirmaster, at Leipzig's St. Thomas Church, where he wrote some of his most profound music. Here too the poet Schiller (1759–1805) wrote his "Ode to Joy," which is now the anthem of the European Community. The authors Gottsched

(1700–1766), Goethe (1749–1832), and Lessing (1729–81) and the musicians Mendelssohn-Bartholdy (1809–47), Liszt (1811–86), and Schumann (1810–56) all spent time in Leipzig where they frequented the historic Zum Kaffeebaum.

The Battle of Leipzig, also called the Battle of the Nations, October 16–19, 1813, saw the armies of Austria, Prussia, Russia, and Sweden pitted against that of Napoleon. After fierce fighting, the French, who were outnumbered two to one, retreated and fled, thus marking the beginning of German liberation from French rule. Following the battle, Leipzig's economy improved and the city prospered throughout the 19th century. During World War II the city was heavily bombed. At the end of the war, the Nazi mayor and his family committed suicide rather than surrender to the Allies. Initially occupied by the Americans, Leipzig was ceded to the Russians. A period of rape and terror ensued until the establishment of the DDR in 1948, when Leipzig became East Germany's second major city.

PLACES TO VISIT

NIKOLAIKIRCHE (St. Nicholas Church). For Christians, a visit to this church ought to be one of the highlights of any German holiday. Almost unknown in the English-speaking world, the Nikolaikirche is a living tribute to the power of God and human courage in the face of an oppressive dictatorship.

The story goes that in the early 1980s, the Communist Party Chairman, Walter Ulbricht, visited his hometown Leipzig, where he saw a small crowd of people near the historic University Church, built in 1409. Delighted to see what he thought was a spontaneous demonstration of support, Ulbricht's mood turned to revenge when he learned that the people were Christians on their way to a weekly prayer meeting, which had begun in 1956. Consequently, he ordered the building of a new university tower on the site of the church. Public protests led nowhere, and the church was demolished to make way for a 34-story architectural monstrosity.

The now displaced congregation was given refuge in the Nikolaikirche, where its weekly Monday evening prayer meetings, held from 5–6, slowly grew in size. Apart from praying for freedom, the prayer meeting became a center of ecological concerns. Air quality in Leipzig had grown increasingly poor due to the unregulated burning of brown coal in nearby power stations. Other destructive industrial practices were also promoted by the regime at the expense of people's health.

By September 1989, the church was completely packed with more than 2,000 worshipers. Then on September 25, people filed out of the church singing "We Shall Overcome." The crowd moved to the site of the University on Karl-Marx Platz and then towards the railway station, causing traffic congestion and general confusion. The following week the march became more organized as the pastor led the people under the slogan "We are the people." This time more Leipzigers joined the march, which began to circle the Ring Road. For the next five weeks, the marches continued with increasing numbers, until a crowd of over 200,000 people were marching around the Ring, which actually marked the site of the old city walls.

At first the crowd encountered fierce opposition from the security police, who used dogs, batons, and water cannon to disperse it. But it soon became clear that the police lacked the will to fire on the crowd or take more serious action, and slowly even the police began to give the demonstrators their unofficial support.

During this time, demonstrations, also linked to prayer meetings, spread to Magdeburg, Rostock, and Berlin. A new spirit of defiance and optimism had entered the hearts of the people. In retrospect it all looks very simple. In reality, at any point the police could have opened fire with live bullets to crush the demonstrations. The crowd even expected to be shot at. But a miracle happened because nothing happened. Resistance to the demonstrators waned, and the government fell. East Germany opened the Berlin Wall, the crowds tore the wall down, and the fall of Eastern European Communism had begun.

Anyone visiting the Nikolaikirche ought not to leave without buying a copy of *Leipziger Demontagebuch* or a similar book on sale in the church. Even if you don't read German, the pictures speak for themselves and remind us that one of the major events of the 20th century was virtually overlooked by the major news networks outside of Germany.

The aftermath of these demonstrations and the fall of the Berlin Wall was not a triumph for the church. Most former East Germans quickly forgot the church after they obtained their freedom. Others wandered in a spiritual vacuum. And the powerful Western Church moved in to merge East German seminaries with those of the West. Consequently, centers of living Christianity, which had withstood Communist oppression, were closed as the radical theology became the new reality.

The Nikolaikirche, first built in 1170 as a Romanesque structure, was transformed into a Gothic church in 1520 and was remodeled in a blend of rococo and neoclassical styles between 1784–97. Today it has a bright and airy interior and a fine organ. In the church's tower are 35 paintings by Adam Friedrich Öser (1717–99). There is also a 16th-century pulpit where, it is claimed, Luther preached.

The University of Leipzig was founded in 1409 and boasts Martin Luther's (1483–1546) opponent John Eck (1486–1543) among its many distinguished teachers. Three in particular deserve mention. These are Constantine von Tischendorf (1815–74), the great evangelical New Testament textual scholar, Franz Julius Delitzsch (1813–90), the Old Testament scholar, and Nathan Söderblom (1866–1931), who received the Nobel Peace Prize in 1930. Söderblom, a Lutheran clergyman, was a pioneer of the ecumenical movement as well as the academic study of world religions from a Christian perspective. He established the Leipzig School of Religion between 1912 and 1914 before returning to his native Sweden.

AUGUSTUSPLATZ, close to the Nikolaikirche, is a large square where you

FAMOUS PROFESSORS AT THE UNIVERSITY OF LEIPZIG

LOBEGOTT FRIEDRICH KONSTANTIN VON TISCHENDORF (1815–74) was hailed by many commentators as "the greatest Christian textual scholar of all time." Von Tischendorf responded to the criticism of the Bible by radicals like D. F. Strauss by seeking historical evidence to refute their negative conclusions. To do this, he made numerous trips to the Middle East, where he discovered thousands of ancient New Testament manuscripts including the *Codex Ephraemi* (found 1843), *Codex Aminatinus* (found 1850), *Codex Claromontanus* (found 1852), and most important of all the *Codex Siniaticus* (found 1844). Thus by hard work he helped restore confidence in the biblical text in the face of hostile rationalist attacks on the historical value of the Bible.

FRANZ JULIUS DELITZSCH (1813–90) was one of Germany's greatest 19th-century Pietist biblical scholars of Jewish ancestry and the author of the massive Old Testament commentary series that bears his name. A conservative who rejected the conclusions of radical criticism, he struggled to defend the integrity of the Bible against rationalist assaults. He founded a missionary society, translated the New Testament into Hebrew, and sought to combat anti-Semitism. He should not be confused with his son Friedrich Delitzsch (1850–1922), who abandoned the faith of his father to embrace radical theories that located the origins of biblical religion in Babylon. It was a lecture by Friedrich Delitzsch that led Kaiser Wilhelm II to abandon his orthodox Christian faith in the late 19th century and eventually develop a friendship with Houston Steward Chamberlain (1855–1927), whose radical views contributed to the rise of the Nazis.

can find the OPERNHAUS (Opera House), NEUES GEWANDHAUS (Philomonic), and the UNIVERSITÄTSHOCHHAUS (Main University Building), which is a huge skyscraper that stands on the site of the former University Church where dissidents originally met to pray for freedom.

RING UND HAUPTBAHNHOF. Normally one wouldn't recommend looking at a city ring road or railway station. But after a visit to the Nikolaikirche, a stroll through Leipzig's streets to the railway station is a worthy pilgrimage as you reflect on the courage prayer gave those early demonstrators.

THOMASKIRCHE (Church of St. Thomas). For music lovers a visit to this church is a must. Here Bach served from 1723–50 and wrote many of his best choral works. Originally buried in the nearby Johanneskirche (St. John's Church), which was destroyed by bombing, Bach's remains were moved here in 1950, enabling visitors to see both his church and tomb.

Founded as an Augustinian monastery and teaching center in 1200, it was built in Romanesque style and remodeled as a Gothic church in 1355. A Baroque tower was added in 1702. Leipzig University was founded in the cloisters in 1409, and the monastery's manuscript collection provided the basis for the university's magnificent library. The cross on the altar was designed in 1720. The church also boasts an 18th-century crucifix and numerous other minor items of interest.

Most important of all is the choir and organ. Visitors often have the pleasure of hearing free organ practices and can attend frequent services and concerts. A fine collection of CDs of organ and choir music are on sale in the church at remarkably good prices, and if you are lucky, you might even meet the organist who frequently wanders around the church casually talking to visitors.

ÄGYPTISCHES MUSEUM (Egyptian Museum) is part of the university and houses a fine collection of Egyptian artifacts which bring alive the world of the Old Testament.

BACHMUSEUM (Bach Museum), opposite the St. Thomas Church, is an excellent museum housing a fine collection relating to all aspects of Bach's life.

NEUES GEWANDHAUS (New Concert Hall). Anyone visiting Leipzig ought to attempt to take in a concert in this most musical of cities. The hall itself was built in 1981 and seats 2,000 people.

ST.-ALEXI-GEDÄCHTNISKIRCHE (Memorial Church of St. Alexi). Opened in 1913, this fine Russian Orthodox–style church commemorates the over 22,000 Russians killed in the Battle of Leipzig.

DT. BUCH-UND SCHRIFTMUSEUM/ DEUTSCHE BÜCHEREI (German National Library). For centuries Leipzig was the center of the book trade. Created in 1912

L

to house all known books in the German language, the library houses over eight million books. Of interest to the visitor is its Book Museum, which has some of the oldest printed books on display.

MUSEUM FÜR BILDENDE KUST (Art Gallery). Opened in 1895 in neo-Renaissance style, the building housed Germany's Supreme Court until 1945. This museum displays some of Germany's greatest paintings in a collection begun in 1837 by the Leipzig Society for the Arts. The museum has over 300 Dutch masters, 15 paintings by Lucas Cranach (1472–1553), 128 works by Dürer (1471–1528), 47 by Max Klinger (1857–1920), and over 900 sculptures. Among its outstanding exhibits are Master Francke's (1380–1430) *The Man of Sorrows;* Cranach's *Junker Jörg* (1521), which shows Luther disguised as a Junker after the Diet of Worms; and Hans Baldung's (1484–1545) *Seven Ages of Women* (1544). You can also see Jan van Eyck's (1390–1441) *Portrait of an Old Man* and a self-portrait by Rembrandt (1606–69).

GRASSIMUSEUM, Johanisplatz. This complex contains three museums. The *Musikinstrumentenmuseum* (Musical Instrument Museum) contains over 3000 musical instruments and reflects Leipzig's rich musical tradition. Although the museum has instruments from the Middle Ages to the present, it concentrates on Bach and the Baroque period.

The *Arts and Crafts Collection* contains an assortment of items of a technical nature from the 15th to 19th century.

Finally, **MUSEUM FÜR VÖLKERKUNDE** (Ethnographic Museum) is one of the oldest in Germany and houses a fascinating collection which illustrates the cultural history of many peoples.

No visit to Leipzig is complete without drinking coffee in the **AUERBACH KELLER,** in the Madlerpassage on the south side of Grimmaische Strasse. Originally built in the 17th century, the walls are decorated with scenes from Goethe's *Faust,* parts of which were both written and set in this café. In *Faust,* Goethe uses a popular story about a man who sold his soul to the Devil to muse about the meaning of life and the fate of man. It is one of the most important texts in the German language.

ZUM KAFFEEBAUM is another of Leipzig's famous meeting places. Here Goethe, Lessing, Liszt, Wagner, and Schumann met with their friends for conversations which created literary and artistic movements that still shape our world.

LICHTENFELS

This sleepy Franconian town was founded in the 14th century and was almost completely destroyed during the Thirty Years' War. It was rebuilt in the 17th century and has a number of buildings from that era. In the 19th century, Lichtenfels became the major wicker-basket producing center and today boasts Germany's only basket-making school. Although unremarkable in itself, the town provides an excellent base for visiting the nearby architectural treasures of the Vierzehnheiligen and Kloster Banz.

PLACES TO VISIT

RATHAUS (City Hall) is a good example of a wood and plaster building, known in German as Fachwerk, designed by Justus Heinrich Dientzenhofer (1702–44).

PFARRKIRCHE "ZU UNSERER LIEBEN FRAU" (Parish Church Dedicated to Our Beloved Lady). This Late Gothic Roman Catholic church has a 15th-century tower and 18th-century high altar that was designed by the Protestant artist Christoph Wilhelm Meuser.

VIERZEHNHEILIGEN (Church of the Fourteen Junior Saints). Set on a nearby hill, the exterior of this Baroque masterpiece is somber and undistinguished.

Once you are inside, the church presents a whole new world full of light and color. The contrast between the plain exterior and the lavish interior is deliberate. Its designer Balthasar Neumann (1687–1753) intended to shock the senses of all who enter the church as a way of conveying to ordinary people the contrast between earth and heaven. So successful was this type of Baroque art which totally engages the senses that many historians attribute the lasting success of the Counter-Reformation to the work of artists like Neumann, whose work drew people to the liturgical richness of the Roman Catholic tradition.

The origin of the church goes back to the mid-15th century when a local shepherd named Hermann was taking his sheep back to their fold. On the way he saw a child crying in the middle of a plowed field. He went to help, but the child had vanished. A few days later, the child appeared again in the same field with two candles burning beside it. Hermann approached, and once again the child vanished. Two years later, on June 28, 1446, the child appeared again. This time Hermann noticed a red cross over its heart. He also saw that 14 smaller children accompanied the child. To Hermann's surprise, this time they did not vanish as he approached but spoke to him, explaining that they were 14 auxiliary, or junior, saints. They also asked him to build them a chapel so that they could assist people through prayer and healing. Later, on July 2, 1446, Hermann and a group of women saw two lit candles descend from the sky to rest on the place where he had encountered the children. Eighteen days later, someone was healed at this very spot, and the local people demanded a chapel be built according to the wishes of the heavenly visitors. At first the local priests were highly skeptical, but as pressure mounted, the abbot of Langheim abbey agreed to recognize the miracle and build a chapel. This decision led to a protracted dispute between the abbot, the local clergy, and the bishop of Bamberg about the building of the church and the distribution of revenues derived from the offerings of pilgrims who had begun flowing to the spot. Eventually, a church was built with the abbot and bishop dividing the spoils between themselves, leaving out the local clergy.

During the Peasants War, the pilgrimage church of the Vierzehnheiligen and the abbey were destroyed by mobs. Later a fortified church was built on the spot of the pilgrimage site. This was replaced by the present structure in the 18th century when, once again, there was a long dispute between the abbot and

bishop over the design and decoration of the pilgrimage church. Eventually, the bishop won out and Balthasar Neuman's plans were used to create the present building, which is generally regarded as one of his masterpieces.

For Protestant visitors, and many American Roman Catholics, the market stalls outside the church selling trinkets, religious books, and numerous pictures of Mary and various saints comes as a shock. These stalls recapture something of pre-Reformation piety. They also evoke the atmosphere of pilgrimage sites established by African Independent Churches in Africa and are useful reminders of the way popular piety has developed outside of Protestant Europe.

KLOSTER BANZ (Banz Monastery) is located exactly opposite the Vierzehnheiligen overlooking the River Main valley. A former Benedictine foundation established in 1695 and designed by Leonhard Dientzenhofer (1660–1707) and completed by his brother Johann Dientzenhofer (1663–1726), it is now a conference and training center for the Christian Democratic Party. Visitors are welcome to join guided tours that display the rich frescoes, altars, and remarkable marquetry, or inlaid woodwork, using different-colored natural woods to create pictures that decorate the chapel.

MAGDEBURG

agdeburg is not high on most people's list of places to visit in Germany. The town was extensively damaged by wartime bombing and is only slowly recovering from 40 years of Communist neglect. Nevertheless, anyone interested in German history or the Reformation has to visit this historic city.

Originally a trading center, first mentioned in 805, the town became the site of a famous Benedictine monastery built by Emperor Otto I, the Great (912–73) in 937. It became an archbishopric in 968 and played an important role as a center for evangelism in Eastern Europe.

As a powerful and rich member of the Hanseatic League, the city prospered and welcomed the Reformation as early as 1524. Almost a century later, Imperial Catholic armies under General Tilly stormed the city on May 20, 1631, after a six-month siege. At the time of the attack, the defenders were engaged in discussions about a possible surrender. They were taken by surprise and quickly overwhelmed after a fierce battle that lasted a few hours. The city fell, and Tilly retired to the cathedral to say Mass as his troops went on the rampage. A fire started and within hours destroyed the entire city, except for the cathedral and one other church. Over 30,000 people perished in the carnage and the fire.

News about the fate of Protestant Magdeburg was seized upon by Gustavus Adolphus and Protestant propagandists as an example of "Catholic barbarity" and quickly spread throughout Europe. Thus, the destruction of Magdeburg became the 17th-century equivalent of the dropping of the atomic bomb on Japan and the fate of the Jews in Auschwitz. The effect of this act and the propaganda that accompanied it was that Protestant kings, princes, independent cities, and even French Catholics rallied to aid Gustavus's army, preventing the conquest of northern Europe by the Imperial forces of Austria and Spain.

Following the end of the Thirty Years' War, Magdeburg was slowly rebuilt. The physicist Otto von Guericke (1602–86), whose experiments proved the existence of a vacuum, was one of the survivors of the siege and eventually became the mayor. Almost a century later, the composer George Philipp Telemann (1681–1767) lived and worked in Magdeburg. Over half of the city, including the old town, was destroyed by Allied bombing on the night of January 16, 1945. Today many fine Baroque and other buildings are slowly being restored to create what promises to be a very beautiful city.

PLACES TO VISIT

WEINKELLER BUTTERGASSE (Wine Cellar Butter Alley) is a unique example of 13th-century architecture that was discovered in 1947 when workmen were clearing away rubble created by Allied bombing. Today it is a restaurant that attempts to recreate a medieval atmosphere.

JOHANNISKIRCHE (St. John's Church), Jakobstrasse, overlooking the river, is a haunting ruin which is being restored as a memorial to war and a reminder of its destructive power. In many ways this church typifies the pathos of Magdeburg's tragic history.

KULTURHISTORISCHES MUSEUM (Museum of History and Culture), Otto von Guericke Strasse 68–73, is an impressive neo-Renaissance type of building designed in 1906 by an Austrian architect Friedrich Ohmann. Inside the vestibule one finds the original magnificent Magdeburger Rider (1240) which, like the Bamberg Rider, is one of the earliest equestrian statues produced in Europe after the fall of the Western Roman Empire. The ground floor of the museum is devoted to the work of Otto von Guericke and provides fascinating insights into the rise of modern science.

M

THE THIRTY YEARS' WAR was one of the most devastating conflicts of all time. It lasted from 1618 to 1648 and brought to an end the Peace of Augsburg (1555) that had regulated relations between Catholic and Protestant areas of Europe. The war was started by a revolt of Bohemian nobles against their elected king, Ferdinand III, of Styria (1608–57), and his replacement by the Protestant Count of the Palatinate, Friedrich V (1592–1632), who was the son-in-law of James I of England (1566–1625). This act disturbed the delicate political balance of Europe and led to an immediate response from the Emperor, who invaded Bohemia and defeated the rebels at the Battle of the White Mountain on November 8, 1620. This success was followed up by further Catholic successes, including the capture of Heidelberg on September 19, 1622. After a series of Catholic victories and the conquest of large areas that had become Protestant, the Swedish king Gustavus Adolphus (1594–1632) landed with an army of 13,000 men at Stettin in Mecklenburg on July 4, 1630. He quickly raised additional troops and marched towards Magdeburg, but for a variety of reasons, including the refusal of the elector of Brandenburg to give his troops free passage through his territories, Gustavus halted after relieving the besieged city of Frankfurt an der Oder. In November 1630, a Catholic army under Tilly laid siege to Magdeburg, which they captured in May 1631. But they were too weak to hold the city and retreated. A series of Protestant victories followed. The main Roman Catholic leader, the pious Count Jan Tserklas Tilly (1559–1632), was mortally wounded on April 15, 1632, at the Battle of Lech. Leadership of the Imperial armies now fell on the mercenary Count Albrecht Wallenstein (1583–1634), formerly a Protestant, and the devout Catholic Count Gottfried Heinrich Pappenheim (1594–1632). On November 16, 1632, the Swedish Protestant army defeated the combined armies of Wallenstein and Pappenheim at the battle of Lützen where both Gustavus and Pappenheim were mortally wounded. The war dragged on for another sixteen indecisive years during which time German-speaking lands were devastated by plague, rape, plunder, and general banditry. Eventually the Peace of Westfalia, signed in Münster and Osnabrück, brought the war to an end in 1648.

MAINZ

ainz was first established as a Roman garrison, Castrum Mogontiacum, in A.D. 38. The site was abandoned for several centuries before a town was reestablished in the 8th century with the creation of a bishopric in 746 by St. Boniface (680–754). It was elevated to an archbishopric in 782 when Mainz became the administrative center of German Christianity. The archbishop was both the primate of the German church and, from 975, the archchancellor of the Holy Roman Empire. During the Middle Ages, the Rheinish League was centered in Mainz, which was known as "the Golden City" because of its great wealth.

Gutenberg (1396–1468) established his printing works here and made the city a center of printing. His world-famous Gutenberg Bible was printed in 1451, and the university was founded in 1466. Nevertheless, the bishop and town council resisted the Reformation. During the Thirty Years' War, the city entered a period of economic decline from which it only slowly recovered in the following century. By the mid-18th century, prosperity had returned, and Goethe was able to speak of Mainz as "our Fatherland's capital." During World War II, over 80 percent of the city was destroyed by Allied bombing.

PLACES TO VISIT

MAINZ DOM (Mainz Cathedral) is a massive red sandstone Romanesque church which contains the tombs of 44 out of 84 German archbishops, many of whom were the most powerful men in German lands during their lifetimes. The cathedral was built between 975 and 1009

M

with two aisles and a nave. Later, in the 13th century, two additional Gothic naves were added. Note the 16th-century statues of St. Willigis (975–1011), who founded the cathedral, and St. Boniface in the side chapel. There is also a famous sculpture of the Madonna, known as the *Schöne Mainzerin,* or Beautiful Madonna of Mainz. Finally, one ought to look at the tombs of Archbishops Diether von Isenburg (1412–86), who founded Mainz University in 1477, and Emanuel von Ketteler (1811–77). Von Ketteler was a leading theorist of Christian Socialism, a movement that developed in 19th-century Britain associated with Wilhelm Maurice and the evangelical writer Karl Kingsley. It sought to promote social reform along socialist lines developed from Christian social teachings. In Germany its greatest proponents were the Catholic Emanuel von Ketteler and Protestant Adolf Stoecker (1835–1909).

The cathedral contains altars in both Renaissance and Baroque styles, as well as rococo choir stalls designed by Johann Philip von Schönborn (d. 1673). There are also two 14th-century pewter fonts. In the crypt are the relics of 22 Mainz residents who have been declared saints.

Next to the cathedral is a fine **Diözean Museum** (Diocesan Museum), which is rich in treasures from the 10th century onwards.

STIFTSKIRCHE ST. STEPHAN (Parish Church of St. Stephen) was built in the 13th century and almost completely destroyed during the war. Today it is well worth a visit to see the impressive new stained-glass windows depicting biblical themes to celebrate the reconciliation of Christians and Jews by Marc Chagall (1889–1985).

GUTENBERG MUSEUM, 5 Liebfrauenplatz. No visit to Germany is complete without seeing the first book to be printed in the Western world, the original Gutenberg Bible, which is on display in a specially constructed strong room in this museum. The museum contains a host of other valuable manuscripts and printed books, equipment, and machinery depicting the history of printing, all providing an essential background to the Reformation.

MARBACH AM NECKAR

A visit to Marbach is important for anyone wanting to understand German theology and culture because one of the giants of German literature, Johann Christoph Friedrich von Schiller (1759–1805), was born here. The astronomer Robias Meye (1723–62) was also born here.

JOHANN CHRISTOPH FRIEDRICH VON SCHILLER (1759–1805) was a gifted poet, playwright, and dramatist. He was a leading figure in the *Sturm und Drang* literary movement. Usually translated "storm and stress," it is more accurate to translate *Sturm und Drang* as turmoil and pressure, or thrust. Schiller's clearly theological plays—notably *The Robbers* (1781), *Wallenstein* (1796–9), *Maria Stuart* (1800), and *The Maid of Orleans* (1801)—strongly denounce intolerance and religious bigotry by vividly illustrating the misery they cause. Other works, like *Wilhelm Tell* (1804), emphasize the theme of freedom and human responsibility. Schiller's historical writings also took up these themes and played an important role in educating Germans about the horrors of such events as the Thirty Years' War and the suffering it caused. Ludwig van Beethoven used Schiller's *The Ode to Joy* for the chorus in his *Ninth Symphony,* which has become the anthem of the European community.

PLACES TO VISIT

EVANGELISCHE ALEXANDERKIRCHE (Protestant Alexander Church) is a pleasant 15th-century church that is worth a short visit.

AM ALTEN MARKT (Old Market). This Late Gothic hall church has its original, very interesting ceiling paintings, a Late Gothic stone pulpit, and a crucifix from the 15th century.

SCHILLERHAUS (Schiller House), 31 Nikolastorstrasse, is now a museum dedicated to the work of Schiller which contains many interesting items and insights into the man and his times.

DEUTSCHES LITERATURARCHIV (German Literature Archive). For casual visitors there is not much to see except a pleasant park and reasonably priced restaurant. But this archive contains a treasure trove of literary documents, books, and manuscripts that are readily available to scholars and authors working on literary projects.

MARBURG AN DER LAHN

Forget about visiting Heidelberg, unless you want to be surrounded by tourists. Instead, go north from Frankfurt am Main to the historic university town of Marburg. It's a wonderful place well off the tourist track and therefore gives the visitor an authentic feel for German university

M

life. Founded in the 9th century, Marburg rose to fame as the greatest pilgrimage center in Germany during the Middle Ages due to the tomb of St. Elizabeth of Hungary.

In 1527, the Landgrave Philip the Magnanimous, or Philip of Hesse, converted to Lutheranism, abolished the cult of Elizabeth, and became one of the strongest defenders of the Reformation. At the same time he established the town university, which became the first Protestant university. Two years later, on Michalmas Day 1529, an important meeting took place in Marburg between Luther and the followers of the Swiss Reformer Ulrich Zwingli (1485–1531). Although Luther treated Zwingli's followers as fellow Christians, he refused to compromise on doctrinal issues, thus perpetuating divisions among Protestants.

In 1901, Marburg University professor Emil von Behring (1854–1917) won the Nobel Prize for his work in developing a vaccine for diphtheria. The first quarter of the 20th century saw a host of leading theologians and philosophers teaching at the university. These men include the biblical scholar Rudolf Bultmann (1884–1976), the historian of religions Rudolph Otto (1869–1937), the philosophical theologian Paul Tillich (1886–1965), the philosopher Edmund Husserl (1859–1938), and his pupils Martin Heidegger (1884–1976) and Karl Löwith (1897–1973). A book that is essential reading for anyone wishing to understand this important period of Germany history is Karl Löwith's *My Life in Germany Before and After 1933*. As you wander around the town you might also see the Rudolf Bultmannstraße (Rudolf Bultmann Street), which gives some indication of how seriously Germans take their intellectuals, including theologians.

During World War II, Marburg escaped relatively unscathed with the result that there are many half-timbered

ST. ELIZABETH OF HUNGARY (1207–31). As a child Elizabeth, the Hungarian king's daughter, was betrothed to the Landgrave Ludwig of Thuringia, who brought her to the Wartburg at the age of four. After an early marriage, Elizabeth became renowned for her piety and good works, particularly the help she gave to the poor. After her husband's death in 1227—either on a crusade or of the plague—she moved to Marburg, where she built a hospital below the castle. Exhausted from hard work, she died at the age of 24 in 1231 and was canonized by the Pope in 1235.

RUDOLF BULTMANN (1884–1976). From 1921 until 1951, Bultmann was professor of New Testament studies at the University of Marburg. Bultmann developed the method of form-criticism as a radical methodological skepticism; with this historical skepticism he combined dialectical theology and the Lutheran doctrine of *sola fide* (faith alone) to create an epistemology that separated history and faith. In his later work, he developed a program of demythologizing the New Testament in terms of the existentialist philosophy of Martin Heidegger. His works include *The History of the Synoptic Tradition* (1921), *Jesus Christ and Mythology* (1960), and *Theology of the New Testament* (1952 and 1955, Vols. 1 and 2). Bultmann's work is unusual in that, unlike many theologians who recast biblical teachings in their own image, he tends to present New Testament teachings accurately before saying why he thinks we cannot believe them today. He then offers his own alternative.

medieval buildings in the town. Because the old city is built on a hill, which is a warren of winding streets, drivers are advised to leave their cars in the new town before exploring the old city on foot. An easy way to reach the Market Square, with its magnificent medieval town hall, is by taking an elevator from the Elwert passage to the old city. You enter near a busy intersection and the river and leave through Elwert's bookshop. You can find numerous bookstores, cafés, and bars where students while away their time in profound conversations about trivia.

ELIZABETHKIRCHE (St. Elizabeth's Church) is the first German church to be built in the Gothic style. Construction began in 1235, under the guidance of the Teutonic Knights, and was completed in 1283. In the church one finds the tombs of the church's patron, Elizabeth of Hungary, and the German First World War hero, Field Marshal von Hindenburg. A statue of Elizabeth stands in the nave. The tomb itself contains a 14th-century bas-relief sarcophagus depicting the saint's death and burial. There are also faded 14th-century and 15th-century frescoes showing scenes from her life. Elizabeth's shrine is a masterpiece of Rhineland art dating from 1250. There is also an Elizabeth window in the chancel with stained-glass medallions depicting her acts of charity. A second statue of Elizabeth, by

M

Ludwig Juppe, dated 1510, is also found in the chancel. In the south transept are the graves of the Landgraves of Hessen.

MARKTPLATZ (Market Place) contains a number of 16th-century half-timbered buildings and the superb **RATHAUS** (Town Hall), which has a finely carved tower by Ludwig Juppe and a wonderful ancient mechanical clock which delights onlookers every hour as various animated figures spring to life.

SCHLOSS (Castle). Overlooking the city is a well-built medieval fortress which now contains municipal offices and the **MUSEUM FÜR KULTUR-GESCHICHTE** (Cultural History Museum). Here one finds numerous items related to Reformation history, including some excellent portraits of leading secular figures who supported Luther, including Philip of Hessen (1504–67). In 1540 Philip entered into a bigamous marriage with the approval of Luther. When the facts became known, a major scandal ensued, resulting in grave harm to the Protestant cause.

STUDENTENMISSION IN DEUTSCHLAND (German Inter-Varsity Fellowship) also has its headquarters in Marburg, at SMD e.V., Universitätsstrasse 30, 35037 Marburg. So does the highly innovative **CHRISTUS-TREFF** (Christian Meeting Point), centered at Christ Haus, Georg-Voigt-Str. 21, Marburg, where a large house has been renovated to create a Christian community and center under the leadership of Dr. Roland Werner. Every Sunday there is an English service with afternoon tea. You can find out all about them at: http://www.christus-treff.org

FREIE THEOLOGISCHE AKADEMIE (FTA) (Free Theological Academy), Schiffenberger Weg 111, in nearby Gießen, 10 kilometers south of Marburg. This is the only graduate-level evangelical seminary in the German-speaking world. All other evangelical institutions are Bible schools unable to offer accredited degrees. There are, of course, numerous theological faculties in German universities. But those that are Protestant are essentially liberal or radical in their outlook. A few are sympathetic to evangelicals, and there are even some evangelicals teaching such things as pastoral theology. German universities, however, keep a tight grip on the teaching of core subjects like the Old and New Testaments through their control of the habilitation process. The result is that theological faculties generally ignore evangelical perspectives. The Academy was founded in 1974 with American help and has over 150 students, a good bookshop, and a library. Today all the key positions are held by German scholars, most of whom studied in Britain or North America.

MARIA-LAACH

This isolated monastery is built by a small lake, actually the crater of an extinct volcano, from which it takes its name. It was founded in 1093 by Heinrich II, count of the Palatinate (11–12th century), as a Benedictine abbey. This magnificent example of Rhineland Romanesque was consecrated in 1156, but only completed in 1220. The name *Maria Laach* means St. Mary's abbey on the lake. In the wake of the French Revolution the abbey was suppressed on August 2, 1802. The church was not used again for another 90 years, although the Jesuits acquired the monastery building in 1863 to establish a theological college which ran until 1872. In 1892 the Benedictines bought back the abbey and its grounds and began the long process of restoration. Since then, Maria Laach has become a center for liturgical renewal and the revival of spiritual life. The six towers symbolize the heavenly Jerusalem.

PLACES TO VISIT

Before entering the church take a look at the **PARADISE COURTYARD**, which is said to be unique in Christian architecture. It symbolizes the innocence of the Garden of Eden. At the center of the courtyard is an ornate fountain supported by two magnificently carved stone lions reminiscent of Islamic art. Carvings on the doorway into the church also represent the Garden of Eden.

Above the high altar is a stunning mosaic of Christ in Byzantine style produced by the Beuron school of artists as part of the church's restoration. Modeled on Sicilian designs, the mosaic conveys a sense of power and majesty. The abbey's founder, Count Heinrich II's tomb, is found in the west choir; there are also some fine stained-glass windows by Rupprecht. Finally, the crypt is well worth a visit.

M

MAULBRONN

The name *Maulbronn* means "mule's watering place." *Maulesel* is the German word for mule, while *Bronn* or *Born* is the old German for *Brunnen* or fountain. Today this is the

only medieval monastery north of the Alps to have been preserved in its original form, making it a United Nations World Heritage site. According to legend, a group of Cistercian monks rested here in 1147 to water their mules. The site was so congenial that they decided to remain there and build a monastery. The Cistercians are a branch of the Benedictine Order founded by Robert de Molesme (1029–1111) in 1098. Bernard of Clairvaux, who entered the order in 1112, was their most famous member. The Cistercians valued manual labor and simplicity of life. All work at the monastery was done by its members, who shunned luxury and idleness. The abbey, which was consecrated in 1178, was originally an Early Romanesque structure to which Late Gothic elements were added. The monastery itself is a complex of 35 buildings with 3 fortified towers surrounded by a wall.

During the Reformation, the monks of Maulbronn embraced Protestantism and turned their monastery into a boarding school in 1556. The conversion of the monks helped preserve the original architectural style, because during the 17th century most surviving Roman Catholic monasteries lost their original appearance due to renovations which transformed them into Baroque buildings. The most distinguished graduate of the boarding school is probably Johannes Albrecht Bengel (1687–1752).

PLACES TO VISIT

THE OUTBUILDINGS are the first things the visitor sees when they enter the monastery complex. Once these buildings housed forges, storerooms, and workshops. Today they contain a restaurant, bookshop, and information office.

THE PARADISE, or porch, added in 1220, stands at the entrance to the abbey church. It is generally regarded as the first example of the Gothic style in Germany.

THE KLOSTER (abbey church) was built as a simple, unadorned chapel in Romanesque style. The impressive fan vaulting was added in the 15th century. This solemn building is divided into two sections by a stone screen. On one side of the screen the lay brothers worshiped; on the other, the monks. On the altar before the screen is a one-piece, hand-hewn,

---

JOHANNES ALBRECHT BENGEL (1687–1752) was born in the small town of Winnenden and educated first at the Maulbronn Academy and then the University of Tübingen. A devout Lutheran, Bengel taught at the seminary in Denkendorf from 1713–41. During this time he produced a critical edition of the text of the New Testament (1734) followed by his famous *Gnomon novi testamenit* (1742), which consists of a commentary on the text of the New Testament in terms of the Greek words used. His writings were popularized in English by John Wesley (1703–91), who held Bengel's work in great esteem.

sandstone crucifix (1473). This crucifix is positioned so that during the summer solstice the rays of the sun fall through a red window pane to create a fascinating glow around the head of Jesus. The carvings on the choir stalls, installed in 1370, depict the events of Christ's crucifixion and interment.

The MONK'S REFECTORY, which is on the opposite side of the monastery, is also in the Early Gothic style with ribbed vaulting and pointed arches. Yet the older solidity of the Romanesque still manages to make its presence felt. The pleasing architecture of the monks' dining room is deliberate because the Cistercians were very frugal, believing that pleasant settings make simple food more enjoyable.

The CHAPTER HOUSE, on the east of the complex, is an example of High Gothic, full of grace and the lightness of being which sets it clearly apart from the more earthy, heavy, Romanesque style.

MEIßEN
(MEISSEN)

M

The castle or Misni, which overlooks a ford in the Elbe, was built around 920 by Heinrich I as a border post and defense against invasion by pagan Slavs. From 968 to 1581, Meißen, which grew into a prosperous town, was the seat of the local bishop and center of mission activity in Eastern Europe. The present castle was completed in 1485. Shortly afterwards, the Wettin dynasty moved its seat of government, accompanied by the bishop, to Dresden.

In 1708, the alchemist Johann Friedrich Böttger (1682–1719) was ordered by Augustus the Strong (1670–1733) to create gold from clay. Instead, he discovered a formula for the creation of white porcelain that until then was a tightly guarded secret known only to the Chinese. Due to large deposits of the basic ingredient, kaolin or china clay, a few miles from the town, Meißen became the center of a thriving new industry. To protect its secret, the ruler of Saxony, Augustus the Strong, established the first porcelain factory in his castle under Böttger's direction. The famous blue onion design, which became Meißen's, was created by Böttger's successor Johann Gregorious Höroldt (1720–55), while two blue crossed swords were adopted as its trademark. So valuable was porcelain in the 18th century that it was known as "white gold." In 1865 the factory was transferred from the castle to its present location in the town.

Meißen was devastated during the Thirty Years' War and again during the Wars of Friedrich II, the Great, and the Napoleonic Wars. Prosperity only returned in the mid-19th century due to the porcelain industry. During the Second World War the town escaped relatively unscathed, although 50 years of Communit neglect caused considerable damage to its ancient buildings.

PLACES TO VISIT

DOM (Cathedral) on the Schloßberg (Castle Mountain) is one of the finest examples of Early Gothic in Germany. It was founded in 1256 by Otto the Great (912–73) and completed in 1410 with three naves and a transept. Before the Reformation, when the area became Protestant, the dom had 50 altars of which only three exist today. The interior contains an excellent collection of medieval furnishings.

The choir contains large carved sculptures of the founder Otto I and his wife Empress Adelheid. John the Evangelist and St. Donatus were created in Naumberg. On the high altar a painting depicts the *Adoration of the Magi*. It is by an unknown 16th-century German painter in the Dutch style.

GEORGSKAPELLE (George's Chapel) contains a superb altarpiece by Lucas Cranach painted in 1534. It depicts Jesus showing his wounds after the Resurrection. The chapel is so named

because it contains the tomb of Duke George the Bearded (1471–1539), who played an important role in the Reformation first by supporting Martin Luther before becoming his main political enemy and persecuting Protestants.

FÜRSTENKAPELLE (Duke's Chapel) houses the tombs of Saxon kings. It contains a series of bronze manufactured in Nürnberg at Peter Visser's workshop by Albrecht Dürer and Lucas Cranach the Elder. The rood screen is a 13th-century creation. Before the screen stands Lucas Cranach the Elder's Laienaltar (Altar of the Lay Brothers).

DOMPLATZ (Cathedral Square) contains a rare collection of medieval buildings that were originally part of the cathedral's monastery. No. 5, the Dean's House, dates from 1526; No. 7, the Priory, dates from 1500; in between is the more modern Canons' House dating from 1728.

ALBRECHTSBURG (Albrecht's Fortress) is a superb example of a medieval castle which was later transformed into a royal residence. The present design is by Arnold von Westfalen (d. 1481) and contains a fine collection of 19th-century Romantic paintings.

FRAUENKIRCHE (Church of Our Lady), off the Market Square, was started in 1455. It is a triple-naved church with excellent star vaulting in the roof. The church contains a rare Porzellanglockenspiel (carillon, or peal, of bells) made from Meißen porcelain, which ring on the hour every hour. The

Late Gothic winged altar depicts the crowning of Mary as Queen of Heaven.

STAATLICHE PORZELLANMANUFAKTUR (National Porcelain Factory). Guided tours of the works have to be booked well in advance. The factory's porcelain museum is open daily and well worth a visit because it helps create a feel for the 18th century, the Baroque, and the Age of Reason.

MÜNCHEN
(MUNICH)

The assumed origin of what is today called München (Munich) goes back to the 9th century when a settlement near a Benedict abbey took as its name the German word for "monk," i.e., Mönch. Over time the old high German name changed to Muniche, and finally it became officially München. In the 10th century a trading, customs, and marketplace named Föhring, 30 kilometers north of München, was destroyed. The Duke Heinrich der Löwe (Henry the Lion) (1129–95) relocated this important market to Munich and granted the settlement customs and minting rights. The first documented mention of Munich was in 1158 when it was referred to as a place where salt was transported across the river Isar, custom duties were collected, and various kinds of coins were made. In 1255 the settlement became the residence of the Wittelsbach dynasty, which ruled Bavaria until 1918. Around 1294 Munich was granted city rights. The rapid growth of Munich during the Middle Ages was caused by trading in salt, cloth, wine, gold, and weapons. In 1503, Munich became the sole capital of Bavaria.

The city was stormed and occupied by the forces of Gustavus Adolphus (1594–1632) in 1632 but avoided being sacked through a payment of 300,000 talers. During the 16th and 17th century Munich became a center for the arts and sciences. Renaissance and rococo styles left their marks on the city while poets, musicians, gold and silversmiths, painters, philosophers, and politicians selected Munich as the place to live. The University of Landshut was relocated to Munich in 1800.

Until 1800, when the population of Munich was 40,000, the town was purely Roman Catholic. Shortly after 1800, the first Protestant was admitted to citizenship in Munich. Since 1821 Munich has been the seat of the Roman Catholic archbishop of Munich-Freising and more recently of a Protestant bishopric. Following World War II many East Prussian refugees settled in Bavaria after they were expelled from their homelands by Russia and Poland.

M

PLACES TO VISIT

The oldest church in Munich is the Romanesque ST. PETER built in the 12th century. It was replaced by a Gothic structure in 1278–94. A fire in 1327 destroyed the church; however, it was rebuilt and reconsecrated in 1386. Its somewhat unusual domed bell tower, "Alter Peter" (Old Pete), is a landmark on the Munich skyline. A statue of the patron saint, St. Peter (1492), carved by Erasmus Grasser (1450–1518), stands in the middle of the church. The decorations, appointments, and paintings were all done by local artists. The Late Gothic main altar (1517) consists of five individual panels by Jan Polack (1435–1519).

The origin of the HEILIGE GEIST SPITALKIRCHE (Holy Spirit Hospital Church) dates back to 1208. It was built at the location of a house of pilgrimage chapel. Duke Otto used the facilities as a hospital, and only in 1327 did work begin on the church, which was finished in 1392. A rebuilding of the entire structure took place from 1723 to 1730, and in 1885 a substantial extension was added to the west side. Only parts of the original frescoes, paintings, and other decorations have survived. A statue of the HAMMERTALER MUTTERGOTTES (Virgin Mary of Hammertal) came from the Abbey of Tegernsee in 1450. In the KREUZKAPELLE (Chapel of the Cross) stands a crucifix from 1510. This chapel is now used as a war memorial. On the west wall of the church is a bronze BURIAL VAULT designed and cast by Hans Krumper (1570–1634) for Duke Ferdinand of Bavaria in 1608.

Another of Munich's landmarks are the two copper onion domes, 99 meters and 100 meters tall, of the FRAUENKIRCHE (Church of Our Lady). A number of old 13th-century buildings were demolished to build the present church, whose cornerstone was laid in 1468 by Duke Sigismund. It was consecrated in 1494, but the distinctive, eye-catching spires were not built until 1524–25. This Late Gothic hall church was built between 1468 and 1488 by Jörg von Halspach. He also designed the town hall. Due to considerable damage to the church during World War II, the church had to be restored according to the original plans in the 1950s. The interior was modernized; in 1994 it celebrated its 500th anniversary.

Since 1821, the Frauenkirche has been the Metropolitan Church of the Southern-Bavarian Churchprovince (Archdioceses), which included the dioceses of Augsburg, Passau, and Regensburg. Much of the richly decorated interior dating from the Middle Ages was lost, stolen, or destroyed during World War II. But the beautiful on-glass-paintings church windows that were created between the 14th century and 16th century were saved. Even today they have lost none of their beauty. The church has one main entrance and four side entrances, two north and two south; the tombstone of the first priest is between the two entrances on the north side. The

SAKRAMENTKAPELLE (Chapel of the Holy Sacrament) contains an altar with a painting of *The Virgin of the Protecting Cloak* by Jan Polack.

The Frauenkirche is the source of the legend of the Devil's footprint. According to tradition, the architect, Jörg Ganghofer, made a pact with the Devil to raise enough money to build the church. The wager was that Ganghofer could not create a church where someone could stand within the building without seeing a single window. After the church was completed, the Devil came to inspect Ganghofer's work and was delighted to see the huge Gothic windows. But once inside, he was taken to a spot where every window was obscured by a pillar. In rage he stamped his foot, leaving an imprint in the stone which, it is said, remains yet today.

EHEMALIGE AUGUSTINERKLOSTERKIRCHE (Former Augustinian-Abbey-Church) was built 1291–94 and the original core is still preserved. Extensions to the building were added in the 14th and 15th centuries. An almost total rebuilding took place between 1618 and 1621. Later the church lost its ecclesiastical status and was used as a custom's office and main police station. Today it houses the DEUTSCHE JAGD- UND FISCHEREI MUSEUM (German Hunting and Fishing Museum). One of the church's paintings by Tintoretto depicting the *Crucifixion,* which once graced the main altar, can be seen in Stift Haug (Haug Convent) at Würzburg.

KREUZKIRCHE, ALLERHEILIGENKIRCHE AM KREUZ (Church of the Cross, All Saints Church at the Cross, 1478–85) is a bare Gothic brick building. The builder, Jan von Halspach, had planned the church as the cemetery chapel for St. Peter's. During the 18th century the inside was decorated in the Baroque style. Noteworthy works of art are the Rottenhammer Madonna (1520) and a tabernacle (1770), which had been taken over from the Karmeliterkirche (Carmelite Church). Very badly damaged during World War II, it was restored and now belongs to the Russian Orthodox parish.

SALVATORKIRCHE (Salvador Church) dates back to 1494. It originally served as a cemetery church for the FRAUENKIRCHE. It is also a bare brick structure; it has a mighty tower with six levels. The inside has been totally refurbished. Today, it is also a Greek Orthodox parish.

JESUITENKIRCHE ST. MICHAEL (Jesuit Church St. Michael), Neuhauser Str. 52, was built 1583–97. After the Reformation, it became a center for the renewal of the Roman Catholic faith and was supported by Duke Wilhelm V, der Fromme (The Pious) (1548–1626). During the construction of the church, one of the towers collapsed. Wilhelm V took this as an omen of the Archangel to built a much larger church than originally planned. The facade of the west

M

outer wall was destroyed during World War II; 26 years later it was rebuilt to its original form showing in the gable the figure of Christ. The church, which houses 10 altars, has a Renaissance-style barrel-vaulted ceiling, 70 meters by 31 meters, which is the largest in Europe apart from St. Peter's in Rome. Among the church's treasures is a crucifixion painted by the Giambologna school. Under the high altar is the Fürstengruft (Tomb of the Nobles) containing the remains of 30 of the Wittelsbacher rulers, including Maximilian I (1573–1651) and Ludwig II (1786–1868).

THEATINERKIRCHE PFARRKIRCHE ST. KAJETAN (Theatine Parish Church of St. Kajetan), Theatiner Str. 22, was built in 1662 for the Theatine monks. The Congregation of Clerics Regular, Theatines, was established by Kajetan of Thiene and Giovanni Pietro Caraffa, the future Pope Paul IV, in 1480 to further the ideals of the Oratory of Divine Love. In the wall niches are placed marble statues of St. Ferdinand, St. Adelheid, St. Maximilian, and St. Kajetan; under the main altar a Fürstengruft (Nobles Tomb) containing the remains of Duke Ferdinand Maria, Max Emanuel, Carl Albrecht, Max III, Joseph, Carl Theodor, King Max I, King Otto of Greece, and Crown Prince Rupprecht. Adjacent to the building is the **THEATINER ABBEY,** which has been used by the Dominican monks since 1954.

EHEMALIGE KARMELITENKLOSTERKIRCHE (former Carmelite Abbey Church),

1654, is in the Karmelitenstraße. This church is now used as the library for the Archdiocesan Ordinariat, the offices of which are located on the grounds of the former abbey.

DREIFALTIGKEITSKIRCHE (Church of the Holy Trinity), Pacellistraße 6, was built in 1704. Legend says that the daughter of a citizen had a vision that the city would suffer disaster unless a church in honor of the Trinity was erected. The city and tradesmen financed the project, and the church was consecrated in 1718 after seven years of work.

FRANZISKANERKLOSTERKIRCHE ST. ANNA IM LEHEL (Franciscan Abbey-Church St. Anne in the Lehel), St. Anna-Straße, was built 1727–30, and severely damaged during World War II. Most of the original paintings and decorations were lost. But an altar by C. D. Asam was partially saved and restored.

KATHOLISCHE KIRCHE ST. JOHANN NEPOMUK, ASAMKIRCHE (Catholic Church of St. John Nepomuk, the Asam Church), Sendlinger Straße, was founded in 1733 and designed in rococo style by the Asam brothers. This church must be seen. The talented Asam brothers, Egid Quirin and Cosmas Damian, who designed many Munich buildings, had a passion for decorating churches. The brothers bought a parcel of land and financed the building of St. Johann Nepomuk as an offering to God for their success as artist architects. Inside and outside, the artistry and craftsmanship are magnificent. The brothers paid great attention to space, light, form, and color in the creation of this masterpiece.

PFARRKIRCHE ST. LUDWIG (Parish Church St. Ludwig), Ludwigstrae 20, was built between 1829 and 1844 in a uniquely German style, known as Rundbogenstil, that combined elements from various earlier styles such as Romanesque and Classical. It served as the University Church for what today is the inner city. The church contains a fresco depicting *The Last Judgment,* which measures 18 meters by 11 meters, making it one of the largest paintings in the world. It was painted by Peter Cornelius (1783–1867), a member of the Nazarene school or brotherhood of painters who sought to recapture the spirit of early Christian art.

ALTER HOF, close to the **RESIDENZ,** was the official residence of the Wittelsbachs from 1253–1474. Its courtyard and half-timbered buildings take one back to pre-Reformation times.

ALTE PINAKOTHEK (Art Gallery), Barenstraße 27. Built between 1826 and 1836, this huge building was designed in Venetian Renaissance style by Leo von Klenze (1784–1864) to house the art treasures of the House of Wittelsbach. It contains a magnificent collection of art treasures from the 14th century to 18th century and is regarded by many as the finest art collection in Europe. It contains 12 Rubens (1577–1640) and 15 van Dycks (1599–1641), as well as paintings by Raphael (1483–1520),

Titian (d. 1576), Brueghel (1568–1625), Hals (1580–1666), Rembrandt (1606–69), and numerous other artists plus German works by men like Hans Baldung Grien (1484–1545), Lucas Cranach (1472–1553), Albrecht Altdorfer (1480–1538), and Albrecht Dürer (1471–1528).

NEUE PINAKOTHEK is a postmodern building opened in 1981 to house 19th-century paintings. Here you can find works by van Gogh (1853–90), Gauguin (1848–1903), Manet (1832–83), Monet (1840–1926), Cézanne (1839–1906), and German painters like Max Liebermann (1847–1935), Moritz von Schwind (1804–71), Karl von Spitzweg (1808–85), and Adolf von Menzel (1815–1905).

When you look at a picture by a man like van Gogh, you will be struck by the way the colors are so much more powerful in reality than in any reproduction. You should also remember that many of these artists started their lives as pious Christians before rejecting their faith under the stress of modern life. Van Gogh, for instance began his career as an evangelist working among very poor miners. The experience of poverty so appalled him that he turned from God to despair, seeking his only comfort in art. Remember too the words of Francis Schaeffer, who wisely said, "Anyone who wishes to understand the world in which we live and the way modern theology has developed needs to take a long hard look at the history of art."

M

Today the NEUE PINAKOTHEK also displays some items from the ALTE PINAKOTHEK COLLECTION including among its many treasures Altendorf's *The Battles of Alexander,* Albrecht Dürer's *The Four Apostles,* Raphael's *Madona della Tenda,* Rembrandt's *Passion,* and Botticelli's (1444–1510) *The Lamentation of Christ.*

GLYPTOTHEK houses Munich's fine collection of Greek and Roman art built in classical style by Leon von Klenze. Among its treasures are the *Tenea Apollo* (6th century B.C.) and the *Barberini Faun* (220 B.C.)

DEUTSCHES MUSEUM was built on an island in the river Isar. This museum of science and technology was founded in 1903 and is arguably the most important of its kind in the world. Anyone wanting to understand the rise of modern science or the impact of technology should make a visit. A host of working models adds to the intrigue of this collection.

HOFBRÄUHAUS, the most famous of Munich's many beer halls, was founded in 1589 and rebuilt in the 19th century. Here Hitler proclaimed his 25 point program in 1925.

RESIDENZ was originally built in 1385 as a residence for the Wittelsbach dynasty. This complex of palaces contains a remarkable SCHATZKAMMER (Treasury), which displays many royal crowns. Among its many religious pieces are the magnificent cross of Queen Gisela of Hungary, and a gold sculpture of St. George killing the dragon. The RESIDENZMUSEUM (Residence Museum)

contains many ornate rooms, including one devoted to the ancestors of the dynasty in which Charlemagne (742–814) is given pride of place.

To the north of the Residenz is the HOFGARTEN (Garden Court) which was laid out by the landscape gardener Heinrich Schön between 1613 and 1617 in the elaborate elegance of geometric balance known as the French style. Destroyed during World War II, it was recreated in 1950.

SCHLOẞ NYMPHENBURG, six kilometers from the city center, is the beautiful summer residence of the Bavarian kings set in extensive parkland. It was initially designed in the 17th century by another landscape gardener, Barelli, in lavish Italian style. Various additions were made over the centuries to create a royal fairyland that evokes the lifestyle of a leisured class. The gardens are set out in the "English style" of the 17th and 18th century.

ENGLISCHER GARTEN (English Garden) near the center of Munich was created between 1789 and 1795 by Ludwig von Sckell following the plans of Benjamin Thompson, Count Rumford, who was born in North Woburn, Massachusetts. Its name comes from the popular style of apparently natural gardens created in England during the 17th century in contrast to fastidious French style. Shortly after the outbreak of the French Revolution, the local ruler, Elector Karl Theodor (1724–99), opened the garden for the enjoyment of the public. Today it is a popular place for recreation and nude sunbathing. Anyone who visits both the HOFGARTEN and the ENGLISCHER GARTEN or SCHLOß NYMPHENBURG is bound to be struck by the sharp contrast between the French and English styles.

DACHAU, 19 kilometers to the northwest of Munich, is the infamous concentration camp that was the first to be established by the Nazi regime after it seized power following the Reichstag fire in May 1933. The British invented the concentration camp during the Second Anglo-Boer War in South Africa, 1899–1902. They interned 120,000 Boer women and children, of whom at least 30,000 died. At first, Dachau was used to imprison political opponents of the regime including Communists, socialists, and Christians, particularly Roman Catholic priests. Later, Jews and other "undesirables" were sent there before being moved on to camps in Poland. The site of the camp is now preserved with Catholic, Jewish, and Protestant memorials. At the end of the war, the camp was destroyed. Later two huts were restored to create a museum that reminds visitors of the horrors of the camp.

ENGLISH GARDEN. During the 17th century, French gardens, such as those found at Versailles, were popular throughout Europe. These gardens were laid out according to intricate geometrical designs intended to emphasize human control over nature. In reaction to the deliberately planned order of the French garden, the seemingly natural English garden became popular in the 18th century. French gardens were carefully constructed to show human skill in contrast to nature. English gardens were deliberately natural, although actually equally artificial. Behind both styles are self-conscious theories about nature and the place of humans in the world that are deeply rooted in changing theological and philosophical views. In his *Art in Crisis* (1957), the Christian art historian Hans Sedlmayr points out that the English garden was developed around 1720 as a deliberate protest against French architectural gardens, which were rejected as "unnatural." From the 1760s a craze for English gardens, which lasted until the 1830s, swept across Europe. This craze was part of a revolt against geometric design and architecture that implied human domination over nature. Thus the traditional and essentially Christian view of the world that saw nature as subordinate to humankind was rapidly replaced by a new relationship between humans and nature. The new relationship, expressed in the English style of garden, was one of subordination, passivity, and the deification of Nature, which was seen as a source of inspiration to be worshiped. This mode of thinking grew out of and helped popularize pantheism.

M

MÜNSTER

St. Ludger (742–809) was sent into the area to convert heathen Saxons as part of Charlemagne's pacification policy. He established a monastery, and in 805 Charlemagne created a new bishopric. A settlement grew up around the church, which gave its name, Münster or Minster, to the town, which was granted a city charter in the 12th century. A hundred years later Münster became a member of the Hanseatic League. The Reformation took root in Münster, where radical Anabaptist sects soon appeared. In 1543 the town was seized by rebels under the leadership of Jan van Leyden. A Christian commonwealth that viciously persecuted property owners was established based on Communist principles and plural marriage. The following year the city was stormed by Imperial troops at the request of Archbishop Franz von Waldeck (1491–1553) with the support of local citizens, landowners, and Lutheran princes. The rebels were slaughtered and their leaders captured. After trials and torture, the rebel leaders were imprisoned in iron cages that were suspended from the tower of the Lambertikirche, where they were left to die. The cages can still be seen hanging from the tower.

In 1648, Münster and Osnabrück were the twin cities where the Peace of Westphalia was signed ending the devastation of the Thirty Years' War. A university, now the third largest in Germany, was founded in 1780. Today the university occupies a magnificent Baroque Schloss that was once the bishop's palace. During World War II, over 70 percent of the old town was destroyed. It was rebuilt to its original glory in the 1960s.

PLACES TO VISIT

DOM OF ST. PAUL, constructed between 1172 and 1267, is a fine example of the transition from Romanesque to Gothic with two broad naves. It contains some magnificent stone sculptures such as the 13th-century Paradise Gate depicting Christ in majesty. The narthex has a secular 13th-century frieze and statues of the apostles. The glory of this artistically rich cathedral is its 14th-century astronomical clock that displays the position of the sun, moon, and stars. It is said that it will remain accurate until 2017. The clock face was finely decorated with religious symbols by Ludger Tom Ring the Elder (1496–1547).

The side chapels contain many interesting tombs. Bishop Clemens August von Galen (1878–1946), who was consecrated cardinal shortly before his death, was an outspoken critic and active opponent of the Nazi regime.

Bishop von Galen's tomb is found behind the high altar. The high altar (1622) itself depicts the life of St. Paul and was carved by G. Gröninger.

THE TREASURY, which is reached from the dom through the medieval cloisters, is particularly rich in ecclesiastical art. It contains richly decorated silver and gold reliquaries from the 11th and 15th century associated with St. Paul and the prophets. There is also a 15th-century altarpiece and a rare 13th-century processional cross.

LANDESMUSEUM (provincial or state museum) on the Domplatz contains a superb collection of medieval religious art including a set of sculptures depicting *The Triumphal Entrance* by Heinrich Brabender. There is also a very interesting collection of *Westphalian paintings,* works by Lucas Cranach the Elder (1472–1553), and local *folk art.*

ST. LAMBERTIKIRCHE (Church of St. Lamberti), on Prinzipalmarkt, is a Late Gothic structure with a magnificent spire. Built between 1237 and 1450, it contains a Jesse tree, depicting the family tree of Jesus, on its south door. Above the church, hanging from its spire, are three iron cages that imprisoned the dying rebel leaders after the failure of the Münster revolt. This ghoulish sight reminds visitors of the barbarisms of an age where torture was regarded as a normal punishment.

RATHAUS (City Hall) is a splendid Gothic building where the Peace of Westphalia was signed in 1648. This treaty that involved every West European nation except Britain brought to an end the Thirty Years' War, which had devastated German territories in Europe. Prior to signing the treaty, Catholic rulers met in Münster for five years debating acceptable terms. The treaty is commemorated by the FRIEDENSSAAL (Hall of Peace), which is a richly decorated room where the treaty was signed by Roman Catholic leaders on October 24, 1648. Protestant leaders signed the treaty in nearby Osnabrück. Apart from recognizing distinct Roman Catholic and Protestant areas, the treaty also ceded Alsace Lorraine to France and recognized the independence of the Netherlands and Switzerland and implicitly encouraged the growth of Prussia as an independent state. Thus the modern European order, which has held sway until our own time, came into being. The room's wooden panels are all originals in the Gothic and Renaissance style. Around the room are portraits of significant figures in the peace negotiations, including the young Emperor Ferdinand III, Philip IV of Spain, and Louis XIV of France.

FRECKENHORST is a small town only 25 kilometers east of Münster that is worth a visit because its parish church of ST. BONIFATIUS (St. Boniface) is one of the few remaining pre-Romanesque fortress churches in Germany. The crypt contains the 13th-century tomb of *Geva,* who founded the local convent. There is also an early stone baptismal font that is richly carved.

WASSERBURGEN. In the district surrounding Münster, one may visit over

M

169

50 water castles. The best, or at least most original, of these is generally thought to be the one in BURGSTEIN-FURT some 35 kilometers from the city.

Anyone interested in visiting castles will find this area a historical paradise.

NAUMBURG

Founded in the 11th century as a frontier post by the Margrave of Meißen on the intersection of several trade routes, Naumburg became a bishopric in 1028. It maintained this role until 1564 when its status changed due to the impact of the Reformation. During the 19th and early 20th centuries, many people regarded Naumburg as the most beautiful town in Germany. Although relatively undamaged during World War II, it was almost forgotten during the DDR when many of its magnificent medieval buildings were allowed to fall into disrepair. Once the renovations that are now underway are completed, Naumburg is sure to become a major tourist destination. Naumberg is also the birthplace of Gustav Warneck (1834–1911).

PLACES TO VISIT

DOM ST. PETER UND ST. PAULUS (Cathedral of St. Peter and St. Paul), Domstraße, is a two-chancel church built in a relatively short time between 1220 and 1250 that combines elements of the Romanesque and Gothic in one unified transitional style. Later additions added a Baroque touch to certain parts of the church. The east chancel, nave, and crypt are Romanesque with Gothic modifica-

tions; while the west chancel, which was built about ten years later, is Early Gothic. The two east towers are Romanesque with Baroque embellishments.

Naumburg is best known for its magnificent sculptures and rood screens created by an unknown artist called the Master of Naumburg (13th century), whom art historians generally consider at least 150 years ahead of his time in terms of the techniques he used. Naumburg Dom is unique in having two rood screens, one in the west and one in the east choirs. The west choir's rood screen is usually considered a masterpiece. It contains a series of carved figures depicting the story of Christ's passion from the Last Supper to his trial. The east rood screen is less impressive but well worth seeing as an example of Romanesque art.

By far the most important examples of artwork crafted around 1250 are the Master of Naumburg's statues of the twelve benefactors who financed the dom's construction. These sculptures are the most famous in all of Germany and are comparable with the classic works of antiquity and the Renaissance. The best known of these statues are the sculptures of Ekkehard II and his wife Uta. Photos

N

GUSTAV WARNECK (1834–1911) was the founder of Missiology in Germany and a great Christian mission theorist. At the University of Halle, he was influenced by Tholuck and later worked for the Barmer Mission, where he developed his views on mission strategy. In 1876 he heard and was impressed by the American perfectionist preacher and one of the founders of the Keswick Convention, Robert Pearsall Smith (1827–98), at a Mission Conference in Brighton, England. This encounter led him to found a Mission Conference in Halle, where he eventually became the Professor of Missions. His many books include *Outline of a History of Protestant Missions* (tr. 1901). Warneck's theories about church growth and the importance of a homogenous community are very similar to those developed by Donald McGavran (1897–1990) and the Fuller School of Church Growth.

of this dignified couple appear in numerous books on medieval art. The serene beauty of Uta, whose gown sweeps over her body, has a lifelike quality that is uncanny.

STADTKIRCHE ST. WENZEL (Parish Church of St. Wenzel), Markt, was consecrated in 1523 as the town church, financed by local citizens as an alternative to the princely dom. This act of defiance against ecclesiastical authority captured the mood of the time immediately before the Reformation when this Late Gothic church was under construction. Inside are two excellent paintings by Lucas Cranach the Elder (1472–1553). These are his *Adoration of the Magi* and *Jesus and the Little Children*.

THE NIETZSCHE MUSEUM was recently opened in a house once owned by Friedrich Wilhelm Nietzsche's mother. The philosopher, who grew up in the area where his father was a minister in the Protestant church, was educated in the nearby Pforta grammar school. A visit to the museum is important for anyone who wants to understand the development of modern atheistic thought.

FRIEDRICH WILHELM NIETZSCHE (1844–1900) is one of Germany's most important philosophers. He developed a passionate hatred of Christianity and profoundly influenced modern thought by his radical rejection of Christianity and the Western intellectual tradition. In *The Gay Science* (1887), he told the parable of the madman that contains the prophetic phrase "God is dead" to describe the condition of modern life. Rejecting the mob, he advocated a heroic ethic that despised women and looked for the coming of the "superman." A brilliant essayist, his work is a profound critique of modernity and modern ideologies which anticipates many 20th-century themes.

NÜRNBERG

(NUREMBERG)

In 1040, the settlement was founded on the north bank of the Pegnitz river by Heinrich III (1017–56), duke of Bavaria and emperor of Germany. The first documented mention of Nürnberg is in 1050. The town was granted market rights in 1062. A fire destroyed the city in 1127; it was rebuilt during 1140–50, expanding to the south bank of the river. According to legend, St. Sebaldus, the son of the Danish king, was a preacher in that region. He worked with St. Willibald and St. Wulibald under the direction of St. Boniface. His relics in St. Peter's Church caused a steady stream of pilgrims to visit the church in the Middle Ages.

Nürnberg became a major trading center with connections to the Mediterranean in the south, the Baltic in the north, Russia in the east, and France in the west. It flourished during the 12th century and 13th century. In 1219, the city received its Great Charter from Friedrich II (1194–1250) to become a free imperial city with large land holdings. Nürnberg was governed by a council of 42 burgers from wealthy patrician families. The wealth of the town attracted trades people and artists as it developed into a center of learning. The Anabaptist Peter Riedemann was imprisoned in Nürnberg in 1540. While in prison he wrote the book *Rechenschaft (Justification);* with the Bible this is the basis of the Hutterite's Doctrine. In 1525, Nürnberg was the first imperial city to embrace the Reformation, and it pioneered religious tolerance in a declaration of 1532, giving citizens the right to follow the religion of their choice.

Philipp Melanchthon (1497–1560) established the prestigious *Gymnasium Aegidianum* (high school) in 1525. A university was founded in 1575 which later was moved to Altdorf, 20 kilometers southeast of Nürnberg. It was one of the poorest universities in Germany in terms of endowments, but the most eminent in terms of achievement.

With the discovery of the Americas, the trade routes to the East lost their importance and the city declined economically. The Thirty Years' War devastated the area, and the custom policies of the larger powers in central Europe hindered Nürnberg's trade. In 1806, the city was absorbed into the kingdom of Bavaria. In 1835, Germany's first railway was built here to the nearby town of

Fürth. The German National Socialist Party (1933–45) made Nürnberg the city for their party assemblies and mass rallies. On January 2, 1945, the core of the city was destroyed in a British air raid that reduced 90 percent of the buildings to ruins. After the war, the city was lovingly rebuilt according to the original plans.

Nürnberg is the birthplace of Albrecht Dürer (1471–1528), painter, engraver, woodcarver, and friend of Martin Luther. Peter Henlein (1480–1542) who invented the pocket watch, and Martin Behaim (1459–1507) who built the first globe, as well as the playwright and poet Hans Sachs (1494–1576) were born here.

PLACES TO VISIT

CITY CENTER. The core of the city retains its medieval character with a splendid Late Gothic RATHAUS (City Hall), built in 1515. The view from the BURG, or castle, lets you see part of the old city wall surrounding the medieval core. The castle was built in the 12th century and extensively damaged in 1420. Most of the present building dates from a 15th-century renovation. The STADTBEFESTIGUNG (medieval city walls) are about five kilometers long with 80 watchtowers, and the four larger, heavily fortified guard towers were built to withstand bombardment by artillery. The distinct red-tiled, steep-pitched roofs of the houses with their unusual Gauben (roof windows) give the town a medieval fairy-tale atmosphere. The skyline is dotted with numerous church steeples, reminding the visitor of the city's Christian past.

ST. SEBALDUSKIRCHE (Church of St. Sebaldus), Winkler Straße 26, is now the main Protestant church in the city. It is the oldest church in Nürnberg. This is a late Romanesque structure started in 1230. The church was widened and remodeled to incorporate Gothic features including new windows and its nave between 1361 and 1379. The remodeled building was 13 meters higher than the original structure and had two chancels. The towers were added in the 15th century. The Sebaldusgrab, grave of St. Sebaldus, is a silver-clad Gothic shrine holding his relics. This artistic masterpiece took 12 years to create. It was the work of Peter Vischer the Elder (1488–1529), whose family were famous Nürnberg artists. With his sons, Vischer designed and built a bronze restraint for the protection and decoration of the shrine. The church's bronze baptismal font is also Vischer's creation. The *St. Peter's Altarpiece* dates from 1485 and was painted at the local Wolgemut studio. There is also a portrait of the Emperor Heinrich II (973–1024) from 1350 and a crucifixion scene by Veit Stoß (1447–1533) dated 1520. Finally, the stained-glass windows in the east chancel are particularly impressive.

LORENZKIRCHE (St. Lorens Church), Königstraße, is a high Gothic masterpiece

N

built at the end of the 13th century. One hundred years later, the west facade with an impressively rich sculptured portal was added. This church is known for its *Englische Gruß,* Angelic Greeting, carved in wood by the sculptor Veit Stoß (1447–1533). The limestone sculpture, the *House of the Sacrament* by Adam Krafft (1460–1509), is 18 meters tall with close to 100 figures depicting the Passion of Christ. The church has a magnificent rose window in the French style while the ambulatory contains further examples of fine stained glass, including a Jesse tree depicting the ancestors of Jesus.

Outside the church is the 14th century SCHÖNER BRUNNEN, or beautiful fountain, consisting of 40 separate figures in a pyramid structure with Moses at the top and the seven Imperial electors and nine Old Testament prophets at its base.

Opposite is the NASSAUER HAUS, the oldest house in Nürnberg.

FRAUENKIRCHE (Roman Catholic Parish Church of Our Lady), main Market Square, was built on the site of a 14th-century Jewish synagogue at the bequest of Emperor Karl IV (1316–78) in 1349. It was elevated to the rank of a court church in 1355. It was here that Karl IV issued his Golden Bull of 1356, which regulated the election of the seven Imperial electors and stipulated that the first Diet of each new emperor should be held in Nürnberg. Artworks by Adam Krafft (1460–1509) include his *Peringsdorffer Epitaph* (1498), depict-

ing the Madonna. The *Tucher Altar,* created in 1440 by an unknown artist of the Nürnberg school who is usually called the Master of the Tucher Altar. Above the balcony is a mechanical clock with figures depicting the acceptance of the Golden Bull by the seven electors.

ST. EGIDIEN, on Egidien square, is the only Baroque church in Nürnberg. Parts of the church belong to an earlier 12th-century Romanesque structure that was destroyed by fire in 1696. The Romanesque features were incorporated in the new building.

DÜRERHAUS (Albrecht Dürer's House), Mauthalle, built between 1489 and 1502, was bought by the artist in 1509 and remained his home until his death. It is one of the few buildings in Nürnberg to have escaped British bombing. The house has been furnished to help the visitor understand the times and the simple life of this great artist.

GERMANISCHES NATIONALMUSEUM (Museum of the German Nation), Kornmarkt, is housed in a former 14th-century Carthusian monastery. It contains a fine collection exhibiting the wealth of the German cultural tradition, including works by Veit Stoß (1447–1533), Tilman Riemenschneider (1460–1531), and Konrad Witz (1400–1444). Albrecht Dürer's (1471–1528) *Hercules Slaying the Stymphalian Birds* illustrates the role mythology played in the Renaissance era. The religious sensibilities of the period are seen in Albrecht Altdorfer's (1480–1538) *The Life of St.*

Florian, while Lucas Cranach the Elder's (1472–1553) portrait of *King Christian II of Denmark* reminds the visitor of the political realities of the time. The role of science in the Reformation era is seen in the museum's excellent collection of scientific instruments, including the world's first globe, constructed in 1491, a year before the discovery of the Americas. The globe was made by the geographer Martin Behaim (1459–1507), who was born in Nürnberg but spent much of his life working on navigational and carto-graphic problems in Portugal. The watch collection reminds visitors that Peter Henlein (1480–1542) invented the pocket watch here around 1510.

Anyone with children, or who is simply interested in childhood, will want to visit the SPIELZEUGMUSEUM (Toy Museum), Karlstraße 13–15, created as a result of Nürnberg's role as a center for the manufacture of toys. The collection is housed in a 17th-century town house and has dolls houses, dolls, railways, and a host of fascinating items.

OBERAMMERGAU

The name *Oberammergau* is derived from local geography. The region west of Oberammergau and Garmisch-Partenkirchen is the Ammer-Gebirge, or Ammer mountain range, a small river, die Ammer, has its source there and empties into the Ammersee, or Ammer Lake, 15 kilometers west-south-west of Munich. The word *Gau* describes a defined region or district. Hence, Oberammergau is the name of the village located at the ober or upper region of the Ammer mountain.

The first documented mention of Oberammergau is in 1633. In the 17th century, a pestilence, what we would call an epidemic, swept through the region killing many people. When the plague was over, the survivors vowed to give thanks to God by staging the Passion of Christ. The first performance took place in 1634. After 1674, the dates were changed so as to fall every ten years beginning with 1680. During the 1770s, religious plays were forbidden throughout Bavaria. The villagers appealed to the elector and the ban was lifted. The play was not performed during World War II. It was resumed in 1950 and has been staged regularly since then, the next performance being in the year 2010. All actors are local people who must have lived in Oberammergau for 20 years.

PLACES TO VISIT

KATHOLISCHE PFARRKIRCHE (Catholic Parish Church), Ettaler Straße, was built 1736–42 and replaced a Gothic church that stood on this site. The main altar and the side altars are late Rococo by artist F. X. Schmädl.

Numerous houses in Oberammergau have so-called Lüftlmalerei (air-paintings) decorating the walls. This is a richly colorful form of architecture depicting religious and secular scenes.

OSNABRÜCK

After defeating the Saxons in 780, Charlemagne built a church and school here as a center of evangelization intended to spread the gospel and educate surrounding heathens. The present cathedral stands on the site of the original church. Within a century, Osnabrück was a center of commerce with the right to mint its own coins. Fortifications were built by Friedrich Barbarossa in the 12th century; subsequently, Osnabrück joined the Hanseatic League. In the 1640s, the city was the Protestant stonghold during the negotiations that led to the signing of the Peace of Westfalia in 1648. One of the conditions of the peace treaty was that in the future Osnabrück would be ruled alternately by Roman Catholic and Protestant prince bishops. The arrangement lasted until it was abolished by Napoleon in 1806. King George I of England, who founded the present Hannoverian/Windsor dynasty, was born here in 1660 (d. 1727). Because of the town's close ties with France, it became a center for French refugees during the revolutionary years of the late 18th century. The anti-fascist,

Christian author Erich Maria Remarque (1898–1970) was born and lived here before fleeing to America in the 1930s. He is best known for his powerful anti-war novel *All Quiet on the Western Front* (1929). The city was badly damaged during World War II but carefully reconstructed. A university was established in 1970.

PLACES TO VISIT

DOM (Cathedral) on Domplatz is dedicated to St. Peter. After Charlemagne's church was destroyed by Saxon raiders, the present structure was built in the 11th century. The octagonal tower was added in the 12th century. The other two towers, one on the northwest and the other on the southwest, were added in the 13th century and 15th century respectively. The nave and choir were also renovated in the late 13th century, and the ambulatory was added two centuries later. Eight wonderful statues of the apostles are to be found in the nave dating from the 16th century. The continual construction and reconstruction means that the dom combines Romanesque and Gothic elements in a unique fashion that is very attractive. In particular, the peal of the bells when heard within the church has a deep, unique sound that is unforgettable. In the 15th century the Dom contained 28 altars. The number of altars was reduced in the 19th century. Leading off the ambulatory are two chapels containing the tombs of bishops. The greatest treasure of the dom is its large triumphal cross from 1250. There is also a 13th-century bronze font. Other artworks include the *Margerethenaltar* in the ambulatory and the *Madonna of the Rosary* in the north transept. Both were carved by an unknown artist during the 16th century in the Gothic style.

DIÖZESANMUSEUM (Diocesan Museum) contains an 11th-century gold cross and the largest collection of chalices in Germany.

RATHAUS (City Hall), on the triangular Markt (Marketplace), is an early 16th-century example of Late Gothic architecture. It was here in 1648 that Protestant leaders from all over Europe signed the Treaty of Westfalia bringing to an end the Thirty Years' War. The FRIEDENSSAAL (Hall of Peace) is a wood-paneled room where one finds the portraits of various Protestant leaders. A copy of the treaty is also on display.

MARIENKIRCHE (Church of St. Mary) is a fine 14th-century Gothic church to one side of the Rathaus also on the Markt. It contains a fine 16th-century altarpiece manufactured by a member of the Antwerp school of artists. The church also contains the grave of the 18th-century statesman Justus Möser (1720–94).

DOMINIKANERKIRCHE (Dominican Church), Bierstrasse, has been converted into a cultural center that often holds art exhibitions. Inside is a rare Late Gothic sandstone bust of Charlemagne.

MUSEUM FÜR KULTURGESCHICHTE (Cultural History Museum) contains a fascinating collection of items relating to local history from prehistoric times to the present, including works by the Jewish artist Felix Nussbaum (1904–44) who died in Auschwitz.

BUCKTURM (Buck Tower), Bierstrasse, is an ancient tower that houses a unique museum of instruments of torture. Among those tortured with these evil devices were Anabaptists and people accused of witchcraft.

PADERBORN

Paderborn derives its name from the name of the spring *Pade,* and the German word *Born* or "source." Hence the source of the river Pade is Paderborn. There are close to 200 springlets under the Cathedral due to a rare geological and hydrographical phenomenon. Archaeological evidence reveals that settlements existed in the area during the 3rd and 4th centuries.

Charlemagne (742–814) maintained an Imperial residence here, and after successfully subjugating the Saxons, he held the first Imperial Diet at Paderborn in 777. In 778, the town became the seat of a bishop, and in the following year Charlemagne met Pope Leo III (750–816), who had narrowly escaped death at the hands of his Italian enemies. Pope Leo III came to ask Charlemagne for assistance in defeating his enemies in Rome. Charlemagne sought the pope's help in establishing an empire. Among the issues discussed was the "birth of the German nation." Consequently, on Christmas Day 800, Charlemagne was crowned by Leo III as Emperor of the Western Empire.

Bishop Meinwerk, who was bishop at Paderborn from 1009 to 1036, was instrumental in founding the Benedictine Abbey Abdinghof and the Canon Collegiat Busdorf. He asked Odilo (962–1048), the abbot of Cluny, to give him 13 monks to establish Abdinghof. The abbey

and a church were finished in 1031. By 1295, Paderborn had joined the Hanseatic League, which gave the citizens the privileges of a free imperial city. The citizens also wanted independence from the rule of the bishop and embraced Protestant doctrines during the Reformation. But the Protestant period did not last, and by 1604, Catholicism had been restored and the prince bishop Dietrich von Fürstenberg (1585–1618) founded a Jesuit University. During the 19th century the great Christian apologist Joseph Kleutgen (1811–83) was educated and taught here before moving to the Gregorian University in Rome.

PLACES TO VISIT

DOM ST. MARTIN, ST. LIBORIUS, AND ST. KILIAN (Paderborn Cathedral), Cathedral Square, was originally founded in 799 as a three-naved Carolingian basilica on the spot where later the cathedral was built. Pope Leo III consecrated an altar to St. Stephen in 815, and in 836,

P

JOSEPH KLEUTGEN (1811–83) was one of the leading 19th-century Roman Catholic theologians and a great Christian apologist who played an important role in the development of neo-Scholasticism. His analysis of modern unbelief was remarkably similar to that of the Dutch Christian thinkers Guillaume Grone van Prinsterer (1801–76) and Abraham Kuyper (1837–1920). Kleutgen argued that the philosophy of Descartes (1596–1650) introduced a radical break into the Western philosophic tradition that led inevitably to unbelief. Only a return to Christian foundations, he argued, could counter the inevitable progress of apostasy. He stressed the importance of the kingdom of God in theology and made devastating criticisms of both rationalism and contemporary radical theology in Germany.

Bishop Baduard constructed a circular crypt for the St. Liborius (d. 397) relics. Fire destroyed the original church in 1000. Its replacement was also destroyed by fire. The present cathedral dates to the 13th century and was almost completely destroyed during a British bombing raid in 1945. After the war it was carefully reconstructed using the original materials and plans. The portal of the Chapel of Mary is generally regarded as the most beautiful part of the building, which is a good example of Gothic architecture. The west tower is Romanesque. There is also a late Romanesque north door and on the south side a fine Paradise porch from the mid-13th century with carved figures depicting the Virgin Mary and the apostles. The window in the south transept depicts scenes from the life of Christ and the parable of the *Wise and Foolish Virgins*. The high altar is a Late Gothic creation, while the pulpit was not added until 1736.

The CRYPT in Paderborn Cathedral contains the relics of St. Liborius and a fine Romanesque cross. St. Liborius was bishop of Le Mans, and a friend of St. Martin of Tours. Upon the death of St. Liborius, his relics were placed to rest at Le Mans. In 836, the relics were transferred to Paderborn, where he was declared the patron of the cathedral, the city, and the diocese. Ironically, St. Liborius was not active in or around Paderborn. Why his relics were brought here is unknown. Nevertheless, the relics made Paderborn an important pilgrimage center. In 1622, the relics were stolen by the duke of Braunschweig, who, in turn, gave them as a present to the duke of Salm. Finally, in 1627, the relics were returned to Paderborn, where they now rest in a valuable shrine.

To the north side of the cathedral is the oldest known hall church in Germany, the BARTHOLOMÄUS-KAPELLE (St. Bartholomew's Chapel), built in the Byzantine style around 1070 by Bishop Meinwerk.

FRANZISKANERKIRCHE ST. JOSEF (the Franciscan Church of St. Joseph) Western Straße; was built between 1668 and 1671 and is generally acknowledged to be the finest Baroque church in Westfalia.

DIÖZESANMUSEUM (Diocesan Museum), Markt 17, has a good collection of ecclesiastical art including the rare Romanesque *Imad Madonna* (1060), named after the bishop who donated this important item. There are also two portable altarpieces by the famed goldsmith and monk Roger von Helmarshausen (d. 1100).

KAISERPFALZ (Imperial Palace), on the north side of the dom, you can find the excavations of Charlemagne's Imperial Palace, the remains of which were uncovered due to Allied bombing during World War II. There is also a reconstruction of a later palace building from the 11th century.

P

POTSDAM

Founded in 993 as a Slavic settlement, Potsdam grew steadily, receiving its city charter in 1317. In the 17th century it became a summer residence of the Hohenzollern rulers of Prussia. Friedrich Wilhelm I (1688–1740) encouraged the settlement of French Huguenots after the Edict of Nantes was revoked in 1685. The presence of these skilled French artisans brought industrial growth and prosperity to the area. Friedrich II (1712–86) made Potsdam his permanent summer residence, building the palace of Sanssouci. Later he built the larger Neue Palais (New Palace) for more formal functions.

During the 19th century Potsdam was occupied by Napoleon's army from 1806–13. Friedrich Wilhelm III (1770–1840) added Schloss Charlottenhof and the Roman baths to the palace complex. The abdication of the Kaiser in 1918 left the palaces empty until they were taken over by the state as public property in 1927. Following the end of World War II, the Americans, British, and Russians signed the Potsdam Agreement at Cecilienhof on August 2, 1945, confirming the new boundaries of Europe. This act, which was given added significance by the presence of Stalin, probably saved the palaces from destruction by the Communist government of the DDR. After the fall of the Berlin Wall

and German unification, extensive renovations began to both the palace complex and the city of Potsdam to restore them to their former glory.

PLACES TO VISIT

NIKOLAIKIRCHE (Church of St. Nicolas), am Alten Markt, was designed by Karl Friedrich Schinkel (1781–1841) and Ludwig Pesius (1803–45) as the largest domed church in Germany. The dome, which is decorated with impressive scenes from the New Testament, consists of four tiers supported by Corinthian columns. It was built between 1843 and 1849 and dedicated in 1850.

MARSTALL (Royal Stables), close to the Nikolaikirsche, on Breite Strasse, now houses the National Film Museum, which provides fascinating insights into German life and thought in the 20th century.

HOLLÄNDISCHES VIERTEL (Dutch Quarter), consists of 134 Dutch-style houses built in the mid-18th century to house workers who had moved to Potsdam. It is in the process of renovation and is well worth a visit because of its homely Calvinist style of architecture.

ALEXANDROVKA SETTLEMENT (Alexander's Settlement) is an area constructed after the Napoleonic Wars for Russian artists who remained in Prussia. The quaint Russian-style houses are in stark contrast to those of the Dutch Quarter. Here also is the **ALEXANDER-NEWSKI-KIRCHE** (Alexander Newski Church), which is a fine example of Russian Orthodox architecture. Inside there are many icons and other symbols of Orthodox piety.

CECILIENHOF PALACE was the last Prussian royal palace to be built in Potsdam. It is an unremarkable mock-Tudor building built for Princess Cecilie and her husband, the crown prince, between 1913 and 1917. Today it is important because this was the site of the Potsdam Conference that divided up Europe between the Communist East and Capitalist West in 1945. Its design also reminds visitors that English style and thought had a great influence on Germany prior to World War I, when the English were held in great respect by ordinary Germans and their rulers, who sought to emulate British fashions.

SANSSOUCI PALACE COMPLEX is one of the absolute musts for anyone visiting Germany. The magnificent park was created by Peter Joseph Lenné (1789–1866), Prussia's greatest landscape gardener after the then popular style of the English garden (see München). The grounds surrounding these palaces are among the greatest in the world. The palace itself, after which the park is named, is Friedrich II's beloved Sanssouci built between 1745 and 1747. The building was designed by Friedrich and built by his friend Georg Wenzeslaus von Knobelsdorff (1699–1753) in the Italian rococo style. To ensure an authentic structure, Friedrich sent von Knobelsdorff on a trip to Italy before construction commenced. This illustrates the immense impact of Italian thought and manners on northern Europe in the 18th century that prepared the way for neoclassicism.

The name *Sanssouci,* meaning "without worry," expresses Friedrich II's goal. It was his retreat from the cares of the world, diplomacy, and war. Here Friedrich relaxed by playing the flute, reading French literature (there isn't a German book in the library), and holding intellectual conversations with his friends, who included the French rationalist philosopher Voltaire. The whole atmosphere evokes the rationalism of the Enlightenment at its best. The dark side, if Voltaire is to be believed, and historians still debate the issue, is Friedrich's unrestrained sex and homosexuality. Here one finds the home of a philosopher king who loved intellectual questions, championed liberty in the abstract, and discouraged the Christian piety and Pietist movement that his father had promoted. More than anywhere else in Germany this palace catches the spirit of the Enlightenment. To go inside this simple one-story palace, visitors must join a conducted tour that is well worth the usual wait.

FRIEDENSKIRCHE SANSSOUCI (Peace Church) stands near the park's main entrance. It was built between 1845 and 1848 in an Italian style inspired by the

P

Basilica of St. Clement in Rome at the wish of the pious Prussian king Friedrich Wilhelm IV. The church was intended to rebuke what the king considered the ungodly arrogance of his famous ancestor Friedrich the Great. The Latin inscription inside the church is from Psalm 26:8 and reads, "Lord, I have loved the beauty of thy house and the place where thy glory dwells." It is intended to remind visitors of their dependence on God. The magnificent mosaic of Christ in the apse, which is above the communion table, is one of the rarest mosaics in northern Europe. It dates from the 12th century and was originally part of the Church of San Cipriano on the Island of Murano near Venice. When Friedrich Wilhelm heard that the church of San Cipriano was to be demolished, he recognized the worth of the mosaic, rescued it from destruction, and brought it to Potsdam.

Visiting the CHINESISCHES TEEHAUS (Chinese Tea House), which can be reached by a leisurely stroll from Sanssouci to the New Palace, is important. This small but highly decorated pavilion reminds visitors of the immense impact Chinese thought and fashions had on the 18th century. Today we hear a lot about ethnocentrism and the insularity of Europeans. This building vividly reminds visitors that in fact Europe has been far more open to other cultures than fashionable post-colonial writers like to assert. Through the writings of Jesuit missionaries and the philosophy of Gottfried Leibniz (1646–1716), the Enlightenment was profoundly influenced by Chinese ideas that rulers like Friedrich II used as a foil to raise doubts about Christian revelation.

NEUES PALAIS (New Palace) was built 1756–63 by Friedrich II after his victory in the Seven Years War (1756–63) against the pious and reforming Austrian Catholic ruler Maria Theresa (1717–80). The purpose of the new building, according to one of Friedrich's quips, was a work of conceit intended to prove to the world that the war had not exhausted Prussia's

GOTTFRIED WILHELM LEIBNIZ (1646–1716) was a German rationalist philosopher, mathematician, and inventor of calculus whose work led to the development of symbolic logic. He is also known for his work attempting to resolve the problem of evil by justifying the actions of God. Technically this is known as theodicy. Leibniz taught that the universe is made up of ultimate entities known as monads. God is the supreme monad responsible for the state of the universe. He is eternal and absolute truth who created this world as the best possible world. Evil is a problem but is to be understood as the consequence of freedom, which makes the world a far better place than if humans lacked the ability to choose.

treasury. This is an imposing, if grandiose, Baroque structure that stands in sharp contrast to the simplicity of Sanssouci. With over 400 rooms all lavishly decorated, it attests to the power of Prussia and the wealth of the king.

CHARLOTTENHOF (Charlotte's Court) to the south was built as a summer residence for the crown prince in 1826. Its design by Karl Friedrich Schinkel (1781–1841) evokes classical themes and mythology, echoing ancient Rome and once again underscoring the influence of the pre-Christian past on the early 19th century.

A one-stop train ride from Potsdam station takes visitors to the **BABELSBERG** film studios which once rivaled Hollywood in producing many excellent films and stars, such as Greta Garbo (1905–90), Marlene Dietrich (1901–92), and the actor/director Leni Riefenstahl (b. 1902). Here many classic films such as *The Blue Angel* and *Metropolis* were made. After the Nazis seized power, the studios were increasingly turned to propaganda purposes. This trend continued under the Communist government of the DDR, making the history of German filmmaking a part of the history of our times. Today the studios are owned by a French company.

QUEDLINBURG

Visiting Quedlinburg is like entering a time warp that takes the visitor back to the Middle Ages. With over 700 half-timbered medieval houses, and more than 1,600 listed buildings—including a castle and an ancient abbey church—that were totally untouched by the Second World War, it is no wonder that UNESCO has declared this unique town a World Heritage site. Although the buildings were allowed to deteriorate during the DDR, a massive renovation program is in place.

Founded by King Heinrich I, the Fowler (875–936), in 925 as an administrative center, it became the site of at least six Imperial Diets. After Heinrich's death, his wife founded a collegiate center to train aristocratic women to administer convents. This college survived until it was abolished at the beginning of the 19th century due to Napoleonic reforms. Throughout the Middle Ages the town flourished as an administrative center and seat of government in Saxony.

Quedlinburg prides itself for being the birthplace of Dorothea Christina Erxleben (1715–62), the first woman to become a medical doctor in 1754 after studying at the University of Halle. It is

183

also the birthplace of the Lutheran theologian Johannes Gerhard (1582–1637) and Christian poet Friedrich Gottlieb Klopstock (1724–1803). The great Christian preacher and the man who inspired the development of Pietism, Johannes Arndt (1555–1621), was the pastor here.

PLACES TO VISIT

ALTES RATHAUS (Old City Hall), a distinctive Renaissance-style building, is now the town museum.

FACHWERKMUSEUM STÄNDERBAU (half-timbered house-building museum), Wordgasse. For anyone interested in knowing how medieval half-timbered houses were built, or how our ancestors lived and worked, this is a fascinating exhibit. It stands in a street full of delightfully ancient houses built in this style.

KLOPSTOCKMUSEUM (Klopstock Museum), 12 Schlossberg, is located in the birthplace of the great German Pietist writer Klopstock, whose Christian poetry provided the composer Handel (1685–1759) with the inspiration for the immortal *Messiah*. His work also inspired early Romanticism.

SCHLOSS (Castle). The grim exterior walls remind visitors that Quedlinburg once stood as a frontier post and center of evangelization for hostile heathen tribes to the east. The fortress was renovated in the 16th century as a Renaissance palace. The Schloss contains various buildings including the RESIDENZBAU (Palace of the Abbess), and the WOHNTRAKT (living quarters), where other nuns lived and worked. Today this building houses a museum of local history.

FRIEDRICH GOTTLIEB KLOPSTOCK (1724–1803). After studying theology at Jena and Leipzig, where he wrote the poem *Messias* (1748) which was used by Handel (1685–1759) for his *Messiah,* Klopstock used his gifts as a Christian poet to struggle against the corrosive effects of rationalism and the Enlightenment. Klopstock is often called "the German Milton" and is generally recognized as the initiator of a late 18th-century northern Renaissance in poetry and literature. His poems include *The Death of Adam* (1757) and a series of *Odes* reflecting on life and religion that were written over many years.

JOHANNES ARNDT (1555–1621) was a devout Lutheran who studied Melanchthon's (1497–1560) works when he was a student at the University of Wittenberg. Arndt was disturbed by the sterile theology that entered the church following the Reformation. Therefore, in 1606, he published his *True Christianity,* which a generation after his death bore fruit in the works of Spener (1635–1705) and Francke (1663–1727).

STIFSKIRCHE ST. SERVATIUS (Parish Church of St. Servatius) was built in 1075 after a fire destroyed the original church. This is an outstanding example of Romanesque architecture with a plain unadorned interior. The 10th-century crypt contains the graves of King Heinrich I and his wife, Mathilde. Although the walls are now plain, it is possible to see traces of earlier paintings on the vaulting of the crypt. The north transept contains the Domschatz, a richly decorated 12th-century reliquary containing relics of St. Servatius. There is also a 13th-century bridal chest containing some of the earliest known heraldic symbols. And look for the priceless Quedlinburg tapestry, the oldest of its kind in northern Europe, depicting the marriage of the mythical figures Mercury, messenger of the gods, and Philology, the queen of knowledge.

MARKTKIRCHE ST. BENEDIKTI (Market Church of St. Benedict), presents another grim fortresslike exterior. The inside, however, was transformed after the Reformation into a fascinating example of north German Baroque that retains a sense of seriousness that is lacking in most Baroque churches.

DOM HALBERSTADT (Cathedral of Halberstadt), one of the finest Gothic churches in Germany, is about 16 miles from Quedlinburg in the town of Halberstadt. Unfortunately the town, which was once regarded as one of the most beautiful in Germany, still bears the marks of almost 50 years of Communist rule and is not very attractive. The dom itself, however, is well worth visiting even though it is rather dark and in need of renovation.

REGENSBURG

Regensburg is situated on the south, right bank of the Danube river, at the confluence of Naab and the river Regen, which flows from the north to Regensburg. The Danube originates in the Black Forest and reaches Regensburg at its highest point north, before proceeding in a southeast direction and finally emptying into the Black Sea. Of interest to American and Canadian readers is the fact that the 49th parallel, the undefended border between Canada and the USA, runs through the city of Regensburg. Standing in Regensburg is like standing on the border between Canada and the USA; between Washington and British Columbia; between Montana and Saskatchewan; or between North Dakota and Manitoba. So you are really not far from home.

Traces of human activity around the present location of Regensburg go back to the Stone Age. Since that time small settlements had been located in this region where, from the north, two rivers, Regen and Naab, empty into the

R

Danube. Its location and easy river crossing made it an ideal commercial center. A pre-Roman, Celtic colony, Radespona, was founded around 550 B.C. It was conquered by the Romans under Vespasian (A.D. 9–79) in A.D. 77. Regensburg's "birth certificate" is an eight-meter (26-foot) long stone slab. On it is inscribed the completion date of the walled complex marking the founding of the city by the Roman Stoic philosopher Emperor Marcus Aurelius (A.D. 121–80). It is dated August 25, A.D. 179. The Romans maintained this encampment of over 6000 troops, which they called "Castra Regina," until the fall of the Western Empire in A.D. 476.

"Castra Regina" became the center of Roman power on the upper Danube under Emperor Domitian (A.D. 51–96), who ruled from 81–96 and insisted on being called "Lord and God." A fortified wall, the Limes Germanicus, was built through Germanic lands. It ran from Hienheim on the Danube, 26 kilometers southeast of Regensburg, to Rheinbrohl, 30 kilometers southeast of Bonn, along the river Rhein. The wall was over 580 kilometers long and was fortified by around 1000 watchtowers. This wall was intended to keep out the Germanic tribes advancing from the northeast towards Roman territory. The wall was maintained until A.D. 300. Ruins of the wall have survived in many places along this ancient frontier.

Unlike most other German cities, particularly in Bavaria and Baden-Württemberg, many of the old houses in Regensburg are built of heavy, large blocks of stone. Consequently, Bishop Arbeo, around 770, described Regensburg as "a city hard to conquer because of the massive, high stone buildings."

According to legend, in the middle of the 7th century, St. Emmeram came from Gallien as a missionary to Bavaria where he founded an abbey. He was appointed bishop of Regensburg, but false accusations against him by the duke of Bavaria forced him to flee. He was murdered by the duke's son and is buried in the Georgkappel in Regensburg. In the 8th century, Bishop Gaubold had the relics of Emmeram placed in a crypt at the Benedictine Abbey, over which St. Emmeram Church was built. In 1659, the relics were placed in a silver coffin and now rest in the treasury of St. Emmeram. Whatever the truth of this story, St. Boniface founded the Regensburg bishopric in 739, and Charlemagne defeated the dukes of Bavaria in 788 to establish a new dynasty.

The patron saint of Regensburg, St. Wolfgang (924–94), was active in the area during the 10th century. Born of a noble family, the Pfufflinger, he entered a monastery at Einsiedeln, Switzerland, where he was ordained, and he traveled as a poor monk and missionary to evangelize heathen peoples. On the recommendation of Bishop Pilgrim of Passau, he was made bishop of Regensburg, where he died and is buried in St. Emmeram.

Throughout the Middle Ages, the city was a center of religious life, with many Crusades starting in Regensburg, including those led by Konrad II (990–1039) in 1147 and Friedrich Barbarossa (1123–90) in 1189. Regensburg freed itself from ecclesiastical rule by prince bishops to become a free imperial town in 1245. Because of its strategic location, on the crossroads between the Black Sea and central Europe, Regensburg was chosen as the city in which to hold many of the Royal Diets of the Holy Roman Empire.

In 1541–42, the Diet of Regensburg led to a peace settlement between Roman Catholic and Protestant rulers. In 1632, the city was stormed by Swedish Protestant forces in the Thirty Years' War. After 1663, Regensburg became the meeting place for all the diets of the Holy Roman Empire until the Empire was dissolved in 1806. The French stormed the city in 1809, during which battle Napoleon was wounded. Two years later Regensburg was annexed by Bavaria. Today Regensburg is the only major city in Germany with over 1,400 Gothic buildings to survive World War II. In 1967 a new university was founded here.

Regensburg's Jewish community is arguably the oldest in Germany. Jews lived in Regensburg during Roman times and were a well established community by 981. During the First Crusade, the local Jews escaped death by embracing Christianity. But the following year, Emperor Heinrich VI (1081–1125) allowed them to reestablish Judaism and gave them the protection of an Imperial Charter under which they were allowed to trade in gold, silver, and other metals as well as become money lenders. They were also given legal protection and the assurance that in any disputes between them and Christians, the trial would be held before judges acceptable to both parties. Consequently, the Regensburg Jewish community avoided many of the massacres that devastated other Jewish groups throughout Germany during the Middle Ages. After the death of Emperor Maximilian (1459–1519), their charter rights were not renewed and they were expelled from Regensburg. The local Jewish cemetery, which was one of the oldest in Europe, was desecrated by the removal of gravestones for use in buildings. The synagogue was demolished and the Neupfarrkirche built on the same site. After 1669, a few Jews were allowed to return to Regensburg, but the community remained small and never regained the status it had during the Middle Ages. Consequently, when the Nazis came to power in 1933, there were only 427 Jews in the city. About half of these escaped Nazi rule, while the others were deported to concentration camps in 1942 where they perished.

Among Regensburg's many claims to fame, it is the birthplace of the artist Albrecht Altdorfer (1480–1538), the writer Georg Britting (1891–1964), and John of Austria (1545–78), who defeated the Turks in the crucial naval battle of Lepanto in 1571.

PLACES TO VISIT

DOM ST. PETER (St. Peter Cathedral), Domplatz. Construction on the present dom began at 1275 after a fire in 1273 destroyed an earlier Romanesque structure. It took several centuries to complete this mighty Gothic structure. The three naves offer seating for over 7000 worshipers. The dom is world famous for its first-class boys choir. Although the towers date from the 14th century, the two spires are a 19th-century addition, completed between 1859 to 1869. Close to the main entrance, the center nave is flanked by statues on horseback; on the left is St. Martin, on the right, St. George. Numerous works of art are found in the church and its chapels. The stained glass in the south transept is 13th century and that in the choir 14th century. The central west pillars have statues of the Virgin Mary and the famed Angel of Regensburg depicted as the angel of the Annunciation. Both works date from around 1280. By the west nave entrance stands a statue of the Devil accompanied by his grandmother! These were placed by the door to remind worshipers that upon returning to the secular world they would be constantly confronted by temptation.

Located around the facade of the dom are a series of sculptures that vividly express anti-Semitism. On the west facade, you will find a sculpture of the Judensau (Jewish pig), intended as a deliberate insult to Jews. Today only a few examples of this once-popular sculpture exist. The carving shows two men, clearly dressed as Jews, suckling at the sow while a third speaks into the sow's ear. On the south facade, you will find a series of sculptures from the Pentateuch including one of Jews dancing around the golden calf. At first this seems like just another biblical sculpture and essentially harmless. But when it is seen in the context of the Judensau, it takes on a different and more sinister meaning. Inside the dom, various stained-glass windows also depict Jews in unsavory ways, reminding the modern visitor how easy it is to stigmatize an entire people through centuries of negative propaganda. We Christians need to be called to repentance for the prejudice of our forefathers.

DOMSCHATZ (Treasury) is located in the south wing of the former bishop's residence. It contains numerous artworks and liturgical items including the rare Ottocar Cross (1430), a reliquary chest made to look like a Venetian house, and the Schaumberg Altar (1534).

DIÖZESANMUSEUM ST. ULRICH (Diocesan Museum of St. Ulrich) is housed in the **ULRICHKIRCHE** (St. Ulrich's Church). It contains further examples of religious art and ecclesiastical treasures including the 12th-century cross of St. Emmeram.

EHEMALIGE BENEDIKTINERKLOSTERKIRCHE ST. EMMERAM (Former Benedictine Monastery Church St. Emmeram), Emmerams Square. Originally an 8th-century Romanesque building, it was transformed in the 18th century by the Asam brothers Cosmas Damian (1686–1739) and Egid Quirin (1692–1750) into a Baroque/rococo jewel. The church is named after the martyred Bishop Emmeram (7th century), who found his last resting place here. The whole monastery complex has grown over the centuries and contains many tombstones from the Carolingian age. The Wolfgang crypt and Emmeram crypt are in the lower part of the structure; the ceiling decorations and paintings are by C. D. Asam.

STIFTSKIRCHE UNSERE LIEBE FRAU ZUR ALTEN KAPELLE (Church of Our Beloved Lady, at the Old Chapel), Alter Kornmarkt. Much of this building dates back to the 9th century and is therefore Carolingian in origin. It was extensively remodeled in the 18th century in Rococo style. The altar room was added between 1441–52. It contains some extraordinary Rococo carvings, and paintings adorn ceiling and walls.

EHEMALIGE DOMINIKANERKIRCHE ST. BLASIUS (Former Dominican Church of St. Blasius), Beraiterweg. This church was built in the 13th century and was one of the first large Gothic structures in Germany. The Albrechtus Kapelle belongs to the adjoining monastery complex.

DREIEINIGKEITSKIRCHE (Church of the Holy Trinity), Schererstraße and Gesandtenstraße, is a Protestant church built between 1627 and 1631. It was here that the Royal Diets of the Holy Roman Empire were held during the 17th and 18th centuries.

SCHOTTENKIRCHE ST. JAKOB (Scotch Church St. Jakob), Jakobstraße, was built by Irish-Scottish monks in 1120. This beautiful church contains some unusual figurines.

NEUPFARRKIRCHE (New Parish Church), Neupfarrplatz, was erected on the site of a synagogue between 1519 and 1540. It originally served as a pilgrimage church "to the beautiful Mary," but was taken over by Protestants as a parish church in 1542.

STADTMUSEUM (City Museum), Dachauplatz, is housed in a former convent built in the 13th century. The museum houses a fine collection of historical and artistic items going back to prehistoric time. Here too is a surviving stretch of the ancient Roman city wall.

STEINERNE BRÜCKE (Stone Bridge), Thundorferstrasse, is Germany's oldest medieval bridge, built between 1135 and 1146, with 16 arches vividly displaying the skill of medieval architects and builders.

R

ROSTOCK

Located on a hill above the left bank of the wide Warnow estuary, Rostock was founded by German settlers in the late 12th century. Prior to that time, a Slavic fort existed on the lower right bank of the river, but the Slavs were driven out by the arrival of the Germans. The town grew around three distinct centers. The Altstadt (Old City) was based on the original stronghold and St. Peter's church. The Mittelstadt (Middle Town) was clustered around the newer Marienkirche built in 1232, and the Neustadt (New City) was centered on the Rathaus (City Hall), built in 1262. The city itself was granted a charter on June 24, 1218, and was one of the founding members of the Hanseatic League. It established northern Europe's first university in 1419. During the Thirty Years' War, the city sided with the Imperial army of Count Wallenstein, who belonged to the local ruling elite. Consequently, it was stormed by Gustavus Adolphus (1594–1632).

A fire destroyed most of the city in 1677. Due to the declining importance of the Baltic trade, the city fell on hard times. Things improved in the 18th century when Rostock became a major port for the export of grain. During World War II, it was extensively damaged by British bombing. The establishment of the DDR in 1948 made Rostock the country's main port; since the Wende, however, the town has stagnated.

PLACES TO VISIT

PETRIKIRCHE (St. Peter's Church), Alter Markt, was the original center of the town and an important frontier church in the Middle Ages that was a base for the evangelization of pagan Slavs to the east. It has an interesting bronze font cast in 1512 and is in the northern German Gothic brick style.

MARIENKIRCHE (St. Mary's Church), Ziegenmarkt, was completely untouched during British bombing. The largest church in the city, it took over 200 years to complete in the northern German Gothic brick style. Originally an Early Gothic structure, the church was turned into a fine example of Late Gothic. From the outside, this transition can be seen in a change in the color of the bricks used in construction. The early bricks were red; the later ones are yellow. This change came about in 1398 when a large part of the earlier structure collapsed necessitating a major rebuilding project. The tower was completed in 1452 by combining two earlier towers. A steeple was added in 1796. The church's most valued treasure is a font cast in 1290. This is the largest surviving medieval font in Europe. The altar, in the Rochus chapel, dates from 1530 and is decorated with carved figures of Saints Rochus (Roch) (1295–1350), Anthony (251–356), and Sebastian (d. 3rd century). All three saints were patron saints of the plague, or rather protection from the plague, reminding us that before the development of modern medicine people flocked to churches for protection during epidemics. One of the glories of St. Peter's is its astronomical clock located above the altar. Originally made in 1475, it was enlarged in 1642 and is the only astrological clock to have survived in its original state in the whole of Europe. The altar itself dates from 1720 and was made in Berlin. The pulpit dates from 1574 and is an outstanding example of Renaissance art. Its canopy is a Baroque addition dating from 1723. The church also contains an excellent organ.

KLOSTER ZUM HEILIGEN KREUZ (Monastery of the Holy Cross) was founded by Queen Margarete of Denmark in 1270. According to tradition, she had visited Rome on a pilgrimage in penance for her late husband's many sins. After leaving Rostock by sea, she was shipwrecked and miraculously saved from drowning. Thereafter she returned to Rostock to found this convent for the training of young women. She lived there until her death a few years later. A large 16th-century painting depicts various scenes from the queen's life. The convent belonged to the Cistercian order and was the only institution of its kind to survive the Reformation in Mecklenburg. It was finally closed in 1920 and restored in 1976 before reopening as the KULTUR-HISTORISCHES MUSEUM (Cultural History Museum). Today there are six well-restored buildings containing fine exhibits of local coins, pewter work, and numerous other items including a good toy collection. KLOSTERKIRCHE (Convent Church) is a three-aisled hall church in the northern German Gothic style with a superb 15th-century high altar.

NIKOLAIKIRCHE (Church of St. Nicholas), Altschmiedenstraße and Lohgerberstraße, is the oldest hall church in northern Germany and was built around 1230. When it was reconstructed after World War II, 20 apartments were created in the roof, making this a unique building.

SCHIFFAHRTSMUSEUM (Sailing Museum), August-Bebelstraße. Before the discovery of America, the Baltic was almost as important to Europe as the Mediterranean. This fascinating museum provides an overview of the Baltic and seafaring from the 8th century to the present and should not be missed.

BAD DOBERAN (Doberan Baths) is 15 kilometers west, slightly outside of Rostock. This small resort town has a narrow-gauge railway that will take you to the sea and some fine neoclassical buildings constructed in the early 19th

R

century. These houses are now in various stages of restoration after being deliberately allowed to decay as a government policy during the DDR.

The main attraction of Bad Doberan is its **PFARRKIRCHE** (Parish Church), the former Cistercian monastery. Construction began in 1176 on a church that is regarded as the greatest example of Northern German Gothic brickwork. Its style and beauty rivals any other in Germany or France. The *high altar* dates from 1310, while the rood screen was made in 1370. The stained glass was made in the 14th century and is superb.

ROTHENBURG OB DER TAUBER

Rothenburg was founded on a sharp bend in the River Tauber. A fort was built here in the 10th century around which a small trading community soon developed. After serving for a time as the capital of Frankonia, Rothenburg was granted a city charter in 1274 making it a free imperial city. During the Reformation the citizens accepted Protestantism. But in 1631, it was besieged by Imperial forces and captured by General Tilly, who intended to raze the town to the ground. According to legend, the mayor offered Tilly a goblet of the best local wine after the general had declared his intentions. This act of humility so surprised Tilly that he offered the citizens a way of escaping their fate. If someone could drink a hanap, 6 pints or 3.2 liters, in one draught he would spare the town. The citizens accepted the challenge and a for-

mer mayor, called Nusch, volunteered. After ten minutes, the monster goblet was empty and the town spared. Nusch then fell into a deep slumber, waking three days later, and the citizens regarded their salvation as a miracle. In the following centuries Rothenburg's economy stagnated, which meant the town avoided further development and maintained its medieval character. During the 19th century, inspired by Romanticism, the citizens recognized the historical value of their town as a living museum and placed strict restrictions on modernization and further development. During World War II, a second miraculous event occurred when J. J. McCloy, who later became the American High Commissioner for Germany, persuaded General Devers to prevent the bombing and shelling of this ancient city. Today Rothenburg is a favorite tourist destination.

R

PLACES TO VISIT

RATHAUS (City Hall) in the city center is a fine combination of Gothic architecture dating from 1250 and with Renaissance elements from 1578.

MITTELALTERISCHES KRIMINALMUSEUM (Medieval Crime Museum), Burggasse 3, reminds visitors of the horrors of medieval justice—or rather injustice—and the ordeals accused people had to face. Anyone wanting to understand the pre-Reformation world should visit this fine museum.

ST. JAKOBSKIRCHE (Church of St. Jacob), Klostergasse, is a wonderful high Gothic church that contains Tilman Riemenschneider's *Heilig-Blut-Altar* (Altar of the Holy Blood), in a side chapel of the same name. This is a masterpiece of wood carving containing a small crystal believed in medieval times to hold a spot of Jesus' blood. The high altar itself is a winged altar carved by H. Waidenlich (15th century) with painted panels by Friedrich Herlin (1430–1500) depicting the legend of St. James. There are also some excellent stained-glass windows illuminating the interior.

STADTMAUER (City Wall). Today you can still walk around the entire city on the ancient defenses and in doing so imagine what it must have felt like to look out on a besieging army such as that of Tilly.

REICHSSTADTMUSEUM (Local History Museum), Klosterhof, is housed in a 12th-century Dominican monastery. You can see an array of local artworks, Nusch's famous goblet, and the remarkable *Rothenburg Passion,* a series of 12 paintings from 1294 depicting the last hours of Jesus. The kitchen of the former monastery has been restored, enabling Rothenburg to boast that it possesses the oldest kitchen in Europe.

SPEYER

The Celts settled in the region around 300 B.C. The Gauls called the town *Noviomagus,* a Celtic word for town. In 47 B.C. Speyer was captured by Julius Caesar. It became a Roman military post in 30 B.C., known as Augusta Nemetum after a Germanic people living in the region. The name *Spira* is found on coins issued in the town during the time of the Merovingians in the 5th and 6th centuries. This name is derived from an older word, *Spiraha,* the name of a brook known today as Speierbach.

Christianity was established by Roman converts early in Speyer's history, and it was made a bishopric in 346. After the fall of the Western Roman Empire, pagan invaders successfully reintroduced heathenism to the area.

S

The present bishopric dates back to 610 after Christian missionaries had reconverted the local people. In 830 Speyer became part of the Frankish empire and attained the status of a free imperial city in 1294. Konrad II (990–1039), whose father was the local count, made Speyer the capital of his empire. After Lothar III (1075–1137) captured Speyer, he assumed the imperial crown and made peace with his enemies in 1134. In 1351, the weavers of Speyer staged one of the first successful strikes in history by refusing to work until they received higher wages. After the loss of Edessa or Urfa in Turkey, which had been captured by Moslems, Bernard of Clairvaux visited Speyer in 1146 and preached in the dom to King Konrad III and an assembly of several thousand knights, whom he convinced to participate in the Second Crusade (1147–49).

Speyer Dom also became a place of pilgrimage because of a painting associated with the Dom's patron saint, the Virgin Mary. The original picture of Mary, regarded as sacred, was destroyed in a fire in 794. But in 930, Pope John XI presented a new picture to the Dom, and this attracted many pilgrims. Large-scale veneration of Mary started in the 13th century when Pope Innocent IV (1243–54) granted indulgences for the observation of certain feast days and rituals associated with Mary. Pope John Paul II visited the cathedral on May 4, 1987.

Over 50 Imperial Diets were held in Speyer. At the Diet of Speyer in 1526, the princes of the principalities were given the right to decide their position on the Reformation. At a second diet in 1529, the Edict of Worms was affirmed against the Reformation, and the followers of Martin Luther (1483–1546) referred to for the first time as "Protestants." The city's economy suffered in the aftermath of the Thirty Years' War and as a result of European wars. The French captured Speyer in 1689, destroying most of the town but carefully preserving the dom. Following the French Revolution, they again captured the town in 1797 and on this occasion deliberately pillaged the dom. This act of barbarism so outraged people all over Germany that during the 19th century, the dom was completely restored through the support of public subscriptions and generous funding from the king of Bavaria.

Jewish refugees from persecution in Mainz were given a home in Speyer in 1084 by Bishop Rüdiger, who granted them what for that time were generous rights. These rights were confirmed and expanded by Henry IV in 1090. During the First Crusade several Jews were killed in riots in 1096. The bishop's intervention protected the community and prevented a massacre. But in 1349, the Black Death provoked further riots, and many Jews were slaughtered. The Jewish community never reestablished itself.

PLACES TO VISIT

The magnificent sandstone **KAISER-DOM** (Cathedral of the Emperor), Domplatz, is the largest cathedral in Germany. It is a significant testimonial to the glory of Romanesque architecture and is the oldest surviving example of a Romanesque church. The dom stands on the site of a 7th-century church. The cornerstone of the present building was laid in 1030 during the reign of Emperor Konrad II and took only thirty years to complete. It is one of the few church buildings which had vaulted ceilings over the central and the side naves from the time it was constructed. The three-chambered crypt, which is described as the largest and most beautiful in Germany, is the resting place of four emperors, three empresses, four kings, and five bishops. The dom was consecrated under Heinrich IV in 1061. In 1689, the soldiers of King Louis XIV burned the cathedral and plundered and desecrated the burial sites; during the French Revolution (1789–92) mobs ransacked the cathedral and destroyed all the altars. Extensive restoration work began in 1957, so that by the time the cathedral celebrated its 900th year, in 1961, the structure looked as it did at the time of the emperors.

For the best view of the nave with its magnificent vaulting and arches, enter by the west doorway. The transept is raised to create a sense of harmony that is astonishing. In the **AFRAKAPELLE** (Afra Chapel of the Sacrament), built in 1110, you can see some exceptionally fine stonework, including a sculpture of Christ carrying the cross and the famed *Speyer Annunciation* from 1470.

DOMSCHATZKAMMER (Dom Treasury) contains numerous objects linked to the kings and queen buried in the dom, including the crown of Konrad II and Heinrich III's imperial orb. The museum also contains important documents dating back the time of the emperors.

KLOSTER ST. MAGDALENEN (Convent of Mary of Magdalene) has a fine Baroque church built in 1708. It is important as the last home of the philosopher Edith Stein, who was murdered by the Nazis.

DREIFALTIGKEITSKIRCHE (Protestant Church of the Trinity), Große Himmelsgasse, was destroyed by the French in

S

EDITH STEIN (1891–1942) was a Jewish philosopher who converted to Christianity in 1922. She entered the Benedictine Order in 1934 in Köln and moved to a convent in Speyer before fleeing to the Netherlands in 1938. She was arrested by the Gestapo, removed from her Dutch convent, and deported to Auschwitz, where she died. She was beatified in 1988. Several of her books are translated into English, including *The Problem of Empathy* (1989).

1689. The new church, designed by J. P. Graber, was consecrated in 1717 and is one of the most important Protestant Baroque churches in Rheinland-Pfalz. A two-story wooden gallery surrounds the main nave. The paintings around the walls are by Guthbier (d. 1713).

GEDÄCHTNISKIRCHE/ RETSCHER-KIRCHE (Memorial Church), Landauer Straße, is a new Gothic church built in memory of the protest against the imposition of Roman Catholicism made by the Protestant princes at the Diet of Speyer in 1529. This is the event that caused the word *Protestant* to be coined.

JUDENBAD (Jewish Ritual Bath), Judengasse. This fascinating 12th-century Jewish mikveh was once part of the Speyer Synagogue and is generally believed to have been built by the same masons as those that worked on the dom. You go down a set of stairs into an underground chamber where you can see the bath that was used for purification of both people and ritual objects. Notice that water runs through the bath all the time. The symbolism here is that of "living waters" and helps Christians understand the rich Jewish symbolism that Jesus drew upon (John 4:10).

HISTORISCHES MUSEUM DER PFALZ (Historical Museum of the Palatinate), Große Pfaffengasse 7, stands out as an exceptionally rich museum because of its regional, cultural, and historical importance.

WEINMUSEUM (Wine Museum), is part of the Historical Museum. Here you will find the history of wine, including a bottle of Roman wine from the 3rd century and numerous examples of wine presses and highly decorated barrels.

The **CITY FORTIFICATIONS** are also well worth seeing, especially the 12th-century gate found in the Maximilian-straße.

STENDAL

The capital of a region known as the Altmark, Stendal was founded in the 12th century by Albrecht I, der Bär (Albrecht the Bear) (1100–1170). It became a member of the Hanseatic League in 1359. Johann Joachim Winckelmann (1717–68), who is regarded as the founder of modern archaeology, was born here. The French novelist Henri Beyle took the name of the town as his pseudonym out of admi-ration for Winckelmann. Today Stendal boasts a unique collection of medieval church windows.

PLACES TO VISIT

ST. NIKOLAUS DOM (St. Nicholas), Hall Strasse, is actually a parish church, not a cathedral. It was founded in 1188 by the Augustinian Order. Built in Gothic style, it has 23 stained-glass windows, dating from 1425–65, that are world famous because they are the best-preserved group of windows in Germany, if not Europe. The church also contains some excellent medieval carving in the choir stalls.

PFARRKIRCHE ST. MARIEN (Parish Church of St. Marien), in the market square, has an excellent high altar by an unknown Flemish artist. Before it stands a replica of the famous medieval sculpture of Roland. The original was destroyed in a storm in 1972.

ST. JACOBI (St. Jacob's Church), Breite Strasse. Although the stained glass here is not as extensive as that found in St. Nicholas, it is nevertheless exceptionally well preserved and worth seeing.

TANGERMÜNDE

Founded in the 12th century at the junction of the river Tanger and the Elbe, this small town, which is rich in medieval buildings, is enclosed by its original 14th-century fortified wall. To enter the town one travels through impressive medieval gates. In 1373, Tangermünde became the major German residence of the Emperor Karl IV (1316–78), who normally lived in Prague. From 1373–78, it was actually the official capital of the Holy Roman Empire. Later it was a favorite residence of the Margraves of Brandenburg.

PLACES TO VISIT

THE TOWN WALLS. These medieval fortifications, which make an enjoyable walking tour, are exceptionally well-preserved, enabling the visitor to gain a vivid impression of life before and during the Reformation.

NICHOLAIKIRCHE (St. Nicholas Church), Lange Strasse, was founded in the 12th century and renovated in 1470 in Gothic style. It is adjacent to one of the town's fine medieval gateways.

STEPHANSKIRCHE (St. Stephen's Church). A short walk away at the other end of Lange Strasse, this church was built in 1184 and remodeled in the 15th century. Later a Baroque tower and altar were added in 1712. The altar is unusual because its centerpiece depicts Christ as the Lion of Judea. The early 17th-century organ was constructed by the Hamburg master Hans Scherer (18th century) and is the only known surviving example of his work.

T

TRIER

There is evidence of human settlements in the valley near Trier in the 3rd century B.C. Trier is Germany's oldest city and claims to possess both Germany's oldest church and pharmacy. Julius Caesar (100–44 B.C.) conquered the city in 56 B.C. while fighting the Belgae, a Gallic people who lived in what is today northern France and Belgium. It was rebuilt as a Roman city in 16 B.C. The Romans named it Augusta Treverorum after Emperor Augustus (63 B.C.–A.D. 14). But it was also called Roma Secunda and Roma Transalpine because it was the largest city, after Rome, north of the Alps in the Western Roman Empire. Citizens of the town had the right to apply for Roman citizenship. By the end of the 3rd century, Emperor Diocletian (245–313) made Treveri the capital city of the Western Roman Empire, and Roman emperors resided here from 286 to 395.

Many of the great buildings such as the Amphitheater, the Barbarathermen, Kaiserthermen, and a bridge across the Mosel were built by the Romans between A.D. 100 and 150. The Porta Nigra (Black Gate), formally the city's north gate, is a weatherbeaten, blackened sandstone structure. It is all that remains of the city's fortifications, which were built in A.D. 260 and once included four major gates and 47 watchtowers. Over 70,000 people lived in Roman Trier, and the amphitheater was capable of holding 30,000 spectators. There are also Imperial Roman baths, which along with many other structures are witnesses of hundreds of years of Roman presence.

During the 3rd century, Trier became a center for the evangelization of northern Europe. Constantine the Great (288–337), who granted toleration to Christians throughout the Roman Empire by his Edict of Milan in 313, lived in Trier from 306 to 314 and is said to have preferred the city to Rome itself. The first bishop was elected in 328. In 470 the city was captured by the Franks. Later, under Charlemagne (742–814), Trier was elevated to an archbishopric. Consequently, during the Middle Ages, Trier was ruled by prince bishops. The Normans destroyed the city in 882, but by the 10th century, it was once more a flourishing trading center. In 1356, electoral rights were conferred on the prince bishops by a papal bull, making them electors of the Holy Roman Empire. The university was founded in 1473. During the following centuries, Trier went into economic decline and came under French rule from 1794 to 1918. It is the birthplace of St. Ambrose (339–97), who converted St. Augustine of Hippo (354–430). Karl Marx (1818–83), the founder of Marxism, was born here.

T

KARL FRIEDRICH MARX (1818–83) was a German Jewish philosopher who was baptized as a child and appears to have been a believing Christian while at boarding school before rejecting all forms of religion as a university student. Deeply influenced by Feuerbach, he saw God as a projection of human needs and sought to explain the persistence of religion in terms of social conditions which create a need for some kind of supernatural belief. He became a newspaper editor and writer who is remembered as the founder of Marxism and modern Communism. After being expelled from Prussia for his revolutionary activities in 1849, he settled in England, where he did most of his writing. His early writings are important because they show a continuity in his thought and use of Hegelian philosophy, which continues into his later works. His most famous but little-read work is *Das Kapital* (1867, 1885, and 1895, 3 volumes). Other voluminous writings include the slim but influential *Communist Manifesto* (1848).

PLACES TO VISIT

DOM (Cathedral), Domfreihof, which is mainly Romanesque, is the oldest cathedral in Germany. The central area dates back to Roman times and was built between 367–83 on the site of a church consecrated in 326 at the behest of the Empress Helena. The original church was one of four churches endowed by Helena. The other three were the original St. Peter's in Rome, the Church of the Holy Sepulcher in Jerusalem, and the Church of the Nativity in Bethlehem. The Franks sacked Trier and its churches in the 5th century, and the Normans wrecked the church in 882. The present dom was built in 1030 and incorporated parts of the older structures to give a sense of space that leads the worshiper to contemplate God as the Creator of the universe.

Inside the dom are Romanesque sculptures of Jesus, John the Baptist, the Virgin Mary, and the Twelve Apostles. There are also numerous tombs belonging to important people and Christian leaders, including 26 archbishops. The Baroque high altar was created in 1699 by Johan Wolfgang Fröhlicher. The dom owns a seamless cloak, the "Holy Coat of Trier," that according to tradition was worn by Christ. The cloak is only displayed on very special occasions and is the Dom's most precious treasure. The Dom's cloisters, which provide an excellent view of both the dom and the adjacent Liebfrauenkirche, also evoke a sense of God's majesty and tranquility. After a fire in 1717, the windows were enlarged, and the dom was remodeled in Baroque style to give the inside of the structure a new look. The treasury is located behind the main altar, and its most treasured relics are the "Holy Coat of Trier" and the richly decorated portable altar of St. Andrew.

T

DOMSCHATZ (Treasury) contains a 10th-century portable altar supposedly containing the remains of St. Andrew and work by local goldsmiths.

BISCHÖFLICHES DOM-UND DIÖZESAN-MUSEUM (Bishop's Residence and Diocesan Museum), Windstrasse 6–8, is housed in a Neoclassical house built in 1830. Here one finds an extensive display of vestments, frescoes, crucifixes, and numerous other liturgical items from Carolingian times to the 18th century.

LIEBFRAUENKIRCHE (Church of Our Lady), located next to the cathedral, is the second Gothic church to be built in Germany in the 13th century. It was modeled on Marburg's Elisabethkirche and built between 1235 and 1260. It is shaped like a rose with twelve petals to symbolize the Virgin Mary. The shape is known as the mystic rose and was greatly loved by Luther. The symbolism also gave birth to a shadowy mystical Christian movement, the Rosicrucians, in the 17th century, from which a number of modern occult groups take their name. The doorways of this church are particularly interesting and richly carved to portray biblical scenes.

ST. ANTONIUS (Church of St. Anthony) is a Late Gothic building known for its magnificent Rococo pulpit installed in 1762, and for the St. Antonius grotto altar.

ST. MATHIAS, Saarstraße, is the oldest Benedictine Abby in Germany and claims the only grave of an apostle north of the Alps. This is St. Matthias, who in Acts 1:26 replaced Judas as a member of the twelve. It is a Romanesque structure built in the 12th century. Under the sanctuary, on a grave plate, rests St. Matthias in a crypt. Under the grave of St. Matthias are the sarcophagi of St. Eucharius and St. Valerius.

ST. PAULIN (St. Paul's Church), Palmatiussstraße, is located at the site of an ancient cemetery. It is a late Baroque church with an uninviting exterior designed by Balthasar Neumann (1687–53). Inside one is dazzled by the exuberant colors and sheer joy of life expressed in its beautifully decorated walls and ceiling. On the ceiling are superb paintings of the martyrdom of St. Paul and of the Theban Legion.

BASILIKA OR AULA PALATINA (Great Hall or Auditorium), Liebfrauenstrasse. Here part of the former Imperial palace which was built by Constantine now houses a Protestant church. Originally built around 310, the building has seen many uses from palace to tribunal to military hospital and barracks. It was reconstructed in 1856 at the behest of Kaiser Friedrich Wilhelm IV (1795–1861), and after World War II, it was turned into a church. This is a magnificent building which enables visitors to grasp something of the glory of ancient Rome and the amazing engineering skills of the Romans. It also provides an insight into the way many early churches looked after the Roman Empire accepted Christianity and secular basilicas were turned into churches.

BAROQUE ROTES HAUS (Red House), Hauptmarkt/Dietrichstrasse, is an interesting example of Renaissance architecture. It bears the inscription: *Ante Roman Treveris stetit annis mille trecentis / perstet, et aeterna pace fruator. Amen.* In English it reads, "Trier existed 1300 years before Rome / May she be granted an equally long life and eternal peace."

THE PORTA NIGRA (Black Gate), Theodore Heuss Allee, is the only remaining Roman gateway in Trier. It is made from massive sandstone blocks bound together by iron rods bonded to the stones with lead. Over time the sandstone was blackened by soot and grime, giving the gate its name. Today this is one of Trier's best-known landmarks. The gate is also known as the Simeonstor (Simon's Gate), because of an 11th-century Greek hermit who often used the ruins as his home. Impressed by the example of Simon's piety, Archbishop Poppo converted the structure into the church of St. Simeon after the hermit's death in 1037. After occupying Trier, Napoleon Bonaparte (1769–1821) heard this story, saw the church, and gave orders to remove all non-Roman additions and thus retain only the original structure.

THE ROMAN AMPHITHEATER, on the slopes of the Petrisberg outside the old city, was built to seat 20,000 spectators. Although ruined, it is still possible to capture a sense of the Roman games where Christians were often pitted against lions and other wild beasts to the delight of the crowds.

KAISERTHERMEN (Roman Imperial Baths), Ostalle, was one of the largest bath complexes constructed by the Romans, whose social life involved a love of bathing. The ruins provide unique insights into the Roman world, especially the sophistication of their technical and architectural achievements.

BARBARATHERMEN (Barbara Baths), Südalle, is another Roman bath complex with an interesting exhibit showing how the complex heating system worked.

SIMEONSTIFT AND STÄDTISCHES MUSEUM (City Museum), Theodore Heuss Allee, adjoining the Porta Nigra, is housed in the former monastery of St. Simeon. It is particularly rich in local history from pre-historic times to the present. Its greatest prize is the *Lotharingian Madonna*, from about 1350. There are also paintings by the modern artist Julius Bissier (1893–1965). Part of this complex includes the unusual BRUNNENHOF cloisters, which are unique in that they are on the second floor above the museum and among the oldest cloisters in Germany.

RHEINISCHES LANDESMUSEUM (Rhineland Museum), Ostalle 44, contains over 150 mosaics of Roman origin and numerous other local archaeological finds from Celtic pre-history to medieval times.

SCHATZKAMMER DER STADTBIBLIOTHEK (State Library and Treasury), Weberbach Str., contains a fascinating collection of ancient manuscripts including medieval Bibles and prayer books which are beautifully illustrated.

T

KARL MARX HAUS (Karl Marx House), Brükenstrasse 10. In a very real sense, Trier witnessed the beginning of the Christian era with the birth of St. Ambrose (339) and its end with the arrival of Karl Marx (1818), whose writings did so much to destroy Christianity throughout the world. Between these two historical figures the drama of church history is enacted. This museum contains numerous original manuscripts and memorabilia connected with Marx. The size of the house gives the visitor a clear understanding of the privileged life Marx lived as a child and the wealth of his family. It also provides clues to understanding the growth of modern unbelief in the revolutionary ferment of the early 19th century.

TÜBINGEN

Although the general area was inhabited as early as the 7th century B.C., the town was not founded until 1078 when it became the capital of the dukes of Württemberg. Eberhard the Bearded (1445–96) founded its renowned university in 1477. The dukes of Württemberg embraced the Reformation and established a Protestant seminary in 1536. During the Thirty Years' War the town was occupied by the Swedish army in 1638 but escaped major damage during both the Thirty Years' War and World War II, although over the centuries several serious fires have destroyed many old buildings. Today Tübingen is a picturesque town with many medieval buildings.

PLACES TO VISIT

EVANGELISCHE STIFTSKIRCHE ST. GEORG (St. George's Church). The master builder Peter von Koblenz built this Late Gothic church in 1470. He added the vaulted ceiling to the main body of the structure and later the stained glass, most notably of St. George. The church is the burial place of many of the dukes of Württemberg, including the founder of the university.

SCHLOß (castle) was originally built in the 11th century and rebuilt in the 16th. It is now part of the university.

AM MARKT, the main market square, has a picturesque 16th-century fountain in the center.

HÖLDERLINTURM (Hölderlin Museum), Bursagasse 6, was the home of the Romantic poet and writer Friedrich Hölderlin (1770–1843). His interpretation of Greek culture in terms of pessimistic tragedy, his introspective subjectivity, and his negative view of the world based on a rejection of Christianity had and still has a deep impact on German intellectuals. The museum helps the visitor gain insight into an important aspect of German, and indeed European, culture.

EVANGELISCHES STIFT (Protestant Seminary), Neckergasse. This former Augustinian monastery was turned into a Lutheran theological college in 1547. Over the years, its faculty moved away from the seminary's original evangelical basis of faith to become a center for radical theology. During the 19th century it was the center of the famous "Tübingen School." It is generally acknowledged to be the most important, in a negative sense, theological movement in the 19th century. The school was led by Ferdinand Christian Baur (1792–1860) and developed a non-miraculous interpretation of Scripture that undermined traditional Christian beliefs. The most radical member of this movement was Baur's student David Friedrich Strauss (1808–74), whose *Life of Jesus* (1835) denied the possibility of miracles, proposing instead a mythological interpretation of the New Testament.

One of the last evangelicals, in the British and North American sense, to teach there was Adolf Schlatter (1852–1938). Karl Heim (1874–1959) also represented a conservative theological position in the faculty, but in general, the faculty of theology at Tübingen and other German universities have managed to exclude conservative evangelicals from key teaching positions through the habilitation process. The only exceptions to this exclusion are pastoral theology and missions.

WILHELMSTIFT (Wilhelm Institute), Collegiumsgasse, is the Roman Catholic seminary, founded in 1817. The Roman Catholic theologian Johann Baptist Hirscher (1788–1865) worked here as an exponent of reform, lay participation in the church, and moral theology. Hans Küng also worked here before moving to his own institution because of the disapproval of church authorities. On the whole, German Catholic theologians, even Küng, are far more conservative than their Protestant contemporaries.

ALBRECHT-BENGEL-HAUS (Bengel House), Ludwig-Krapf-Straße 5. Since the 17th century, the church in Baden-Württemberg has been a stronghold of Pietism. At the same time, the training of pastors for the ministry is controlled by university faculties of theology that are strongholds of liberal and radical teachings. To help Christian students cope with hostile theological environments, Pietists have established a number of student residences in major university cities where extracurricular evangelical instruction is given alongside the required university courses in theology. The Albrecht-Bengel-Haus in Tübingen is one such residence. Here Christian students can live in a community and take extracurricular courses intended to counter the corrosive effect of their theological education. Until

T

INFLUENTIAL PROFESSORS AT THE UNIVERSITY OF TÜBINGEN

JOHANNES ALBRECHT BENGEL (1687–1752) was a leading German Pietist theologian who taught at the University of Tübingen, where he encouraged the study of the New Testament in the original languages. His work contributed to the development of modern biblical scholarship and a greater understanding of New Testament times.

FERDINAND CHRISTIAN BAUR (1792–1860) was a German theologian and founder of the Tübingen School. He was a disciple of Schleiermacher and greatly influenced by Hegel's philosophy of history. He caused great controversy by suggesting there was an essential conflict between the views of St. Paul and the disciples of Jesus. This interpretation came from his application of Hegel's theories to the New Testament.

DAVID FRIEDRICH STRAUSS (1808–74) was a radical German theologian and one of the founders of biblical criticism. His book *The Life of Jesus* (1835) caused a storm by its denial of the supernatural and his use of myth, which he defined as a story contrary to the laws of nature, to reinterpret the Bible in secular terms.

ADOLF SCHLATTER (1852–1938) was a biblical scholar and theologian who upheld an evangelical perspective similar to British and North American evangelicalism. He was Professor of New Testament in Tübingen from 1889–1922. His last work was *Wird der Jude über uns Siegen? (Will the Jews Rule Over Us?)* (1936), which was a slim booklet subtly attacking Nazi propaganda in terms of Christian faith.

KARL HEIM (1874–1959). Coming from a Pietist background, Heim became a leading conservative Lutheran theologian who resisted both scientific secularism and Nazi neopaganism. His work on science and religion is widely acknowledged to be among the most insightful in this complex area and includes his book *Christian Faith and the Natural Sciences* (1935). Heim was also a very strong supporter of Christian missions, missionary activity, and the study of missions.

recently, the Albrecht-Bengel-Haus was led by Dr. Gerhard Maier, the author of *The End of the Historical-Critical Method* (1974) and *Biblical Hermeneutics* (1994). Presently the director is Dr. Rolf Hiller.

KLOSTER BEBENHAUSEN (Bebenhausen Monastery), six kilometers north on Wilhelmstraße, was founded in 1180. It is a classic example of a Cistercian monastery. Originally Romanesque, many Gothic elements were later added.

ULM

The region around Ulm bears marks of human activity back to the Stone Age. Evidence of a settlement around 5000 B.C. and another one in 1500 B.C. has been found near Eggingen about 5 kilometers southwest of Ulm. Ulm is first mentioned as a king's palace or residence in 854. The favorable river location not only brought wealth to its citizens but also invaders that forced the city fathers to build a defensive wall in 1027. After years of rule by noble families—first the Salier, 1024–1125, and then the Staufen, 1138–1268—the citizens obtained a charter making Ulm a free imperial city in 1274.

Beginning at Ulm, the Danube is navigable. As with many other cities along the river, the merchants of Ulm used to transport their goods along the Danube. The goods were mainly Barchent, a cotton-flannel cloth, sent downriver to Vienna and further on. Because it was a cheap means of transport, the barges used were made to last one trip. The barge, called a Schachtel (flimsy box), was then sold at the final destination for building

and firewood. Hence the term "Ulmer Schachtel" is used to denote something that can be used once and no more.

For the music lover, Hans Sachs (1494–1576) was a citizen of Ulm, a German poet, musician, shoemaker, and Meistersinger (Master Singer). He is one of the main characters in Wagner's opera *Die Meistersinger*. Sachs wrote the poem *Die Nachtigall von Wittenberg (The Nightingale of Wittenberg)* in praise of Martin Luther. Shortly after the Reformation, in 1524, the Protestant princes of Germany met at Ulm to plan their strategy against the Catholic powers allied with Karl V (1500–1558). The Agreement of Ulm between the German Catholic League and the Protestant Union was signed in 1620. Later, Ulm intervened in the Thirty Years' War in favor of the Holy Roman Emperor Ferdinand III (1608–57). The Treaty of Ulm in 1647 provided that the electors of Bavaria and Cologne would remain neutral until the end of the war.

Albert Einstein (1879–1955) was born here, as was the astronomer

U

Johannes Kepler (1571–1630). Kepler published his *Rudolfinische Tafeln (Rudolphine Tables)* in Ulm in 1627. These tables calculate planetary motion and give the locations of more than a thousand stars.

PLACES TO VISIT

ULM DOM (Ulm Cathedral), Münsterplatz, was begun in 1377 and proceeded slowly. Work stopped during the Reformation, and the building was not completed until 1890. It is one of the more imposing church buildings in Europe with 5,100 square meters (1.15 acres) of covered area that can hold 20,000 worshipers. The spire is 161 meters (528 feet) high, making it the tallest church spire in the world. Architecturally the dom is incomparable. The main portal, built in 1430, on the west side, has elaborate carved figures and decorations. It is a masterpiece of church building and art. The stained-glass windows are 15th-century works that create a solemn, festive atmosphere. On the center post of the west entrance is the *Schmerzensmann* (the man in pain), painted by Hans Multscher (1400–1467) in 1429. The carved choir stalls were completed between 1469 and 1471 by Jörg Syrlin the elder (1425–91). They are generally recognized as the best wood carving of this type in Germany. The stall carvings represent Christ, the apostles, martyrs, and Old Testament figures. Those on the sides of the stalls represent figures from Greek antiquity and mythology. Before the Reformation, the cathedral had 60 altars, most of which were later destroyed by rioting Anabaptists. Notice what appears to be a second pulpit above the real pulpit. This is intended to remind the preacher that the real minister of God's Word is the Holy Spirit, who speaks to human hearts through the sermon.

DREIFALTIGKEITSKIRCHE (Church of the Holy Trinity), Neue Stral, was built 1617–21 and is now an ecumenical meeting place for Christians in Ulm.

RATHAUS (City Hall) dates, in part, back to 1360. Its astronomical clock was installed in 1520. The SCHWÖRHAUS (House of the Oath) reminds visitors of the tradition that the mayor and all guild members had to swear the oath to adhere to the City Statutes.

ULMER MUSEUM (Ulm Museum), Marktplatz 9, contains artifacts from the Late Gothic period to the present.

The former Benedictine ABBEY WIBLINGEN lies five kilometers south of Ulm and belongs to the city. In the 11th century, the dukes of Kirchberg endowed the abbey, which acquired a Holy Cross relic in 1099. It is said that the founders of the abbey brought the relic from the Holy Land. From the 12th to the 18th centuries, Wiblingen Abbey was a major place of pilgrimage. The Holy Cross Brotherhood was founded in 1692 and is still active today. In 1806, the abbey was secularized and abolished as a living religious institution, which slowed the flow of the pilgrims.

The former **CLOISTER CHURCH,** which is now a parish church, was designed and built in the 18th century in the late Baroque style. Although a relatively low building, the ceiling is cleverly painted to give the impression of great height. The Holy Cross relic is now located on the main altar. The larger-than-life crucifix used to be kept in the Ulm Cathedral. In the abbey library a 1744 painting by Franz Martin Kuen depicts the heavenly wisdoms. Other items depict the sciences, virtues, and the worldly powers.

WEIMAR

The name *Weimar* is derived from *Wimares, Wihmari,* or *Wimar,* which mean "blessed place," "holy bog," or "blessed lake." The city lies in the valley of the river Ilm, surrounded by protective hills. It is the former residence of the princes of the Grand Duchy. The favorable soil conditions attracted settlers very early in human history. Human and animal skeletal remains have been found in the area that date back to the early Stone Age, approximately 10,000 B.C. Evidence of Illyric and Celtic presence points to around 800 B.C. with numerous archaeological finds. The rulers of this territory were the barons of Weimar. Wilhelm I of Weimar (928–68), who ruled 949–61, is the first documented ruler. The baron of Weimar is first mentioned in a document dated 975 when Emperor Otto II (955–83) held an assembly of princes in the baron's castle. The barons resided in the castle and continued to do so well into the 11th century. From then on they used the castle of Orlam Onde near Jena. In 1060, they added the name "Orlam Onde" to their family name.

In 1218, the first settlement was located at a more elevated plain, to avoid floods, moors, and bogs. This core settlement grew around the Jakobskirche, which is first mentioned in 1168. Not far from the Jakobskirche, a Cistercian cloister was founded in 1240. A war between the barons of the region lasted from 1342–46. The Orlam Onde Weimar rulers were defeated by the Wettiner who then ruled the region in the 16th century when Weimar came under the control of the dukes of Thuringia.

The town of Weimar is first mentioned in a document dated July 9, 1245. In a later document, from 1262, the seal of the town is mentioned. In the 13th century, the German Ritterorden (Order of Knights), know as the Teutonic Knights, sent its representatives to Weimar. They stayed there as administrators of the church and schools until the introduction of the Reformation in 1522. Martin Luther stopped at Weimar during his travels in 1518 and 1521. Later he visited again, giving sermons in the ducal palace and in the St. Peter and St. Paul Church.

In 1617 a literary association *Die Fruchtbringende Gesellschaft* (The Fruit-bearing Association) was founded for the promotion of the German language by Prince Ludwig von Anhalt-Köthen (1579–1650). Christoph Bach (1613–61) and later his nephew Johann Sebastian Bach (1685–1750) were both active musicians at the court of Weimar. Here Johann Sebastian composed many of his best-known compositions before he left in 1717 to move to Leipzig. Literature, music, and theater played an increasingly important role in Weimar during the 18th and 19th centuries. Weimar is best known for the two giants in German literature: Johann Wolfgang von Goethe (1749–1832), who moved to Weimar in 1775, and Friedrich von Schiller (1759–1805). They were friends of Duke Carl August (1757–1828). Both men are buried side by side in the grand ducal family vault. Goethe, Schiller, Herder (1744–1803), and Wieland (1733–1813) all worked here. Franz Liszt (1811–86), who directed the court orchestra while living with Princess Caroline von Sayn-Wittgenstein, made Weimar known throughout central Europe. In July 1919, after the end of World War I, the National Assembly adopted the constitution of the new German Republic in Weimar. Weimar was chosen as the European City of Culture for 1999.

JOHANN WOLFGANG VON GOETHE (1749–1832).

To most English-speaking people Goethe is a vague name if they have heard about him at all. To Germans, his name is synonymous with an entire era, the *Goethezeit* (Goethe time, or period). As a young man, Goethe was educated by a Pietist and strongly influenced by his devout mother. In later life, he retained a respect for Pietism, although he had moved away from Christian orthodoxy through the influence of the philosophers Spinoza (1632–77) and Kant (1724–1804) to develop his own form of pantheism. Goethe is best known for his play *Faust* (1808), which develops an old German legend about a man who makes a pact with the Devil in return for immortality. He rose to fame through his novel *Die Leiden des jungen Werther (The Sorrows of Young Werther)* (1775) that ends with the hero committing suicide. After its publication, a spate of suicides followed. Goethe was shocked, because he intended his work to be a morality play. Thereafter, he changed his style of writing and moved away from Romanticism to neoclassicism.

W

JOHANN GOTTFRIED VON HERDER (1744–1803) was a German Lutheran scholar and leader of the Romantic movement who was influenced by the philosophy of Kant (1724–1804) and even more by the Christian philosopher Johann Georg Hamann (1730–88), who strongly rejected Kant and the ideas of the Enlightenment. His studies of the *Synoptic Gospels* (1796) and the *Gospel of John* (1797) led him to conclude that they could not be harmonized and helped launch 19th-century German biblical criticism. His philosophy of language argued that the language of a people encapsulates its historical identity and underlying unity. This view greatly influenced German Nationalism, although Herder was essentially liberal and cosmopolitan in his outlook. His most influential works were his *Outlines of a Philosophy of History of Man* (1800) and *Treatise upon the Origin of Language* (1827). He took his work as the superintendent of Protestant churches in Weimar very seriously and sought to encourage education, piety, and pastoral care among the clergy.

PLACES TO VISIT

JAKOBS-KIRCHE (Jacob's Church), Karl-Liebknecht Strasse, was built on the foundation of the first church erected in 1168. Johann Wolfgang von Goethe was married here to Christiane Vulpius, October 19, 1806. The grave of Lucas Cranach the Elder (1472–1553) is on the southwest side. The adjoining cemetery is the oldest in Weimar, which contained the grave of Friedrich von Schiller from 1805 to 1827, when his remains were moved to the prince's tomb in the new cemetery. The church has a large painting of Luther (1483–1546) by Lucas Cranach on the wing of the altar.

HERDERKIRCHE (Herder's Church), also known as **STADTKIRCHE ST. PETER UND ST. PAUL** (City Church of St. Peter and St. Paul), Am Herderplatz, was built in 1250 and was twice burnt down. It was first rebuilt between 1498 and 1500 in the Late Gothic style. Today it is a Baroque church following rebuilding in 1735–38. Protestant services have been held here since 1524. Martin Luther gave many sermons here. Johann Gottfried von Herder (1744–1803), the great German philosopher and poet who was the father of Romanticism, was the local church superintendent of Weimar and the court preacher. Although his views contributed to the development of biblical criticism, Herder was essentially a conservative theologian who valued pastoral work. His efforts as superintendent of churches in Weimar did much to revive the church. Artworks by Lucas Cranach the Elder and Cranach the Younger decorate the walls of this important church.

GOETHEHAUS (Goethe House Museum), Am Frauenplatz, is a Baroque structure, built in 1709, where Goethe

W

lived for over 47 years. Numerous artifacts, collections, books, graphics, paintings, and drawings that shed light on Goethe and his times can be viewed here. The house contains Goethe's library of over 5,400 volumes.

GOETHE-NATIONALMUSEUM
(Goethe National Museum). Few people are as talented as Goethe, who besides being a poet, philosopher, and very busy statesman, was also a scientist. The museum, which is housed next door to the Goethe house, contains a fascinating collection of scientific instruments and related items.

SCHILLERHAUS (Schiller House Museum), Schillerstraße 12. Schiller bought the house in 1802 and lived there until his death in 1805. The house contains many artifacts and personal items. Goethe and Schiller are the two greats of German literature. Unlike Goethe, Schiller retained far more of his original Christian orthodoxy while teaching history at the University in Jena and preaching in local churches. His study of the *Thirty Years' War* (1802) and plays like *Mary Stuart* (1800) and *Wallenstein* (1799) bring home the irony of Christian history in Germany, and the problems Christians had to face in light of the terrible disasters that followed in the wake of the Reformation. Schiller's most famous poem is his *Das Lied von der Glocke* (The Song of the Bell), which was once hailed as a masterpiece, but is usually neglected today. Through observations about the casting of a bell, Schiller reflected on human life and its trials.

GOETHE-SCHILLER-ARCHIV
(Goethe-Schiller Archives) are housed in the Duke's Palace and contain a wealth of literary remains and manuscripts.

WIELAND MUSEUM, devoted to the life and work of Christoph Martin Wieland (1733–1813), is being moved from its present location to Wieland's birthplace outside of Weimar. Ask at the tourist information for directions to this museum. Wieland was an important German author and Enlightenment philosopher who turned from his early Pietism to hedonism under the influence of English writers. His works contributed to the decline of Christian orthodoxy in German universities and encouraged the growing fascination with pre-Christian classical antiquity. As tutor to Duke Carl August (1757–1828), he was responsible for bringing Goethe to Weimar and played an important role in creating the German neoclassical and later Romantic movement.

CRANACHHAUS (Cranach House) is where Luther's friend, Lucas Cranach, spent the last year of his life living with his son-in-law and working on his last masterpiece, *St. Jacob's Altar*. It also housed Weimar's first bookshop, opened in 1725, which was restored in 1972.

WEIMAR SCHLOSS (Weimar Palace) was originally a moated castle that was renovated during the 17th century in Renaissance style by Johann Moritz Richter (1620–67) and again as a neoclassical palace

W

THE ENLIGHTENMENT is a movement characterized by the historian Ernst Troeltsch (1865–1923) as the beginning of the really modern period of European culture. It had its roots in Protestant Christianity and found its clearest expression in the work of Kant, who defined "the Enlightenment" in his book *Religion Within the Limits of Reason* (1793) as "man's emergence from a self-inflicted state of minority." Kant wrote, "Have the courage to make use of your own understanding is therefore the watchword of the Enlightenment." The Enlightenment originated in the Netherlands and England in the mid-17th century but reached its highwater mark in French rationalism and materialism, finding political expression in the French Revolution. Its richest philosophical and political results were achieved in Germany under the influence of Kant. Although many branches of the Enlightenment were self-consciously anti-Christian, a distinctive form of Enlightenment Christianity developed in Protestant countries. Other branches of Protestantism were influential in promoting concerns similar to those of the Rationalists. Enlightenment Christianity as such was characterized by a retreat from dogmas, sacraments, and ceremonies, faith in providence, obligation to "virtue," and a tendency to subordinate Christian dogmas to current ideas from science and culture.

in Goethe's time by the Berlin architect Heinrich Gentz (1766–1811). Apart from the building itself, which is well worth a visit, the Schloss houses the exceptionally rich *Weimar Art Collection* that should not be missed. The *Deutsche Nationale Forschungs-und Gedenkstätten* (German National Research Collection and Museum) is also kept in the Schloss. It has a unique collection of important manuscripts from this crucial period of history.

DEUTSCHES NATIONALTHEATER (German National Theater), Theaterplatz, is a modified neoclassical building built in 1779. Here Schiller's play *Wilhelm Tell* (William Tell) was first performed in 1804. In 1919 the ill-fated Weimar Republic was born here.

LISZTHAUS (Liszt House), Belvederer Allee, is actually an apartment in this gardener's lodge. Franz Liszt lived here with the love of his life, Princess Caroline von Sayn-Wittgenstein, while he was conductor of the local orchestra before moving on to Rome, where he eventually became a Roman Catholic priest.

A memorial to those who died in the notorious concentration camp of BUCHENWALD has been set up on the site of the camp eight kilometers west of Weimar. At its height, the camp held over 250,000 prisoners. Over 60,000 people, including

W

211

11,000 Jews, died in the camp, which mainly held German opponents of the regime. Among the many who died here was the German Communist leader Ernst Thälmann (1886–1944), who organized opposition to the Nazis in Hamburg, and the Christian leader Paul Schneider (1897–1939), who was martyred for his attacks on Nazi ideology in books and sermons. In 1990, mass graves were discovered in the area that were identified as people killed by the Russians after the end of World War II. Although many of the people imprisoned by the Russians were Nazis, they also eliminated Christian and democratic opponents of Communism.

WITTENBERG

The origin of the name *Wittenberg* is unknown. All we know is that the town is first mentioned in a document dated 1180. At that time, it sat on an uneasy frontier between German and Slav where missionary bishops sought to spread Christianity among an essentially pagan people. The most likely suggestion about the origin of the name Wittenberg is that the town takes its name from a hill or bank of white sand on the shores of the River Elbe. Wittenberg is, of course, forever linked to the tempestuous career of the Augustinian monk and Protestant Reformer, Martin Luther.

Martin Luther (1483–1546) was undoubtedly one of the most important men in history and the greatest German theologian and biblical scholar. He reluctantly launched the Protestant Reformation in 1518 as a result of his study of the Bible, where he discovered the principle of justification by faith. Those churches which today take the name Lutheran, with around 45,000,000 members worldwide, are named after him. They follow his theological teachings and his guidelines for the establishment of ecclesiastical organizations.

Ordained as an Augustinian priest in spring 1507, Luther taught moral philosophy at the new University of Wittenberg. In November 1510, Luther and another monk went on pilgrimage to Rome, where he was shocked by the worldliness of church leaders. The sale of indulgences provoked him to protest against the practice, leading to his posting of his 95 *Theses* on October 31, 1517. This act led directly to the Reformation. Originally he sought internal reform of the Roman Catholic Church and taught that Scripture alone is the source of religious authority for the Church. Catholic theologians, led by John Eck (1486–1543), rejected his suggestions and began the active persecution of Luther's followers. The Reformation which followed quickly spread throughout Europe.

W

After defending his views before Emperor Karl V (1500–1558) at the Diet of Worms in 1521, Luther took refuge disguised as a young noble in Wartburg Castle, where he completed his translation of the New Testament into German. In 1522, Luther returned to Wittenberg, where he continued teaching and writing and attracted a large international following. Inspired by Luther's teachings, a Peasants' Revolt broke out in 1524, which was crushed in 1525, the year in which Luther married a former nun, Katharina von Bora.

Luther's teachings spread quickly through Europe where various Reformations took place with differing degrees of success. In Germany, a religious settlement was reached through the Diet and Confession of Augsburg in 1530

KATHARINA VON BORA (1499–1552) was the beautiful and talented wife of Martin Luther. She was described by the humanist Erasmus of Rotterdam (1469–1536) as "remarkably gracious." After her mother's death around 1505, she was placed in a nunnery by her new stepmother whom she appeared to irritate. At the age of 16, she entered the Cistercian Order as a novitiate at Nimbschen Cloister where her aunt Margarete von Haumbitz was the abbess.

By 1522, a number of nuns had read Luther's gospel tracts and accepted the gospel of salvation he preached. As a result, they plotted to leave the nunnery and flee to Wittenberg. This was a very dangerous undertaking which brought with it the penalty of death in the event of failure. Nevertheless, plans were carefully laid and an escape effected.

Once in Wittenberg, some of the former nuns joined their families. Others quickly found husbands from among the former monks who had flocked to Wittenberg to hear Luther's preaching and join the movement for Reformation. Katharina appears to have lived at the home of Lucas Cranach for some time during which she refused several offers of marriage.

Then she became engaged to Jerome Baumgaertner from Nürnberg, but his family objected to the marriage and the engagement was broken off. Finally on June 13, 1525, she married Martin Luther in Wittenberg. The wedding was attended by Lucas Cranach and his wife, Luther's parents, and a small group of close friends.

The marriage was an exceptionally happy one which produced six children. As a poor preacher and university professor, Luther's possessions were few. But the elector gave him the Luther House as a wedding gift, and Katharina proved a diligent housekeeper and businesswoman who emulated the Bible's image of a good wife found in Proverbs 31.

W

and the Peace of Augsburg of 1555, which allowed each king, prince, or duke to determine the religion of his realm. Although Luther hoped to reform the Roman Catholic Church, his actions led to the creation of new churches throughout Europe, something Luther never intended. His translation of the Bible into German not only caused a religious revolution, but effectively created a new high German common language understood by all.

Since World War II many writers, notably William Shirer in his *Rise and Fall of the Third Reich* (1962), have popularized the thesis first argued by Peter F. Wiener in *Martin Luther: Hitler's Spiritual Ancestor* (1945), that Luther's anti-Semitism led directly to the Holocaust. Ironically, this was an argument used in Nazi propaganda, and there is no doubt that at certain times in his life Luther expressed violently anti-Jewish sentiments. But, as Gordon Rupp shows in *Martin Luther—Hitler's Cause—or Cure* (1945), one cannot link Luther to the Nazis, whose views he would have certainly rejected. More recently, the German-Jewish historian Frank Eyck in his *Religion and Politics in German History* (1998) gave a favorable picture of Luther while pointing out the ambiguity of his views about the Jews. What seems clear is that while Luther sometimes reflected the prejudices of his day and certainly wanted to convert Jewish people, he was not a proto-Nazi. It should also be remembered that out of Luther's teach-

ings John Calvin (1509–64) developed a theology that respected Judaism and led his followers in the Netherlands and England to reject anti-Semitism and welcome Jewish immigrants.

Wittenberg entered modern history when Friedrich III the Wise (1463–1525) became ruler of Saxony in 1486. He decided to make Wittenberg his residence and set about developing the town. A pious and just ruler, he returned from pilgrimage to the Holy Land in 1493 and began to amass what became the greatest collection of relics in Germany. In 1502, Friedrich enlarged an existing theological college to found the University of Wittenberg.

After Martin Luther's (1483–1546) protest against indulgences in 1518, Friedrich became Luther's protector. Following the Diet of Worms, he arranged a mock kidnapping of Luther and secretly hid him in the castle of Wartburg by Erfurt. For political reasons, Friedrich never declared himself a Protestant, although on the day of his death he took communion in both kinds—bread and wine—according to Lutheran teaching. He was succeeded by his brother John (1526–32) and later John's son, John Friedrich, known as the Steadfast (1532–54). Both of these men were pious Lutherans. In 1547 John Friedrich's forces were defeated by a Spanish Catholic army at the battle of Mühlberg. He was imprisoned for a number of years by the Emperor Karl V (1500–1558), who sought to restore

Catholicism to the whole of Germany through the force of arms.

At the beginning of the 16th century, in 1500, Wittenberg had 392 houses and a population of 2,146 people. These population figures compare well with other German towns like Dresden, whose population at the time was 3,200, and Leipzig, which had a population of 4,000. In those days most of the houses appear to have been mud huts with thatched roofs. Martin Luther's colleague, Philipp Melanchthon (1497–1560), described Wittenberg as "a spot which has no houses, only tiny cottages, simple huts built of mud and covered with straw." A building boom soon changed things dramatically as many of the fine Renaissance houses, such as those seen today in the Market Square, were erected.

The first thing the visitor sees is the tower of the Castle Church. The present tower dates back to the late 19th century and looks like a Prussian helmet of the type frequently worn by Kaiser Wilhelm II (1859–1941). This odd architectural feature distinguishes Lutherstadt-Wittenberg from surrounding villages. Initially Wittenberg, or Lutherstadt-Wittenberg as it is now known, is unimpressive. Yet in many ways its very obscurity and lack of pretension saved this historic town, which became the home of Martin Luther and the center of the Reformation, from destruction, thus preserving a unique historical site.

PLACES TO VISIT

LUTHERHALLE (Luther's house) charges a small admission fee which is worth every penny. The Luther House is one of those rare places far richer in history than their unimposing exterior suggests. Built by Friedrich the Wise in 1504 to provide housing for 13 Augustinian hermits, it is a magnificent example of late medieval architecture.

Restored as a museum in the late 19th century, the Luther House contains the richest collection of Reformation artifacts in the world. Apart from many physical objects associated with Martin Luther, there are numerous contemporary portraits of the Reformer and his contemporaries by such great artists as the Cranachs. An entire floor is devoted to a magnificent collection of Reformation-era books of untold value. A magnificent collection of coins, medals, and woodcuts makes this incredible museum worthy of an entire day's visit. For many years, the Luther House was the home of Katharina von Bora (1499–1552), who ran Luther's household with remarkable efficiency and success.

MELANCHTHON'S HOUSE. A few doors along the high street from the Luther House is the home of Luther's great assistant, the Reformation scholar Philipp Melanchthon (1497–1560). Less of a museum and more a home than Luther's House, this interesting building was erected in 1536 for Melanchthon, who first arrived in Wittenberg as professor of Greek at the new university in 1518.

Here the visitor gets a vivid insight into 16th-century life and the work of the man who became known as the "teacher of Germany" because of his extensive educational work. Inspired by a reforming zeal and theological studies, Melanchthon sought to reform German schools, thus making education accessible to all and enabling people to read the newly translated German Bible of Martin Luther.

An unusual feature of this house is the reconstructed medieval garden complete with an authentic herb garden such as the one Melanchthon was known to have grown. A stone table, said to be the very one used by Melanchthon, sits under a yew tree which is said to be original. Throughout the house itself, most of the furnishings and room decorations are authentic and can be traced back to the time of Melanchthon, making this house rare indeed.

STADTKIRCHE ST. MARIEN (St. Mary's City Church). Crossing the narrow street in front of Melanchthon's House, the visitor should walk toward the center of the town and turn right into Kupferstrasse. One block further, turn left into Mittelstrasse, which leads directly to the City Church of St. Mary where Martin Luther frequently preached, where he was married in 1525, and where his six children were baptized.

Despite the ravages of numerous wars, Wittenberg's oldest building is still an impressive sight. Today the church is hemmed in by houses, but in the past it stood alone in the center of a large square. The church is characterized by its twin Gothic towers topped by octagonal turrets, which were added in the 16th century. The earliest parts of the church date from the 13th century, although its central nave was consecrated as late as 1439.

The church's Gothic font, which was used in the Luther baptisms, is generally regarded as the church's richest treasure. It is well worth examination as a superb example of bronze work by the famous Nürnberg artisan Herman Vischer. The font is supported by columns depicting the twelve apostles. The symbolism reminds a child's parents and godparents that the gospel alone is the source of our salvation. During the Napoleonic wars, two of the apostles statues were stolen and had to be replaced by replicas in 1864. All the others are original.

Around the inside walls of the church are numerous carvings in wood and stone as well as paintings by such artists as the Cranachs. The other pride of the church, in addition to its font, is the Reformation altarpiece executed by Lucas Cranach the Elder and consecrated in 1547. The center of this magnificent work of art is his famous depiction of *The Last Supper.* Here Martin Luther is portrayed as an apostle of Christ. He can be recognized as the disciple receiving the cup of wine from a servant. This detail is important because it illustrates one of the most contentious issues of the Reformation debate. Luther argued that

W

GREAT PAINTERS OF THE REFORMATION

LUCAS CRANACH THE ELDER (1472–1553) is generally regarded as Martin Luther's closest friend, the greatest painter of the Reformation, and one of the most innovative painters of all time. He was born in Kronach, which was then ruled by the prince bishop of Bamberg. His father, whose name was Moller, was also an artist, but none of his works survive. Around 1500, Lucas traveled to Vienna, where he attended the university and painted some excellent portraits of the rector Stephan Reuss, his wife, and several other university people. During this time it is thought that he met the painter Altdorfer, who seems to have been influenced by Cranach's style, and began to produce woodcuts.

The elector of Saxony, Friedrich the Wise, invited Cranach to the city of Wittenberg in 1504 as his court painter. The elector had recently established a new university and was seeking to make Wittenberg the "Venice of the North." From the nature of the invitation, it's generally assumed that by this time Cranach had established a considerable reputation as an artist. Apart from acquiring considerable wealth, Cranach was granted the coat-of-arms which became the symbol of his work.

In Wittenberg, Cranach established a thriving school of painting, employing numerous apprentices. He also established the local pharmacy, held a monopoly on the sale of wine, established a printing press, and bought several houses. He joined the city council in 1519, a post he held to 1549. From 1537–45 he was the Bürgermeister (mayor) of Wittenberg.

After the defeat of Elector John Friedrich of Saxony by Roman Catholic forces at the Battle of Mühlberg in 1547, Cranach followed his master into exile in 1550, living first in Augsburg and then Innsbruck. He died in Weimar at the age of 81 on October 16, 1553.

LUCAS CRANACH THE YOUNGER (1515–86) was the second son of Lucas Cranach the Elder, and a worthy successor to his father whose art and woodcuts helped spread the message of the Lutheran Reformation throughout Europe. Born in Wittenberg in 1515, he rose to prominence after the death of his elder brother, John, in 1536.

A pupil of his father, he continued the work of the Reformation by illustrating Martin Luther's work. He died in exile in Weimar in 1582 after hostilities between Roman Catholic and Protestant forces had destroyed the peace of the area.

W

Christ's intention as taught in the Bible is for all Christians to celebrate communion, known as the Mass by Roman Catholics, by receiving both bread and wine. The Roman Catholic Church rejected this insight, restricting the communion wine to ordained priests, thus emphasizing a division within the Christian community between priests, who were holy, and the laity, who were in effect second-class citizens. Countering this view, Luther argued that the Bible teaches the priesthood of all believers, saying that all Christians are alike in the sight of God and that no one has a special relationship with God.

Other figures seen in the series of pictures which make up the altarpiece are Friedrich the Wise and Melanchthon. Indeed all the people in the pictures were contemporaries of Cranach. By using his fellow citizens in his art, Cranach was proclaiming the significance of the gospel to his contemporaries. In modern language, Cranach contextualizes the gospel by showing that its message applies today to people who were recognizable to anyone who looked at his pictures. A striking feature of this painting is the conception of the Last Supper taking place at a round table. The theological significance is that in this way everyone in the picture can look into each other's eyes in trust and sincerity. Thus the truth of the gospel as the basis for true community is vividly illustrated. On the outside of the church are many medieval sculptures and stone reliefs, some from gravestones formerly found in the the church square but deconsecrated in 1772 and added to the church wall.

Outside, high on the east facade of the church, in bas relief, is a Judensau that was sculpted in 1305. Here a Jewish rabbi looks under the tail of a pig as other Jews suckle at its breasts. There is also a mock Hebrew inscription that reads "the name of god." A big debate took place in 1988 about whether or not to remove this insult from the church wall. The town council wisely decided that rather than remove it, a memorial plaque should be added commemorating the persecution of Jews who were first expelled from Wittenberg at the beginning of the 14th century and reminding visitors of the terrible fate of Jews during the Second World War. The plaque is now below the Judensau and serves to remind Christians of this dark side of Christian history and that even Luther was not immune to anti-Semitism.

THE MARKET SQUARE. Leaving St. Mary's, a small alley takes you into the Market Square, which contains an impressive 16th-century Rathaus (Townhall), surrounded by rows of equally historic town houses, some of which now house shops. At either side of the Market Square are statues of Martin Luther and Philipp Melanchthon. Across the street at the southeast corner of the square is the Goldene Adler, or Golden Eagle Hotel. One of the oldest hostelries in Germany, it was built in 1524 and was a favorite meeting place of both Luther and Melanchthon.

THE CASTLE CHURCH. Continuing to walk along the Schlossstrasse away from the Luther House, one comes to the end of the street and the Schlosskirche (Castle Church). It was here on October 31, 1517, that Martin Luther inadvertently launched the Reformation by nailing his 95 *Theses Against the Sale of Papal Indulgences* to the church door. At the time Luther wanted to initiate an academic disputation. Instead, he launched a revolution grounded in the dynamic biblical message of justification by faith.

Unfortunately the original church door was destroyed in 1760 during the Seven Years' War along with much of the church. But after further destruction at the hands of Napoleon's troops, the church was fully restored in 1885, complete with a bronze door with the 95 *Theses* written on it.

Inside the church are statues of Friedrich the Wise and Friedrich the Steadfast, who did so much to protect the Reformers. Beautiful stained-glass windows based on designs found in a collection of woodcuts by Albrecht Dürer depict the life of Christ. Here also Martin Luther's grave can be seen.

THE CRANACH HOUSE. Visitors to Wittenberg cannot avoid hearing or reading about the Cranach family of painters. The town of Wittenberg is presently restoring the home of Lucas Cranach the Elder (1472–1553), who is possibly the greatest of all German artists. Unfortunately, the complete restoration will take many years. Nevertheless, many of the paintings and woodcuts by Lucas Cranach the Elder and his son Lucas Cranach the Younger (1515–86) can be seen in various locations around town, including a large collection in the Luther House.

The Cranach heritage was enormous, even though many modern art historians tend to play down the unique contribution of the Cranach school of art. To many it is simply a minor development in northern German art. To others it is a puzzle which they clearly find difficult to evaluate. Many comment on the influence of Martin Luther on the Cranachs, but then downplay their religious zeal by making inane comments about the fact that both artists painted nudes.

The issue of nudity is in fact one of the key factors in evaluating the art of the Cranachs. Unlike other painters of their time, they found no contradiction between their deep piety, close friendship with Luther and his colleagues, and an affirmation of life. Indeed the Reformation freed them from the constraints of Catholicism, which divided the world between the sacred and profane. Yet most modern art historians find this simple point impossible to grasp.

The many derogatory comments about the slimness of Lucas Cranach's nudes, which some suggest shows they are entirely imaginary figures, overlook the fact that he could, and did, produce paintings like *The Suicide of Lucretia* (1518) and later woodcuts which show women of quite different proportions. These works are conveniently overlooked by his critics. Too many modern writers like to dismiss Cranach's art in terms of what they imagine as a repressed sexuality brought on by his desire not to offend Luther.

In fact, nothing could be further from the truth. The Cranachs were pious artists who delighted in God's creation. They painted the world as they saw it in vivid and truthful ways. If many of the women in these pictures are particularly slim, it is not because they distorted reality. Rather, they reproduced the proportions of their models, whose physiology is common in Germany, if not North America.

Criticism of the Cranachs and Martin Luther in terms of their supposed suppression of sexuality really exposes the ignorance of the critics. Nobody who has read Martin Luther's works can possibly condemn him for repressing sexuality. After rejecting the monastic life, Luther became a champion of marriage and, as his *Table Talk* and other writings show, was no prude.

In actual fact, the Cranachs were artistic geniuses, as earlier generations of German writers readily recognized. Indeed their unpopularity with the literary elite is a good gauge of modern secularism. Following the Reformation, the Cranachs were seen as great Christian painters. But from the late 18th-century Enlightenment to today, their art has been increasingly criticized or ignored because it preaches the gospel too clearly for modern intellectuals.

The remarkable realism of their paintings is disturbing to the modern mind. This is because they have no difficulty depicting pain and death, love and life, God and man, in ways that clearly proclaim their own faith. Such is the power of their work that it resembles the music of Bach as a living testimony to the power of the gospel.

It should also be noted that the Cranachs were also the first modern advertising experts and masters of propaganda. Without their woodcuts, which vividly illustrate Luther's work and a host of other Reformation writings, it is doubtful if the Reformation would have made quite the impact it did on Luther's contemporaries.

It was the Cranachs who took a scholarly dispute, Luther's posting of his *95 Theses,* and gave it national and international importance. Without their work, Luther's scholarship could easily have ended as unread books gathering dust in a remote German library. Instead, through their meaningful illustrations they turned Luther's rediscovery of the Bible into a tidal wave which rocked Germany and the world.

To do this, the Cranachs produced the first comic books, which proclaimed the rediscovery of the gospel of grace by

W

Martin Luther and in doing so made the teachings of Luther and the Bible accessible to even the most illiterate peasant. Both the Luther and Cranach houses display numerous superb examples of these fascinating publications.

Above all, the Cranach family left behind a rich record of the Reformation and its leaders in their many portraits of Martin Luther, his family, and his friends. Without their work, we would be hard pressed to know what Luther and many of his contemporaries looked like. Portraits such as Luther disguised as *Junker Jörg* after his flight from the Diet of Worms provide a unique historical record of events which changed the world.

WOLFENBÜTTEL

This picturesque town was the residence of the dukes of Brunswick from 1432–1753. Undamaged during World War II, Wolfenbüttel has remarkably preserved the atmosphere of a capital of a small mid-European state within the Holy Roman Empire.

PLACES TO VISIT

In the town center you will find numerous FACHWERKHÄUSER (half-timbered houses) that evoke the atmosphere of a bygone age. Look out for the biblical quotations and numerous decorations on their walls and beams. Many excellent examples are to be found in the STADTMARKT (Market Square). Here too you can see the home of Justus Georg Schottle, or Schottelius (1612–76), who launched the German obsession with philology that in many ways led to the development of biblical criticism in the 18th century.

SCHLOß (Palace) was founded in the 12th century as a fortress for Heinrich der Löwe (Heinrich the Lion) (1129–95). It was transformed into a Baroque palace in the 17th century when it also became a center for the arts.

HERZOG-AUGUST-BIBLIOTHEK (Herzog August Library) was founded in 1572 by Augustus der Junge (August the Young), who collected over 150,000 volumes, making it the largest and most important library in Europe. Today the library houses over 600,000 volumes and is a major resource for scholars. The library has a wonderful exhibition where you can see some of its valuable manuscripts, including the 14th-century *Saxon Mirror* and the 15th-century *Story of Melusina.* Most important of all is the 12th-century *Helmarshausen Gospel,* which was probably produced for Heinrich the Lion. The gospel itself was sold to a private collector after World War II. In 1983, it was auctioned at Sotheby's in London, and the State of Niedersachsen, Lower Saxony, paid an all-time record of 10,000,000 pounds

W

GOTTHOLD EPHRAIM LESSING (1729–81) was a key figure in the German Enlightenment. He was a philosopher, publicist, playwright, critic, and art theorist. Lessing worked for the free and democratic development of the German people and their culture and was highly critical of the possibility of historical knowledge, especially of religious events. His publication of fragments of work by Herman Samuel Reimarus (1694–1768), who questioned the possibility of historical knowledge and raised serious doubts about the historicity of the Gospels, led to the development of German biblical criticism. Through the publication of Reimarus's work, Lessing became the father of higher criticism by rejecting the miraculous elements of the Bible and indirectly charging biblical writers with fraud. Thus he prepared the way for the work of critics like David Friedrich Strauss (1808–74).

to recover the manuscript, making it the most expensive book in the world.

LESSINGHAUS (Lessing's House). From 1770 to 1781, this splendid Baroque house was the home of the philosopher and writer Gotthold Ephraim Lessing (1729–81), who is the father of modern biblical criticism and author of such important plays as *Nathan the Wise* (1779).

HAUPTKIRCHE (Parish Church), Kornmarkt, was built in 1608 as a Protestant church in the Gothic style. It has high windows and some wonderful vaulting.

WORMS

Worms lies on the west, left bank of the Rhine River. Originally called by the Celtic name Borbetomagus, the settlement was renamed after a tribe in that region as Civitas Vangionum by the Romans, when the Roman General Drusus erected a fort around 14 B.C. on a flood-free stretch of the Rhine. A settlement quickly grew up around the Roman garrison to create a prosperous town. A bishop of the Vangiones from Worms attended a church council at Cologne in 347. During the time of the migration of the nations in 413, the Burgundians were permitted to settle on the west, left bank of the Rhine. There they founded a kingdom with Worms as their capital city under their king Gunther, who is a major character in the ancient German saga the *Nibelungenlied*. Shortly afterward, the Burgundians converted to Arianism. Their decision to embrace this heresy brought them into conflict with the Romans, who in turn called upon the Huns to wage war against the Burgundians, who were defeated and the city of Worms destroyed in 436.

Later Worms was rebuilt as Wormatia and became an episcopal see, or the seat of a bishop. It is first mentioned in documents in 614. A royal palace, occasionally used by Charlemagne (742–814), was built in the 8th century. The Normans plundered Worms in 861, but the town was rebuilt and the power of the bishops of Worms gradually increased. In the year 1000, Worms, which had been the seat of a bishop since the 4th century, came under the control of the local bishop. The wealth of the city increased after 1074 when Emperor Heinrich II (973–1024) gave the city the right to impose customs duties on travelers using the Rhine.

The 11th century Bishop Burchard (1000–1025) destroyed the Frankish castle and replaced it with a new cathedral that proclaimed the growing power of the bishopric. In September 1122, the investiture controversy between the Roman Catholic Church and the emperor was brought to an end through the Concordat of Worms. In 1200, the citizens of Worms freed themselves from the rule of the bishop. They joined with the citizens of Mainz in 1224 to form the confederation of the Rhine.

An Imperial diet was held in 1495 for the purpose of reforming the

Church, and an "Eternal Peace" was proclaimed on the basis of its decisions. In all, approximately 100 Imperial diets were held in Worms, including the most famous, the Diet of Worms, in 1521, which was called by Emperor Karl V (1500–1558) to allow Cardinal Aleander (1480–1542), the papal nuncio (ambassador), to examine Martin Luther for possible heresy. Luther was found guilty and banned by Aleander from the Holy Empire. After the Diet, Luther fled in disguise to Wartburg, where he began the translation of the Bible into German.

Worms became a Protestant city during the Thirty Years' War, when the city suffered severe damage. In 1689, Worms was almost completely destroyed in a fire that ravaged the city. The city was annexed to France in 1797, but it was returned to German rule in 1815. During World War II, over 65 percent of its buildings were destroyed by British bombing, but most were restored in the 1960s.

During the Middle Ages, Worms was known as "Little Jerusalem" because the city's tolerant policy toward Jews encouraged Jewish settlement. Many Jewish intellectuals lived or studied in Worms, including the great Talmudic commentator Solomon ben Isaac of Troyes (1040–1105), who is also known as Rashi. With Mainz and Speyer, the Jews of Worms formed a protective league. In 1096, tragedy struck the Jewish community when members of

223

the First Crusade (1096–99) came to Worms and slaughtered at least 800 Jews despite the efforts of the bishop to protect them. During the Second Crusade (1147–49), the Jews were given refuge in local fortresses and protected in exchange for paying higher taxes. But during the Black Death of 1390, they were accused of poisoning wells and brutally attacked. Further persecution occurred in 1615. This was followed by a long period of acceptance and improvement with the ghetto being abolished in 1852. The 1930s brought renewed persecution with the advent of Nazi rule and the destruction of a community of over 1,000 people, of whom 462 died in concentration camps.

PLACES TO VISIT

DOM OF ST. PETER (St. Peter Cathedral), Domplatz 1, is an almost perfect example of high or late Romanesque architecture. The cathedral was started by Bishop Burchard in 1181 and completed in 1230. Until the 13th century, several changes were made to the original design. Today the cathedral, with its four towers, is an impressive structure and a masterpiece of medieval art. The south entrance has a richly carved Gothic doorway with sculptures depicting the four evangelists and the church triumphant. The richly decorated wooden choir stalls date from 1760. Balthasar Neumann (1687–1753) created the high altar in 1740. Reliefs of *Daniel in the Lions' Den* and *Habakkuk and an Angel* are located in the first chapel on the south side, the chapel of St. Anna. The chapel of St. Georg (St. George) is a Renaissance construction, while the baptistery of St. Nikolaus is Gothic, completed in 1325. The dom also contains nine imperial tombs beneath the choir.

ST. MARTINSKIRCHE (St. Martin's Church) Ludwigsplatz, was formerly known as the Collegiate Church St. Martin. This is the main Roman Catholic parish-church, and some of the Romanesque structure dates back to 991. The richly decorated Gothic portals are from the 13th century.

PAULUSKIRCHE (St. Paul Church), Paulusplatz, was also built by Bishop Burchard at the beginning of the 11th century in Gothic style, although most of the present building comes from the 13th century. The archway, at the south, contains stonework from the very first building, as does the tower. Originally this church was part of a Dominican monastery. Next to the church are 13th- and 14th-century cloisters.

LIEBFRAUENKIRCHE (Church of Our Lady), Liebfrauenring. Wine lovers must visit this ancient three-aisled church which gives its name to the famous Liebfrauenmilch wines that grow in the area. It contains some excellent sculptures and a superb 14th-century painting of the Madonna.

KUNSTHAUS HEYLSHOF (Cultural Museum Heyls Court) contains a rich collection of artworks that belonged to

W

the von Heyl family. The garden of the museum was once part of the bishop's palace and still contains parts of the ancient city walls. Among the many treasures of this collection are Rubens' (1577–1640) *Madonna and Child* and a statue of Adam by the sculptor Konrad Meit (1480–1551), who was a native of Worms and one of the few German artists to completely adopt the Italian Renaissance style.

DREIFALTIGKEITSKIRCHE (Church of the Holy Trinity) was built 1709–25. Its modern glass mosaics depict Martin Luther before the Diet of Worms.

LUTHERDENKMAL (Luther Monument), unveiled in 1868 to commemorate the Reformation, is largely the work of Ernst Rietschel (1804–61), but was completed after his death by a group of other artists. This impressive bronze sculpture depicts Martin Luther in a neoclassical pose as the prophet of German nationalism. The monument also depicts such important Reformers as Pietro Valdo (Waldo) (1140–1217), John Wycliffe (1320–84), John Hus (1370–1415), and Girolamo Savonarola (1452–98), as well as Philipp Melanchthon (1497–1560), Johann Reuchlin (1455–1522), Landgrave (Duke) Philip of Hessen, the Magnanimous (1504–67), and the elector of Saxony, Friedrich the Wise (1463–1525), who gave Luther protection in the Wartburg after his trial at the Diet of Worms. The women sitting around symbolize the towns of Speyer, Augsburg, and Magdeburg, which were among the first to embrace Luther's teachings.

JUDENFRIEDHOF (Jewish Cemetery) is one of the largest Jewish cemeteries in Europe and one of the oldest Jewish sites in Germany, with one tombstone bearing the date 1076.

SYNAGOGE (Synagogue), first built 1034, was severely damaged during the Crusades. A new synagogue was built in the 12th century in Romanesque style, possibly by the same workers as those who constructed the dom. The new building incorporates stones from the older buildings, including an inscription which can still be seen today that names the original founder. Although often desecrated in subsequent centuries, it became the oldest synagogue in continuous use in the world. It remained a place of worship until November 9–10, 1938, when it was burnt down by the Nazis during Kristallnacht, the night of broken glass. Following the end of the war, the synagogue was restored through the efforts of American servicemen to create a unique memorial to Jewish life in Germany. It is an important place to visit for anyone wishing to understand both German and Jewish history. The synagogue complex includes a teaching room known as the **RASCHI-KAPELLE** and an underground ritual bath for women known as the **TAUCHBAD**. There is also a fascinating museum of Jewish history.

WÜRZBURG

Around 1000 B.C., a Celtic structure for the protection of settlers and travelers had been built at the site of the present Marienberg fort on the west side of the Main river. The site of the present town was occupied by the Romans who built a fort. In 704, the "Castellum Virteburch" was mentioned for the first time in documents. The old Latin name for the town was Wircebirgum. In the 12th century, the name Herbipolis was used, probably with reference to herbs gathered in the area used for beer or other beverages.

Würzburg was a major German pilgrimage destination. The first bishop of Würzburg, St. Kilian, was of Scots-Irish descent. With two of his friends, Kolonat and Totnan, he was martyred by local pagan tribesmen in 689. St. Kilian is the patron saint of Würzburg and Heilbronn as well as the patron saint of wine growers. His feast day is June 8. Bishop Burkhard (d. 754) built a chapel over the spot where the murders took place. Würzburg was made a bishopric by St. Boniface in 741. In 705, Duke Hetan II built the Marienberg on the west side of the Main river. This round church is the oldest such stone structure in Germany. Charlemagne was present at the consecration of the first cathedral in 788. The first stone bridge over the river Main was built in 1133. The bishops of Würzburg moved their residence into the fortified Marienberg castle in 1253.

Over the centuries, a stream of important people have visited Würzburg. Bernard of Clairvaux came here in 1146. Friedrich Barbarossa (1123–90) was married here in 1156. Albertus Magnus (1200–1280), the teacher of Thomas Aquinas (1224–74), visited in 1262. Martin Luther (1483–1546) was a guest at the Augustinian Monastery in 1518. Gustavus Adolphus (1594–1632) of Sweden visited in 1631, and Empress Maria Theresa (1717–80) and her husband visited in 1745.

Tilman Riemenschneider, known as the Master of Würzburg, the famed sculptor and carver, came to Würzburg in 1484. He became a member of the city council and later lord mayor from 1520–21. Because of his participation in the Peasant Revolt (1524–25), Riemenschneider was severely punished by the local bishop. The demands of the peasants were free choice of parish, i.e., place of residence, limiting the amount of the tithe, abolition of serfdom, and free hunting and logging. They were unsuccessful and defeated at great cost to human life by the princes' armies. Later even heavier burdens were laid upon the peasants.

W

Julius Echter von Mespelbrunn (1545–1619), the bishop of Würzburg, advocated reform of the Roman Catholic Church according to the Tridentinum (Council of Trent) (1545–61). He also founded the University of Würzburg, which acted as the hub of the Counter-Reformation. On March 16, 1945, Würzburg was almost totally destroyed during an air raid. It was carefully rebuilt according to earlier plans after the war.

PLACES TO VISIT

FESTUNG MARIENBERG (Fortress of Mary's Mountain), overlooking the town, was built around St. Mary's chapel to become the fortified residence of the prince bishop from 1201 to 1719. Its central feature is the Round Tower, built about 1200 as the main keep. The castle was turned into a Renaissance palace by Julius Echter in the early 17th century. During the Thirty Years' War, it was again converted into a fortress. The armory is the MAINFRÄNKISCHES MUSEUM (Frankish Museum) and contains a rich collection of artworks by Tilman Riemenschneider and Veit Stoß (1447–1533). Many tales are told about the building of the castle, including ones about secret tunnels which are supposed to run from it to both local inns and the Residenz. According to tradition, these tunnels were used by the bishop's troops to quell rebellions and resistance to what at times could be oppressive rule.

RESIDENZ (Bishop's Palace or Residence) was designed by Balthasar Neumann (1687–1753), who completed the construction of this Baroque masterpiece between 1719 and 1744. It is a must on any visit to this part of Germany. The Residence is one of the most opulent Baroque structures in Germany. The grand staircase, the imperial hall, and imperial apartments with their Rococo stucco work and period furniture are unequaled. This exaggerated display of wealth and power served as residence for the prince bishops of Würzburg. The court chapel, in the south wing, is a masterpiece of Baroque architecture, utilizing wood and stucco work, marble, paintings, and stained-glass windows.

To visit you must join a guided tour that takes about an hour but is well worth the time. Although extensively damaged during World War II, renovations have restored the main hallways and rooms to provide visitors with a glimpse of the power and majesty of prince bishops during the 17th and 18th centuries. In particular, notice the immense fresco above the main and very impressive grand staircase that shows the entire world coming to pay homage to the bishop. In this Baroque fantasy, even Rome is subordinate to the spiritual power of Würzburg. When it was built, critics said that the roof over the staircase would easily collapse. Yet it, and its fresco, survived the bombing of World War II that destroyed many other parts of the palace.

DOMKIRCHE ST. KILIAN (St. Kilian Cathedral), Domplatz, is one of the largest

Romanesque churches in Germany. A church was built on this spot in 788 that was consecrated in the presence of Charlemagne. Construction began on the present Domkirche in 1040. Further changes were made in 1133 and then again shortly before it was consecrated in 1187. The basic form is that of a cross. Four towers grace the building to form an impressive silhouette against the skyline. The east tower was built of red and green sandstone in alternating layers for visual effect. In the south transept is the modern Altar of the Apostles by Hans Weber that incorporates four 16th-century statues by Riemenschneider. The crypt contains the grave of the founder Archbishop Bruno. There are also 15th-century cloisters.

SCHÖNBORN KAPELLE (Beautiful Chapel), in the dom, was designed by Balthasar Neumann as a funeral chapel for the prince bishops of Würzburg. The inside has many fine examples of the Baroque stucco artwork. Here too the burial niche of Tilman Riemenschneider is located beside many of his carvings, such as Christ and the apostles. The many tombs span over 700 years of church history beginning at 1190 to 1979. A bronze baptismal font dated 1279 is associated with Meister Eckehart (1260–1327). It is the only one remaining from that era in southern Germany. One of the dom's bells, the Lobdeburg Glocke (Praise the Castle Bell), was made in 1275.

ST. BURKARD, Alte Mainbrücke, was founded by the first bishop of Würzburg.

It was originally called the Andreas Kloster (St. Andrew's Monastery); the name of the monastery was changed in the 11th century and relocated to the present spot at the foot of the Marienberg, west of the Main river. It is a Romanesque building, and part of the west wall is the original masonry. Emperor Heinrich II (951–95) was present at the consecration. After the Thirty Years' War, the inside of the church was redecorated and completed in Baroque style. After 1464, it was used for charitable purposes. In 1803 it became a parish church. One of the treasures of the church is a bust of the Madonna by Tilman Riemenschneider that is carried at processions.

NEUMÜNSTER (New Minster), St. Kilians Platz, served as Würzburg's cathedral from 1950 to 1967 while the dom of St. Kilian was being restored after bomb damage. This church is the destination of thousands of pilgrims who come from all over Germany to visit the tomb of St. Kilian. The first church was built over the graves of Kilian, Kolonat, and Totnan. It was erected in the 9th century by Bishop Adalbero and extended in the 11th century when it became the Romanesque basilica that remains as the main structure of the present church. It has an eight-cornered Romanesque dome. The onion-shaped top was added during the Rococo period. A Tilman Riemenschneider sandstone, *Madonna,* can be seen over the side altar. On the right is another Riemenschneider, *Christ on the Cross,* which shows Christ with his

W

hands off the cross and crossed over his chest. According to legend, Christ was holding on to a Swedish soldier who tried to desecrate the cross during the Thirty Years' War.

FRANZISKANERKIRCHE (Franciscan Church), Neubaustrasse, was founded in 1221 at a time when St. Francis was still alive. It was the first Franciscan church in Germany. A wooden carving of the Pieta made in 1510 by Tilman Riemenschneider can be seen above the organ.

EVANGELISCHE DEUTSCHHAUSKIRCHE (German Protestant House Church), Zellerstraße, is of Early Gothic design with a late 13th-century Romanesque tower. It was originally built by the Teutonic Knights.

WALLFAHRTSKIRCHE ST. MARIA (Pilgrimage Church of St. Mary), Auf dem Nikolausberg, was built by

Neumann between 1747 and 1750. It is located on a hill high above the town. Because of its location and pleasing features, it is frequently visited throughout the year. The set of stairs leading to the church represents Christ's passion.

UNIVERSITÄTSKIRCHE (University Church), Neubaustraße, was consecrated in 1591 and is built of red sandstone in the Renaissance style.

ST. PETER, Petersplatz. The west towers of this Romanesque basilica built in 1100 were retained during the Baroque renovations in the 18th century.

RATHAUS (City Hall), built in the 12th century, used to be the residence of one of the local lords and a residence for the bishop. The present building is a good example of Renaissance architecture with a pleasant courtyard and decorated facade.

XANTEN

This town is an important historical site for European history since it was the north base for Roman legions stationed on the frontier to prevent the invasion of Roman lands by Teutonic tribes from the east of the Rhine. A Roman fort was first established here in A.D. 15. Eventually the nearby town of Colonia Ulpia Traiana had a population of over 10,000. The name Xanten comes from the Latin *Ad Sanctos* meaning "a memorial to the saints." In 1933, a double grave from the 4th century was found under the crypt. Examination of the corpses showed that both men had died violent deaths, supporting the tradition that the dom was built over the grave of early martyrs. Norbert of Xanten (1080–1134) was born here.

PLACES TO VISIT

The **DOM** was built on the site of an earlier Romanesque church in 1163.

NORBERT OF XANTEN (1080–1134). The younger son of a rich noble family, he became canon of Xanten but lived a dissolute life at the Court of Henry V (1086–1125) until his sudden conversion in 1115 when, like Luther, he was caught in a thunderstorm in a wood. Following this dramatic event, he became an itinerant preacher, an efficient evangelist, and a church reformer. He founded the Premonstratensian Order to revive the church in 1120.

This is one of the lower Rhineland's most striking Gothic churches. It was built on the site of an earlier church that housed the relics of St. Victor (d. 303). The original church was established by St. Helena (250–330), the mother of Constantine the Great (288–337), who was born in Trier and converted to Christianity at the age of 60, after which time she endowed many churches. Part of the towers and west side belong to the original building. Consequently it was an important pilgrimage center in medieval Germany and even today has over 20 altars, many of which are important works of art.

The high altar houses the shrine of St. Victor and illustrates his life and that of St. Helena. It was redesigned in 1530 by Bartholomäus Bruyn the Elder (1493–1555). The altarpiece itself was finely carved in 1536 by Heinrich Douvermann (1480–1544). The choir stalls date from 1240. Outside the dom are some fine cloisters.

DOMSCHATZ (Treasury) contains a good collection of ecclesiastical objects and rare gold and ivory carvings.

REGIONALMUSEUM (Local History Museum) has some interesting exhibits from pre-Roman, Celtic times, to the present.

ARCHÄOLOGISCHER PARK to the north of the town is the Roman town of Colonia Ulpia Traiana, the only Roman city north of the Alps that was not built upon in later centuries. Therefore, it is a unique archaeological find that is being reconstructed and turned into a major archaeological exhibit. This is well worth visiting because here one sees the layout of a Roman city with its baths, amphitheater, walls, etc.

ZITTAU

Originally a fortified frontier post, Zittau was founded in 1228 by the Bohemian King Otokar I (1155–1230). The first mention of the town occurs in 1275. In 1346, the citizens, or more accurately the town council, joined the republican Lusatia League that included Bautzen and several other local cities. In 1369, the Celestine Order of monks built a cloister at Oybin near Zittau. Later, in 1513, the city built a fortified wall and zwinger around the town; parts of this wall are still visible today. Although plundered by Austrian troops during the Thirty Years' War, the town recovered quickly to become the center of a textile-producing region. Following the Treaty of Vienna in 1815, the town was ceded to the Prussian province of Silesia. Today it is the center of a tourist area close to Herrnhut and the Zittau mountains which may be visited on a quaint narrow gauge railway.

PLACES TO VISIT

PETER-UND-PAUL KIRCHE (Church of St. Peter and St. Paul) was formerly a Franciscan monastery built between 1270 and 1280, in the transitional Romanesque and Early Gothic style. It was transformed into a Baroque church in the 17th century. The high altar and the pulpit, from 1668, are fine examples of highly ornate Baroque craftsmanship.

JOHANNIS KIRCHE (Church of St. John), Johannisplatz, was renovated in neoclassical style in 1837 and is a good example of Karl Friedrich Schinkel's (1781–1841) constructive use of neoclassicism.

The grand neoclassical **RATHAUS** (City Hall) and several other buildings in the city center were designed or redesigned by Schinkel, giving Zittau an Italian look.

STADTMUSEUM (City Museum), Klosterstraße, is housed in a former Franciscan monastery and contains items of local interest, including some valuable Bohemian glass.

OYBIN, 10 kilometers south, is a magical spot graced by the impressive ruins of a castle and Celestine monastery. (The Celestine Order was founded as a branch of the Benedictine Order in 1254.) During the 18th century these ruins inspired J. Ch. Schmied, when he visited Oybin, to decorate the Dorfkirche (Village Church).

Z

GLOSSARY OF ART AND ARCHITECTURE TERMS

BAS RELIEF: A three-dimensional sculpture on a flat background that protrudes minimally from its background. They appear on tombs and as plaques on walls.

BYZANTINE: In art and architecture, this term describes the style that developed in the Eastern Roman Empire centered on the city of Constantinople. The Greeks founded the city in 667 B.C. at the entrance to the Bosphorus and named it Byzantium. Later, when it became the "New Rome" of the Emperor Constantine (288–337), in 330, the name was changed to Constantinople. For over a thousand years a unique Christian civilization flourished under the protection of the Eastern Empire. In 1453 the city fell to the Turks, who renamed it Istanbul. Byzantium is therefore identified with the civilization developed by the Eastern Orthodox Church.

CAROLINGIAN: Designates the second Frankish dynasty; also the name given by historians to the art and architecture of the 8th century that is associated with Charlemagne and his immediate era.

FRESCOES: Paintings made on plaster to decorate walls and ceilings. They were popular in Roman times and during the Baroque period. A few Romanesque and Gothic frescoes survive.

HALL CHURCH: A spacious Gothic-style church designed for congregational use where the nave and aisles are approximately equal in size and the roof is the same height. The interior is lit, or illuminated, by light coming from the side aisle windows. St. Elizabeth in Marburg and the Frauenkirche in Nürnberg are good examples of hall churches.

MOSAIC: A colorful picture created out of small pieces of glass or stone used to decorate ceilings, walls, or floors.

SARCOPHAGUS: This term comes from the Greek word for "flesh eating" and is used to describe limestone coffins used to store bodies. Over time, artists began to decorate the outside of these coffins so that they became major works of Christian art.

GLOSSARY OF RELIGIOUS TERMS

COUNTER-REFORMATION: A reform movement in Roman Catholicism during the 16th century which sought to purify the church and combat the Protestant Reformation. It was characterized by a revival of artistic, educational, and missionary activities.

EVANGELICAL: Pertaining to the gospel; one who is devoted to the good news, or evangel, of God's redemption in Jesus Christ. In the English-speaking world evangelical Christians are committed to the inspired Scriptures of the Bible as the divine rule of faith and practice. They affirm the fundamental doctrines of the gospel, including the Incarnation, virgin birth of Christ, his sinless life, substitutionary atonement, and bodily resurrection as the grounds of God's forgiveness of sinners, justification by faith alone, and the spiritual regeneration of all who trust in Jesus Christ. In the German-speaking world *Evangelische* denotes those who are Lutheran or Protestant and implies membership of a mainline church. Thus German "Evangelicals" often hold liberal and radical theological views which are quite unevangelical to English-speaking Christians.

FOUR VIRTUES: Traditionally virtue was defined as "those things which confer goodness and make the acts of individuals good." The four virtues represent different types of virtue. They were the (1) *heroic virtues,* where an extraordinary amount of perseverance is shown in one's task; (2) *infused virtues,* which are virtues bestowed by God; (3) *moral virtues,* or those habits of life that enable a person to strengthen their character through prudence, justice, religion, obedience, fortitude, humility, chastity, temperance, and meekness; and (4) *natural virtues,* or those habits that are acquired by frequent repetition. Natural virtues include those listed above under moral virtues and are things that the natural man can develop without acknowledging God's grace.

HERETIC: Someone who commits heresy. In its loose sense, heresy refers to the conscious, willful rejection of any doctrine held to be normative by a group or institution. Roman Catholicism defines a heretic as any baptized person who, wishing to call himself a Christian, denies the truth revealed to the church. Until the 19th century, Protestants generally regarded heresy as the willful rejection of any truth taught in the Bible. With the rise of biblical criticism, defining heresy became a problem because the notion of a canon and orthodoxy itself came under increasing criticism. Although originally a religious term, it is common today to talk about political, scientific, and other forms of heresy to mean deviation from the status quo or accepted orthodoxy.

INDULGENCES: The practice which emerged in medieval Roman Catholicism, based upon the belief that the church had the power to forgive sin. Thus priests were believed to have the power to forgive the sins of individuals who made appropriate contributions to the church or undertook pilgrimages or other sacred duties. Initially, the practice was intended to encourage people to live exemplary lives. But it quickly degenerated into the belief that we received forgiveness of sins through our good works and contributions to the institutional church.

During the late 15th century and early 16th century, when the Renaissance popes were beautifying the city of Rome, the sale of indulgences became a way of raising funds to pay artists like Michaelangelo. Martin Luther's protest against the sale of indulgences in Germany led to the Protestant Reformation.

JUSTIFICATION BY FAITH: While preparing lectures on St. Paul's letter to the Christians in Rome, the New Testament book of Romans, Martin Luther rediscovered St. Paul's teaching about justification by faith. This is a technical theological term used in the New Testament to signify the act by which God restores humans to a relationship with himself based on the individual's acceptance of the suffering of Jesus on the cross. The Bible teaches that Christ died for our sins and that humans may enjoy the fruits of his sacrifice through faith in him.

At the time of the Reformation, Protestant and Roman Catholic theologians disagreed as to how the doctrine of justification was to be interpreted. For the Roman Catholic, it means making just the sinner through the infusion of supernatural grace that blots out sin to regenerate the soul and make the soul worthy of God the Creator. For the Reformers, justification is an act of divine forgiveness brought about by faith alone on the basis of the propitiatory sacrifice of Christ on the cross of Calvary.

PILGRIMAGE: A journey made for a number of reasons, including the religious purposes of strengthening one's faith or one's body. Through pilgrimage, individuals are linked to the wider Christian tradition and history. The cities of Rome and Jerusalem were traditional centers of pilgrimage, although smaller sites were also very important. Places of pilgrimage often contain relics of saints or the founders of religious orders.

PRIESTHOOD OF ALL BELIEVERS: The Protestant teaching developed by Martin Luther states that all Christians share a common priesthood. It is based upon the New Testament teaching that under the "new covenant" initiated by God through the sacrifice of Jesus on the cross, no other sacrifices are needed to placate divine wrath. Therefore, there is no longer a need for an earthly priesthood to offer sacrifices to God. Rather, all believers offer their lives to God as a living sacrifice.

PROTESTANT: A name given in the 16th century to supporters of Martin Luther who sought the Reformation of the Catholic Church and protested against what they saw as spiritual abuse. Protestants sought to reform the church on the basis of the authority of the Bible.

REFORMATION: A term that has come to mean any religious movement which reforms a preexisting tradition to restore its primitive purity or orthodoxy. More specifically, it is associated with the religious movement that began with the protest of Martin Luther (1483–1546) against the sale of indulgences in Germany in 1517. The Reformation led to the creation of independent churches which renounced the claims of the papacy and sought to return to a thoroughly biblical Christianity. The Reformers taught that the Bible is the only source of faith and doctrine. They rejected transubstantiation, indulgences, and the worship of saints and the Virgin Mary. Instead, they emphasized justification by faith and proclaimed the priesthood of all believers. Known as Protestant, because of Luther's protest against widespread corruption in the Roman Catholic Church, the Reformation quickly spread throughout northern Europe and made significant inroads into southern European countries where it was eventually defeated by the Counter-Reformation and the Inquisition, which ruthlessly persecuted Protestants as heretics who were burnt at the stake. The movement broke into several branches led by Martin Luther (1483–1546), Ulrich Zwingli (1485–1531), Menno Simons (1496–1561), John Calvin (1509–64), and the Anglican tradition originating in England.

RELICS: In medieval theology, relics were sacred objects associated with a saint or martyr that were believed to have miraculous power through their contact with the person. The corpse or parts of the body of a saint or martyr were first-class relics. Clothing and intimate personal items were second-class relics. Finally, anything that was touched by a saint or martyr was a third-class relic. Anyone caught buying, selling, or manufacturing counterfeit relics was liable to excommunication. The Roman Catholic Church continues to value relics as an important aid to devotion and spiritual healing. Protestants reject their use, claiming that they deviate from Scriptural teachings about salvation.

RELIQUARY: During the Middle Ages, relics were collected by bishops and princes and stored in reliquaries (repositories) within shrines, where they could be adored by pilgrims.

VESTMENTS: Ecclesiastical garments worn by Roman Catholic, Eastern Orthodox, and some Anglican and Lutheran priests or ministers. Vestments are changed according to the season of the church year. They are highly symbolic and are intended to help worshipers remember the seasons and events in Christ's life.

THE CHRISTIAN
TRAVELERS GUIDES

"In an era that often overlooks the significance of the past as such, and certainly the Christian past, Professor Hexham's well-crafted guides for heritage tourists truly fill a gap. Don't leave home without one!"

—J. I. Packer, Author of *Knowing God*

By describing and interpreting the religious significance of people, places, and events in various countries, Irving Hexham illustrates the incredible impact Christianity has had on Western Civilization. Each guide is organized alphabetically according to the names of the cities and sites. The Christian Travelers Guides will help you deepen your faith by bringing to life the struggles and triumphs of great Christian leaders and common believers through the living witness of places where the saints once walked.

THE CHRISTIAN TRAVELERS GUIDE TO FRANCE

Irving Hexham, General Editor;
Written by Mark Konnert, Peter Barrs, and Carine Barrs

- Relive the experience of the Huguenots and the creators of such masterpieces as Chartes and Notre Dame.

    Softcover 0-310-22588-4

THE CHRISTIAN TRAVELERS GUIDE TO GERMANY

Irving Hexham, General Editor;
Written by Irving Hexham and Lothar Henry Kope

- Experience the church's struggle against Nazi paganism, ponder the sorrow of the Thirty Years' War, and see where the modern missionary movement was born.

    Softcover 0-310-22539-6

The Christian Travelers Guide to Great Britain

Irving Hexham, General Editor;
Written by Irving Hexham

- Come into contact with the Venerable Bede, who almost single-handedly preserved European civilization in an age of death and destruction, become a pilgrim with John Bunyan in his beloved Bedford, and see where John Wesley preached against slavery and converted thousands.

Softcover 0-310-22552-3

The Christian Travelers Guide to Italy

Irving Hexham, General Editor;
Written by David Bershad and Carolina Mangone

- Experience a wealth of art and architecture stretching back to the early church and the age of martyrs, travel where Christians died in the arena, and see where great artists such as Michelangelo depicted unforgettable scenes of biblical truth.

Softcover 0-310-22573-6

Pick up a copy today at your favorite bookstore!

We want to hear from you. Please send your comments about this book to us in care of the address below. Thank you.

ZondervanPublishingHouse
Grand Rapids, Michigan 49530
http://www.zondervan.com